THE
COMPLETE
BLADESMITH

THE COMPLETE BLADESMITH

Forging Your Way to Perfection

JIM HRISOULAS

PALADIN PRESS

BOULDER, COLORADO

Also by Jim Hrisoulas:

Forging Damascus: How to Create Pattern-Welded Blades (Video)

Master Bladesmith: Advanced Studies in Steel

Pattern-Welded Blade: Artistry in Iron

The Complete Bladesmith:
Forging Your Way to Perfection
By Jim Hrisoulas

Copyright © 1987 by Jim Hrisoulas

ISBN 0-87364-430-1
Printed in the United States of America

Published by Paladin Press,
a division of Paladin Enterprises, Inc.
Gunbarrel Tech Center
7077 Winchester Circle
Boulder, Colorado 80301, USA
+1.303.443.7250

Direct inquiries and/or orders to the above address.

PALADIN, PALADIN PRESS, and the "horse head" design
are trademarks belonging to Paladin Enterprises and
registered in United States Patent and Trademark Office.

Illustrations by Joyce Morris and Melinda Sherbring
Photography by:
William De Savage: Figure 104
Dan Fitzgerald: Figures 25, 102, 103, 105, 106, 127, 157, 158, 159
Stephen Jacobsen: all other photos

Endsheet photo: Three different knives made by Sean McWilliams: a
utility/cam design (top), a traditional bowie (middle), and a drop-
point hunter, all with stag antler grips. Photo courtesy of Dan
Fitzgerald.

Front cover photos: Stephen Jacobsen
Back cover photos: Stephen Jacobsen (left) and Dan Fitzgerald (right)
Back flap photo: Stephen Jacobsen

Contents

Foreword

The Complete Bladesmith is a result of over seventeen years' experience in forging blades. There are no "secrets" to learn, no hard rules engraved in stone to follow. What works for you may not necessarily work for someone else. If something isn't working, then you aren't doing anything wrong; you just aren't doing it right. The old adage, if it works don't fix it, applies to forging blades.

This text was written not only for the novice bladesmith, but also for those already forging their own blades who are seeking additional information on the subject.

There has been a great deal of misinformation spread about bladesmithing, and most people have been led to believe that it is the most difficult way to make a blade. Nonsense. If you know by which end to hold a hammer, then there is no reason you cannot forge a good blade.

Good blades are becoming more difficult to obtain. It seems that the custom-blade market values looks and finish more than the ability to cut and hold an edge. A good blade is one that will cut, and cut,

and then cut some more. It doesn't have to be pretty (although I will admit it is nice if it is) to get the job done. On the other hand, you can have the most beautiful blade in the world that won't hold an edge for two minutes. But what good is it as a knife if it doesn't cut?

The blade is the heart and soul of a knife—a blade must cut and hold the edge it is given. It is not difficult to forge a blade to this end, though it can be labor-intensive in some cases. Anyone can forge a blade, and a good one at that, if he puts his mind and heart into it.

I hope this book aids those who wish to learn the art of bladesmithing and wish to follow the ways of the forge and the hammer in their quest for the perfect blade. I have tried to make this volume as complete as possible. However, only you, the reader, will be able to determine whether or not I have succeeded.

I will leave you with this: *Illegitimate non carburundum*.

Jim Hrisoulas

Acknowledgments

Special thanks to:

Mr. Bob Engnath, for putting up with me and my demented ideas.

William and Jean De Savage for talking me into writing this book, and for the help with the scrimshaw chapter.

And last, but not least, my beloved wife, Deb, who has put up with me, and allowed me to pursue my dream of forging the perfect blade.

CHAPTER 1————————
The Workshop and Tools of the Trade

As with any craft, a work space and the appropriate tools are needed. This work space can be elaborate or simple. Regardless of the type of shop you establish, certain basic needs must be met.

The first and most important consideration in setting up a shop is adequate ventilation. The place must have sufficient airflow through it or you will have some potentially serious problems. Even a small forge fire can produce a vast amount of carbon monoxide gas, and in a closed area this can be quite fatal.

In addition to the need for a lot of fresh air for the forge, the grinder will produce a large quantity of very fine grit from the steel. There is also the hardwood dust and other airborne particles to which you will be exposed. You should wear a respirator/filter while you are grinding—but good ventilation will cut down on the amount to be filtered out.

The second need is for proper lighting in the proper places. The area around the forge should be dim, but not dark. This general lack of lighting around the forge will enable you to see the colors of the heated steel better than would a brightly lit room. This is especially important when welding, as any error in temperature judgment, as discerned by color of the steel, can cause a failure of the steel.

Other areas of the shop will also need good lighting as you will need to be able to see in detail what you are doing while grinding, fitting, and such.

The very best lighting is natural background lighting, though this is not always feasible. The best artificial lighting is overhead fluorescent tube fixtures. For grinding operations, the best possible lighting is an arrangement above and slightly behind the grinder. With the lighting arrayed in such a way, you can easily see the material on which you're working.

Once you have found a suitable place to work (and it really isn't all that difficult, as I first started out underneath my carport), you will find that getting set up really doesn't take as long as you first thought.

The bladesmith's shop hasn't changed much over the past few centuries. The only real innovation has been the addition of electrical power. The actual techniques and processes still remain much the same. The majority of today's smiths started out as one-man operations stashed away in a corner of a garage or some other out-building.

The layout of the shop is a personal matter and is best left to the individual smith. As long as the anvil is close to the forge and there is a tub of water close at hand, design the floor plan as you see it. You may use the layout of my shop, shown below, as a guide.

As you can see in Figure 1, the anvils and the two forges are in close proximity to one another. The reason is that the less heat lost while moving from forge to anvil the better. This is critical when welding as the working time is short for a good weld. This close proximity between anvil and forge also saves steps and space. A good starting distance is six feet from the center of the forge to the anvil stand.

Note also that the slack tub (water) is close to the

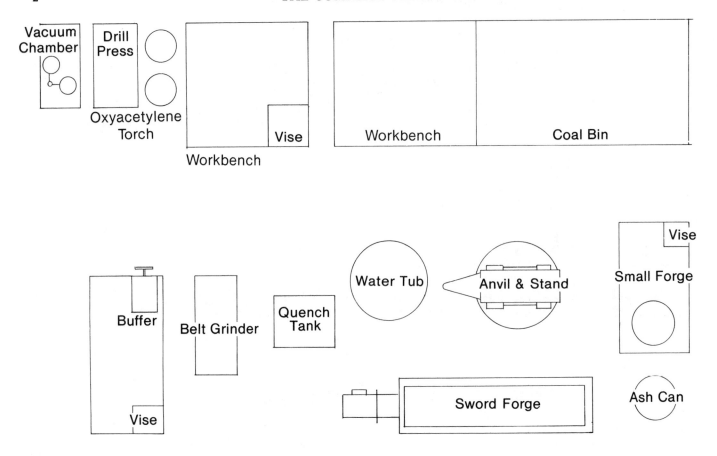

Fig. 1. Shop floor plan

anvil and forge since water will serve a number of purposes. Play around with different layouts and determine which one works best for you. However, I strongly suggest that you lay out the forge areas so you do not have to reach over the fire or any hot steel while you are working.

If you are building a shop from the ground up, I suggest that you have at least one socket wired for 220-volt current, as a 220-volt grinder is a real boon when you need to remove a lot of material quickly. Also, put the electrical sockets at least fourteen inches above the floor (workbench height is even better), and use the outdoor-type sockets—those with the little cover and rubber gasket—as this will prevent any electrical problems if you have a liquid-spill.

As with any shop, it must be kept in reasonable order. Some shops are so clean that you wonder if any work is ever done there. On the other hand, some are so cluttered that one needs a skip loader to clear a path from the forge to the anvil. My shop tends toward the latter. But, unless my loving wife takes pity upon me and decides to help out by cleaning up my smithy, in which case it takes me a week to find anything, I know exactly where everything is all the time.

A safety tip: Any shop is no place for animals or small children. Their presence can be hazardous even if the child is about trying to help daddy. Keep them out of the shop and out of harm's way.

TOOLS OF THE TRADE

The tools used by today's modern bladesmith are not all that different from those used one thousand years ago. The forge, hammer, and anvil are still there. Granted, with the electric marvels such as belt grinders and electric forge blowers, the task has become somewhat easier.

The bladesmiths of old, nonetheless, have earned my respect and admiration. I have tried to make a simple blade using only hand tools and it can be done quite well indeed, but it is very hard work. I will cover the basics of the older ways as well as the new in this book. I feel that all bladesmiths should try to do a blade without any power tools at all so they can see what it was like to be a smith in the days of yore.

Every craft has its own hazards. Bladesmithing can be quite enjoyable, but do not enjoy it so much that you get careless and negligent. Wear adequate eye protection at all times. It doesn't take but a tiny mistake to be seriously injured for life. I would rather have slightly impaired vision due to my wearing safety goggles while working than to have my vision permanently damaged due to my being "inconvenienced" by wearing protection.

This also applies to clothes. *Do not* wear polyester, nylon, or other synthetic material. These materials burn hot and fast and melt into the skin. Cotton pants and shirts are best. When forging, a leather apron will keep almost all of the sparks and cinders off your clothes. A good pair of leather safety boots, worn under the pant legs, are the best footwear.

Forge

The forge, simply put, is the heat source that the smith uses to get the metal to the desired temperature. It can be simple or elaborate in construction. One can be easily built from readily available materials or purchased new.

In this day and age, there is a choice of three differently fueled forges: gas, electric, and coal. Each has its own advantages and drawbacks.

Electric forges are very expensive, not only to acquire but also to operate, as they require a vast amount of electricity to heat up. This type of forge is the cleanest of the three when it comes to lack of harmful elements that can be absorbed from the forge into the steel. In most of the electric furnaces, the interior atmosphere can be controlled so some of the state-of-the-art stainless steels can be used. As far as temperature control, electric forges are excellent. Such forges, however, are not very energy efficient when used for small amounts of forging and heat-treating since the power drain is immense when first starting to heat up the interior (compared to the other two systems).

The electric furnace is the primary heat source for most of the professional heat-treating firms that need the control and the ability to do a greater amount of volume.

Gas forges can be built by the individual smith, but they require careful planning and thought. They are not overly expensive when purchased, and they do have some real advantages over coal. Gas forges do not produce the great clouds of smoke and soot, nor do they produce clinkers that have to be cleaned out of the fire or any flying ash or cinders. They require a rather steady supply of gas (natural, LPG, or propane). Gas forges burn clean, although they do tend to oxidize the steel more than the coal forges do. I have also found that they tend to heat up the steel quickly, which can present a problem when welding. Many smiths swear by the gas forge and will never go back to coal.

The gas forge would be a good choice for someone who's concerned with the smoke and aroma of a coal fire. They do get hot enough to weld with, although more flux is required than with a coal forge. Gas forges are readily available from most blacksmith/farrier supply sources. The costs are comparable to coal forges.

The *coal forge* is perhaps the one forge most people think of when the word "blacksmithing" is mentioned. Coal-fired forges are easy to build, maintain, and use. There are also a number of them on the market at reasonable prices, both in portable and shop models.

The coal forge offers a range of versatility that the other forges cannot. On the average, a coal forge will probably outlast the other two types of forges by a considerable length of time.

Welding and forging are easily accomplished using a coal fire. (As you can tell, I am rather biased in favor of a coal forge. I have used one for many years and I am quite pleased with it.) They do have some drawbacks. Coal is not as available as it once was, although it is still being sold by the farrier/blacksmith supply houses. The coal forge also puts out a dense black smoke when first lit. Then there are the clinkers, ash, and cinders to deal with. But the smell of the coal, the smoke, and the steady glow of the fire stir the imagination and bring the romance of days long past back to life. To me the best "first forge" is the coal-fired forge.

As previously stated, there are numerous coal forges on the market, and most of them are big enough to do everything except sword-length blades. In case you want to build your own forge, there are several plans in this book.

I have had great success using an old cast-iron diesel truck brake drum and an electric squirrel cage fan on a rheostat. It gets hot quickly and will easily heat a large piece to working temperature. The costs are within reason, even for a longer sword-length forge.

The enclosed plans are for the fire pot/blower assembly only. The rest of the forge can be housed to suit individual needs or desires.

I have written this book with the concept of using a coal fire. The techniques used are readily adaptable to gas or electric heat sources as the forging processes are basically the same.

Besides the electric blower, you can obtain a hand-cranked blower, which also works well, though trying to get enough blast going to do a billet of pattern-

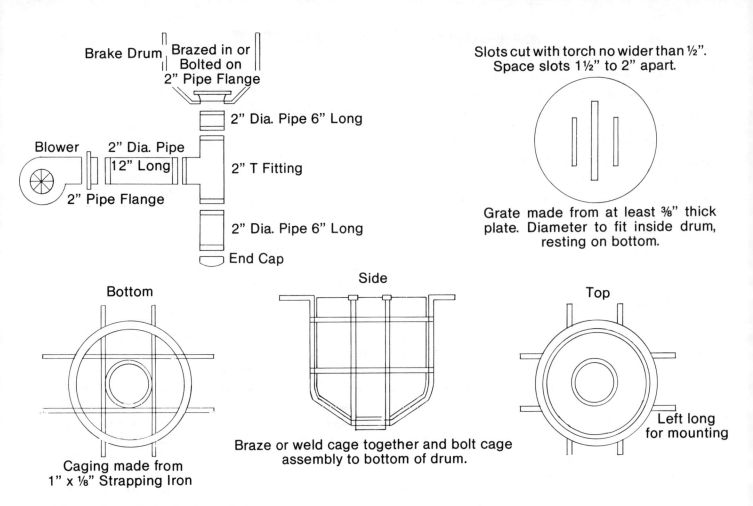

Brake Drum Brazed in or
Bolted on
2" Pipe Flange

2" Dia. Pipe 6" Long

Blower   2" Dia. Pipe
          12" Long   2" T Fitting

2" Pipe Flange

2" Dia. Pipe 6" Long

End Cap

Slots cut with torch no wider than ½".
Space slots 1½" to 2" apart.

Grate made from at least ⅜" thick
plate. Diameter to fit inside drum,
resting on bottom.

Bottom

Side

Top

Caging made from
1" x ⅛" Strapping Iron

Braze or weld cage together and bolt cage
assembly to bottom of drum.

Left long
for mounting

Fig. 2. Plans for brake drum forge

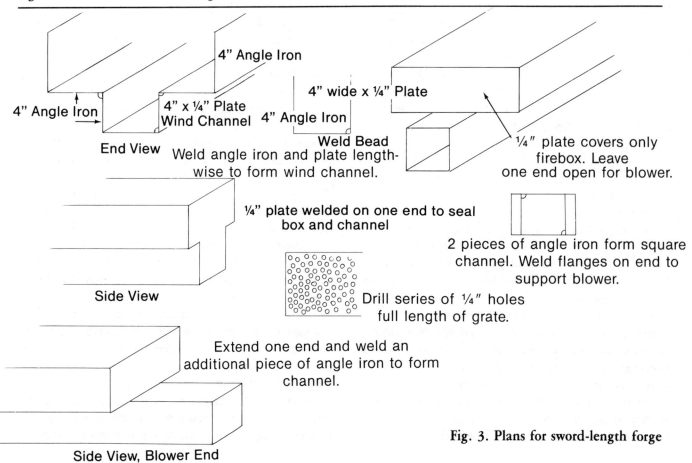

4" Angle Iron

4" Angle Iron   4" x ¼" Plate
                       Wind Channel

End View

4" wide x ¼" Plate

4" Angle Iron

Weld Bead

Weld angle iron and plate lengthwise to form wind channel.

¼" plate covers only
firebox. Leave
one end open for blower.

¼" plate welded on one end to seal
box and channel

Side View

2 pieces of angle iron form square
channel. Weld flanges on end to
support blower.

Drill series of ¼" holes
full length of grate.

Extend one end and weld an
additional piece of angle iron to form
channel.

Fig. 3. Plans for sword-length forge

Side View, Blower End

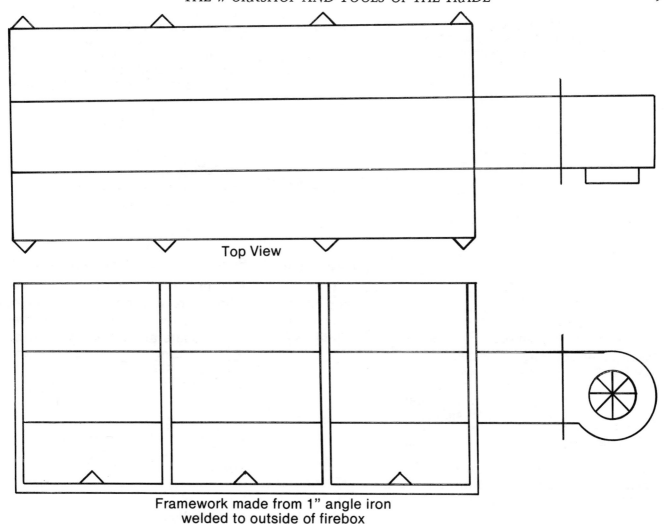

Top View

Framework made from 1" angle iron
welded to outside of firebox

Fig. 4. Further plans for sword-length forge

welded steel can be quite a chore.

There is one real drawback to a hand-cranked forge (other than the one mentioned above) and this is that the size of work that can be done in them is limited. This size limit should be taken into consideration when building or purchasing a forge.

You don't need to settle for an electric or hand-cranked blower. If you have the desire to do it "the old-fashioned way," you can use a bellows instead.

Bellows are the "traditional" air supply for the smithy. They are easy to make and can be a lot of enjoyment while working, though they do take up a lot of floor space unless mounted overhead. The plans below can be adapted to suit almost any size forge. Always make the bellows larger than you think you'll need. As for installing them, just replace the blower with the bellows and you're all set.

As with any tool, different parts of the forge serve different functions.

1. The *duck nest*, or *fire pot*, is the place where the actual fire is burning and where the iron is placed to get hot.

2. The *tuyere*, or *tue iron*, is the airflow pipe that enters the duck nest. It is usually covered by a grate.

3. The *wind channel* leads from the blower into the tue iron.

4. The *ash dump* is a space usually directly below the grate and well below the line of the tue iron. The ash dump is usually opened by a hinged door to allow removal of any debris that may have fallen through the grate.

5. The *hearth* is the entire upper section of the forge. It serves as a ready-reserve area for coal/coke.

Fire Tools

The fire will need to be cared for from time to time. This care can run from adding more coal to removing clinkers. The following tools really come in

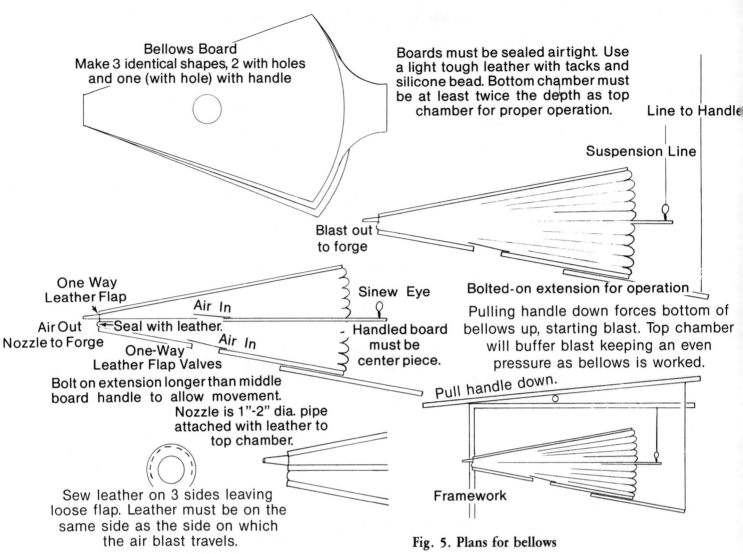

Bellows Board
Make 3 identical shapes, 2 with holes and one (with hole) with handle

Boards must be sealed air tight. Use a light tough leather with tacks and silicone bead. Bottom chamber must be at least twice the depth as top chamber for proper operation.

Line to Handle

Suspension Line

Blast out to forge

One Way Leather Flap

Air In

Sinew Eye

Air Out Nozzle to Forge

Seal with leather.

Handled board must be center piece.

Air In

One-Way Leather Flap Valves

Bolt on extension longer than middle board handle to allow movement.
Nozzle is 1"-2" dia. pipe attached with leather to top chamber.

Bolted-on extension for operation

Pulling handle down forces bottom of bellows up, starting blast. Top chamber will buffer blast keeping an even pressure as bellows is worked.

Pull handle down.

Sew leather on 3 sides leaving loose flap. Leather must be on the same side as the side on which the air blast travels.

Framework

Fig. 5. Plans for bellows

handy, are easily made, and work well.

1. The *fire poker* is used to locate clinkers, clean the grate, or for any other purpose you find for it. Make it out of one-fourth inch to three-eighths inch round or square mild steel stock, eighteen inches or longer.

2. The *fire rake* is an L-shaped tool used to move the fire around inside the forge, break up the coal, and to help locate and remove clinkers. Make it out of one-eighth inch by one inch mild steel rectangle bar stock.

3. The *fire tongs* are specially shaped tongs used to remove clinkers and other debris from the fire.

4. The *coal shovel* is used to place additional coal into the fire and to clean out the forge.

5. The *water dipper* is used to cool off parts of the work while in the forge, control the fire size, and to dampen the green coal when it's first added to the fire. This item is easy to make from a tin can and a piece of hardwood that is to be used for the handle. Just brad or wire the two together. Punch a few holes in the bottom of the can with a small nail and you're all set.

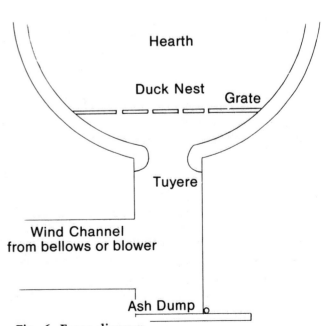

Hearth

Duck Nest

Grate

Tuyere

Wind Channel from bellows or blower

Ash Dump

Fig. 6. Forge diagram

Hammer

The smith's hammer is an extension of his hands with which he forms the hot steel to his will, giving it the shape he desires. The hammers used in bladesmithing are very similar to everyday hammers except for one important feature: they are "crowned."

Crowning is done to a hammer to give it a rounded edge along the edge of the hammer's face. This smooth edge will prevent any sharp angles from being struck into the surface as in the case of a misdirected blow. Such hammer marks can really mess up the surface of the steel and will have to be ground out later. All the hammers used in forging should be crowned to prevent these ugly marks from occurring.

There are several different types of hammers that will be useful to the smith:

1. The *ball peen* hammer can be used for hollowing, peening rivets, shaping, and general forge work. It is available in a range of weights, though a two-to three-pounder is suggested.

2. The *cross peen* hammer is perhaps the one most used in forging. It has either a square or octagonal face with a wedge-shaped peen opposite. This wedge is set at a 90-degree angle to the handle and should be rounded some before use. The cross peen hammer is used for most heavy forging work such as drawing out, upsetting, shaping, and the like. A two-and three-pounder will suffice.

3. The *straight peen* is the same as the cross peen except that the wedge is set in line with the handle.

4. The *double-end sledge* hammer is used for very heavy forging and where a lot of metal must be moved. It has two identical faces and usually weighs between five and twenty pounds. Its handle is around thirty-six inches long and is used by the smith's striker or helper.

5. The *double-faced single jack* hammer is a smaller version of the sledge hammer. The weight varies between two to five pounds with a handle similar in length to that of the cross peen. It can be used for welding and some shaping. A two- or three-pound hammer will suffice for most work.

6. The *brass head hammer* is not used for actual forging but for use with the anvil tools, such as cut-off hardies. By using a brass hammer, you can prevent the hardy from becoming damaged in case you strike through the steel unexpectedly. The brass hammers usually come in two- and three-pound weights. Get one of each.

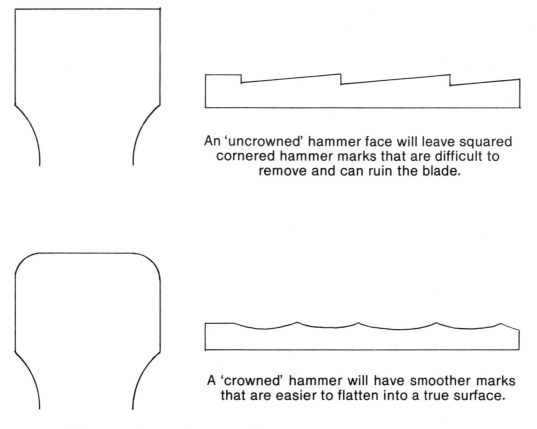

An 'uncrowned' hammer face will leave squared cornered hammer marks that are difficult to remove and can ruin the blade.

A 'crowned' hammer will have smoother marks that are easier to flatten into a true surface.

Fig. 7. An uncrowned hammer (top) and a crowned hammer (bottom)

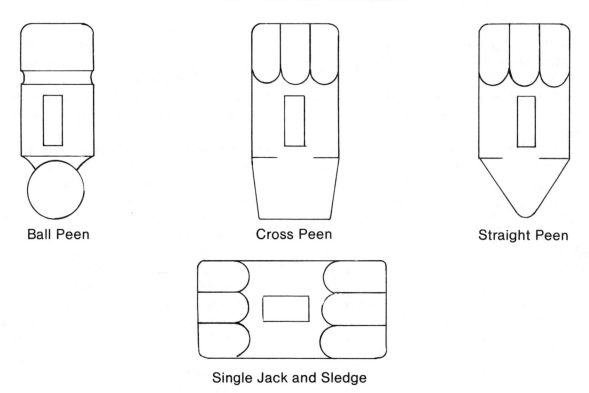

Ball Peen   Cross Peen   Straight Peen

Single Jack and Sledge

Fig. 8. Hammers

For most forging and welding, I use a three-pound cross peen; for other forge work, I have several different cross and ball peen hammers.

7. The *flatter* and the *set hammer* are not hammers, but tools to be used with the hammer to flatten and smooth out the surface of the iron. The flatter is about three inches square, looks like a large sledge hammer, and is set on top of the steel and struck with the hammer to smooth out the surface of the metal. The set hammer is similar to the flatter but is smaller (one-and-a-half-inch square) and is usually used for squaring shoulders and cor-

ners of blades.

Regardless of the types of hammers you prefer, they should all have good hardwood handles, hickory or ash being the best. Most hammer handles come with a sealing varnish on them. This finish should be sanded off and the handle soaked in oil for two to three weeks. I have soaked every hammer I have ever had in my tempering oil (head and all) for a month or so and have only had to replace one handle in five years. In addition to preventing handle breakage, this treatment also prevents splinters from arising and cutting into your hands.

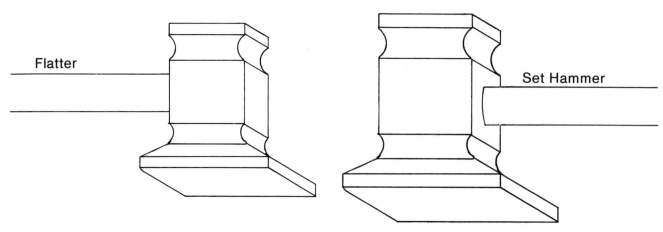

Flatter

Set Hammer

Fig. 9. Flatter and set hammer

Slack Tub

The *slack tub* is a real must for all smiths. It is a large tub of water which is useful for cooling tools, workpieces, and hands (steel *does not* have to be red to be hot, and you'll be dunking your hands frequently until you learn this). It is wise to keep an extra bucket around in case a fire gets out of control.

A good, solid oak whiskey barrel, cut in half, will make an excellent tub. These are available from most nursery and garden supply stores. Galvanized steel will also work. Make sure that the barrel holds at least ten gallons and is not near any plastic containers. A plastic bucket is totally worthless around hot metal — drop a piece of hot steel into a plastic bucket of water and you will be mopping the floor.

The slack tub should be conveniently close to the work area but not so close as to cause a problem. I have mine on a wheeled framework so I can move it around. This is really convenient when I want to dump it and change the water (the water should be changed on a regular basis). Put a dash of dish soap or baking soda in the tub to help keep it fresh and to prevent any critters from taking up residence. I have also found that it will reduce rusting of the steel placed in the water.

Quenching Tank

The *quenching tank* contains the oil (or other hardening medium) used in the heat treatment of the blades. It should be made of metal with a lid. Size depends on the length of the blades you will be making. I recommend that it be tall instead of wide so as to allow a vertical (point down) quench. It should be at least six inches deeper than the blades are long to allow proper cooling of the steel.

Anvil

The anvil is perhaps the best known of all of the bladesmith's tools. It is usually made of cast low-carbon steel with a higher-carbon steel face welded onto the body.

The anvil in use by the modern blacksmith is usually referred to as the London pattern. (The difference between this and the farrier's pattern anvil is that the latter is not built to take the greater impact of general forging work and should only be used for very light forging procedures.)

A good anvil must have a solid base with a smooth face on top. A *horn* or *bick*, a conical appendage, extends from the side of the face with a smaller flat area or *pad* separating the two.

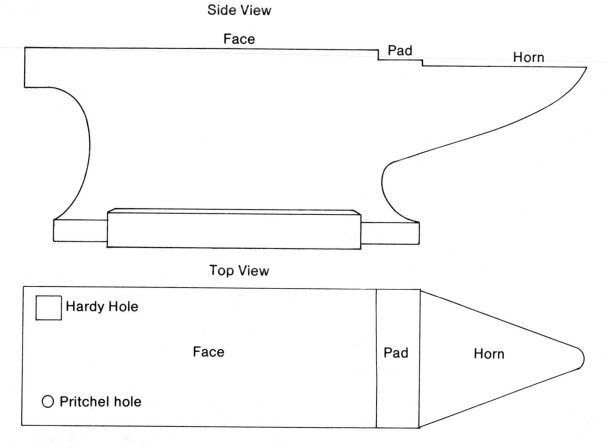

Fig. 10. Diagram of the "London" pattern blacksmith's anvil

Generally the anvils in use today are between twelve inches and seventeen inches in height and run between 150 to 500 pounds. (I suggest that for really serious work, an anvil of at least 200 pounds be used. The heavier the anvil the better, as it will absorb more of the hammer's energy and will rebound the hammer less.)

When trying to acquire an anvil, you will find that those available from blacksmith/farrier suppliers are quite expensive. On the other hand, an anvil purchase is a once-in-a-lifetime investment — a good anvil will literally last a couple of lifetimes. But if you don't wish to buy an anvil, you may also be able to find one at flea markets, swap meets, and antique stores. If you can get a used anvil in reasonably good shape, go ahead, but if it's scarred with deep gouges, cracks, and dents in the face, pass it up.

There are numerous anvils that are being produced outside of the United States that are attractively priced, but the quality is very poor. The best anvils available are imported from England, Sweden, or Germany. The easiest way to tell if an anvil is good is to strike it lightly with a hammer on its face and horn. If it rings clear and sharp when you strike its face and slightly duller when you strike its horn, then it is probably a good quality anvil that could last a few hundred years if used properly.

It is possible to reface an old anvil, but this is usually beyond the capabilities of most craftsmen as it involves regrinding and heat-treating the entire anvil. There are craftsmen who can do this, but the process is expensive. You will be better off in the long run to get a good anvil at a fair price than to get an old beast which may require significant reworking.

As for the anvil, you will see that there are two holes in the face. One hole is round and is called the *pritchel* or *punching hole*. This hole is about three-eighths inch to five-eighths inch. The other hole is square in shape and is called the *hardy hole,* and is used to hold the anvil tools or *hardies*. The *hardy hole* is square to prevent the tool from turning, and is from three-fourths inch to one and one-fourth inch square.

It is advisable that the first one-fourth to one-third of the length of the anvil edge back from the horn be round. These radii of curvature will help prevent grooves from being cut into the steel's surface when forging sharp bends. An edge radius of one-eighth inch to one-fourth inch is quite enough. (I have on my anvil an edge one side one-eighth inch and the other one-fourth inch.)

The pad of the anvil, also called the *table*, is usually left unhardened and is used for chisel cutting. To use a chisel on the face can cause deep scratches and gouges in the working surface of the anvil. These marks will be transferred to the surface of the metal being worked and can cause a mess on the finished forging. (You can also use a piece of heavy mild steel scrap under the work if you prefer to chisel on the larger surface of the anvil's face. This will protect the smooth surface.)

The horn of the anvil is left unhardened and is used for all sorts of shaping and curving.

If you cannot find an anvil, a serviceable working surface can be made out of an old piece of railroad track. A lot of work can be done on a surface such as this, although you will be pushing it when it comes to the heavier work.

MAKING A RAILROAD TRACK ANVIL

A short length of railroad track can be used for an anvil, and if properly made, it can be quite serviceable, though rather small.

The first thing you are going to need is a piece of old railroad track. You can often find odd pieces lying around railroad rights of way and wherever track repairs are going on. The railroad industry will not appreciate it if you go out and cut a small section out of one of their tracks, so don't even think about it! Usually if you ask a railroad worker, you'll obtain a piece gratis.

After you have acquired a section of track, you must find out whether or not the steel used in its construction is heat-treatable. The easiest way to do this is to cut off a small section of the track, heat it to a cherry red, and quench it in water. If it hardens enough to pass the file hardness test, then it is usable for an anvil.

You can shape the track to just about any shape you wish. I have found that if you follow the design of a normal blacksmith pattern anvil, you will not be too far off on design and function. Of course, you can do all sorts of "custom" designs for specific purposes which can really come in handy if you also wish to do specialized work, such as armor.

To start out on this project, use either a cutting torch or a grinder to remove the steel from under the horn section so you will be able to properly shape the curves and tapers. I strongly suggest using a cutting torch.

After the cutting is finished, grind the cuts smooth and refine its shape. Use either a very coarse belt (thirty-six grit) or an abrasive auto-body grinder to grind it to shape. This will take a little bit of time, so

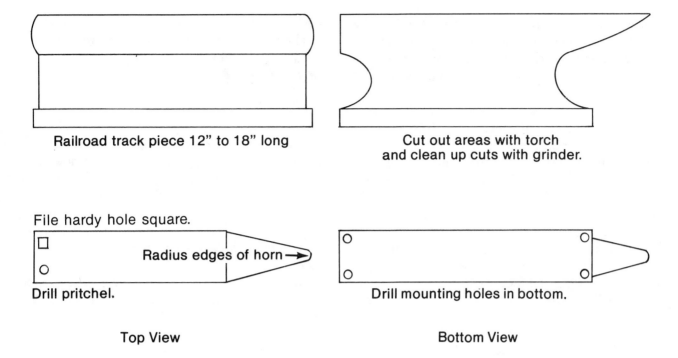

Railroad track piece 12" to 18" long

Cut out areas with torch
and clean up cuts with grinder.

File hardy hole square.

Radius edges of horn →

Drill pritchel.

Drill mounting holes in bottom.

Top View

Bottom View

Fig. 11. Railroad track anvil

don't rush it.

After you are satisfied with the shape, put in the pritchel and hardy holes. A three-eighths-inch hole is all that is required for a pritchel as this hole is to remain round. For the square hardy hole, a three-fourths-inch hole is drilled and then filed into a three-fourths-inch square. You do not have to put these holes in the anvil if you do not foresee using a hardy or doing any hot punching.

You may also wish to drill some mounting holes to bolt the anvil down to its base. You can also use these holes to attach a handle made from a one-fourth-inch diameter rod to aid in handling the piece in heat-treating.

With the holes drilled and filed and the anvil shaped, now comes the heat treatment. You will need a large fire to heat the anvil. There will be high volume of steel to heat-treat and bring up to temperature—more volume than most small forges can heat. You can probably make a long grate out of a piece of four- to six-inch cast-iron pipe cut in half lengthwise and drilled through with three-eighths-inch holes to make a long grate.

Build a large fire with at least a four- to five-inch bed of coals. Place the anvil topside down into the fire and heap the coals over it until the top is buried in the bank of coals.

It will take a considerable length of time to get this amount of steel up to temperature. Take it slow until

the piece is hot enough to harden. If you cannot get it hot enough, there is always the option of having it heat-treated by a commercial heat-treating firm (check the yellow pages in your area).

When the piece is at the proper temperature (cherry red), cool the handle with a wet rag and remove the anvil and quench it in a metal trash can filled with salt water. Let the anvil down as far as you possibly can without touching the bottom of the trash can. The bubbling and steaming will be quite heavy but not at all uncomfortable.

When the piece is cooled, polish the face and place the anvil back into the fire (the fire should be cleaned of clinkers, and burning clean and hot) right-side up.

Draw a temper on the anvil face to a very light straw color and quench. Do not worry about the horn as it will be annealled to a soft blue temper. Take your time, and go about it slowly.

If you have had enough of the hassles that such a big fire causes, you can temper the anvil in your kitchen oven. Set the anvil on the bottom of the oven on a cookie sheet and set the temperature at 325°F. Let it bake for a couple of hours.

When the temper on the face is completed, draw the horn back (let the horn cool slower than the rest of the anvil) to a blue temper with a blowtorch. Take your time and watch the color change. Be sure that the temperature bleeding does not run into the face or you will anneal it as well. When the horn is annealled, quench the entire anvil again to prevent the face from becoming softened. Then polish the surfaces with gradually finer grits of abrasives until a 240 grit is reached and you are ready to start to work.

Of course, you can always have the heat treating and tempering professionally done if you do not wish to do it yourself, but it is expensive. I prefer to do these things myself, as this way I know that it was done to my own satisfaction, and not in the quickest and easiest route to get the job done.

You will be limited by the size of the railroad track anvil as to the kind of work that you can do on it. You can do a great variety of work, but do not expect to do heavy forging or shaping on such a small anvil. This anvil is a good tool for starters, so they can get the feel of forging without a large monetary outlay for an anvil.

MOUNTING THE ANVIL

An anvil must be mounted on a sturdy and rugged base in order to be used to its best advantage. It also must be the proper height. The face of the anvil should just touch the smith's knuckles when he is standing normally, his arms at his sides, hands curled into fists. When placed at such a level, the hammer should land flat upon the piece being worked instead of at an angle. This way the telltale hammer marks

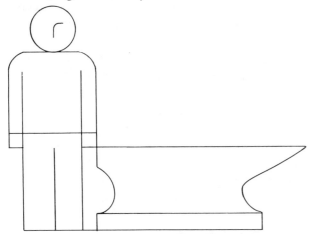

Fig. 12. Elevation of anvil surface is knuckle level.

are kept to a minimum. A good base can be made out of a cut-down oil drum, filled with sand to the proper level, with the anvil resting on a solid hardwood block. I have used this arrangement for years and have found it to work very well.

The anvil needs to be placed close to the forge so the steel will not lose too much heat when it is moved from the forge to the anvil face. Let it ring true and loud when working. (If your neighbors complain, the ringing can be cut down considerably by the use of an

old automobile fan belt with a five- to-ten-pound weight attached to it. Simply slip the weighted belt over the horn and you will be surprised at how much the ringing is reduced.)

Hardies and Other Anvil Tools

Hardies are the tools that fit into the square hole in the anvil face. These wedge-shaped tools are used to cut or groove the steel by driving the bar down onto the wedge with the hammer. They can be straight, curved, or any other shape that may be desired.

Bicks are also used in the hardy hole and are shaped like scaled-down versions of the anvil's horn. They can also be shaped to the smith's needs and wishes.

Fullers are "top and bottom" tools. The top tool usually has a handle like that of a hammer, and strikes down upon the bottom half, which is secured in the hardy hole. The fullers are similar to chisels, but instead of being sharpened for cutting, the surfaces are rounded for making depressions in the steel. These tools are used to groove, flute, and form collars/shoulders in the steel.

Swages are similar to fullers but instead of grooving the metal, they are used to change the cross sections of rods and such (i.e., change a square to a hex, a round to a triangle, etc.).

Punches and *drifts* are tools used to form holes and/or enlarge them. The punch actually removes a *slug* of metal from the hot steel whereas the drift will expand the already existing hole to a larger diameter or to a different shape.

Hot and *cold* chisels are used to cut the iron. The hot chisel is used while the steel is red-hot and will make a smaller and cleaner cut than the cold chisel. The cold chisel is used only on soft, unheat-treated steels or iron.

The hot chisel usually has an edge bevel of approximately thirty degrees whereas the cold chisel has about 60-degree bevel.

The above tools can be easily made and should be made of a medium-carbon steel that has been hardened and tempered to a light blue.

Tongs

The tongs are a means by which the metal is held upon the anvil. They are indispensable. The most commonly used tongs in the shop are called *single pickups*. There are numerous types of tongs, one for every purpose or use imaginable: round-jawed, curve-jawed, rivet, bolt, and straight-lipped. The list goes on and on.

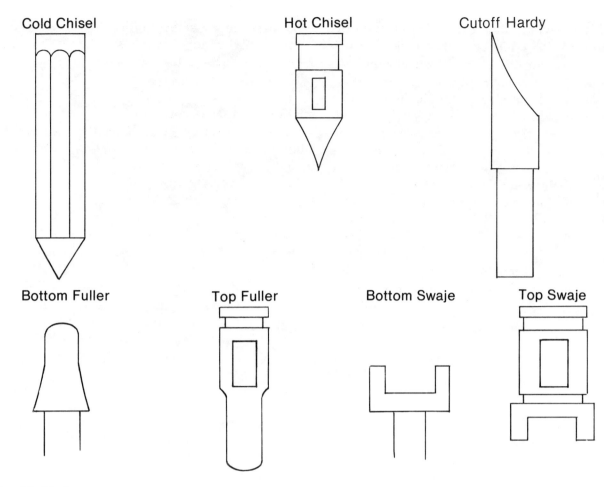

Cold Chisel

Hot Chisel

Cutoff Hardy

Bottom Fuller

Top Fuller

Bottom Swaje

Top Swaje

Fig. 13. Tools

Nevertheless, the single pickups will be the ones most used in the shop. Tongs should fit the work being held and should be sturdy and well made. If they are not the correct tongs for the purpose, the steel could slip out and fly up when struck with the hammer. A face full of 1,500-degree steel is an experience that should by all means be avoided.

Some smiths make a hook out of one handle and fit a steel ring around the tong handles so they can be locked closed. I have tried this and found it to be more trouble than it is worth.

A good pair of tongs should have handles of no less than eighteen inches and be made of a tough and shock-resistant steel that can withstand the constant heating, cooling, and strains of everyday use.

You will find that you will need several different pairs of tongs. In addition to the single pickups, you will probably need the following tongs.

1. *Square-lip* tongs are used to hold square stock and are available in one-fourth inch square and larger.
2. *Round-lip* tongs are used to hold round stock and come in almost any size that you will need. These tongs are a real aid if you are forging round stock

down into a different shape.

3. *Vise grips* or the self-locking pliers have a place in the shop, but they should never be used in the place of tongs as they may open accidentally at the wrong moment and cause all sorts of problems.

It is a good idea to never leave the tongs in the fire, and to cool them down from time to time in the slack tub. (You will be surprised as to how quickly they get hot while working.)

The Oxyacetylene Torch

This handy little gadget really makes it easier for you to do various things: weld, braze, anneal, straighten, and cut. Cutting steel is where you will probably use this torch most. This is especially true if you are salvaging carbon steel from plowshares, saws, or the like. And using this sort of "raw" material is where the bladesmith has the stock-removal guys (those who simply grind an alloy bar into a blade) beat out. If you want to make a local bend and do not want to fire up the forge, the torch will usually be able to do it.

You can also do some heat-treating on the smaller

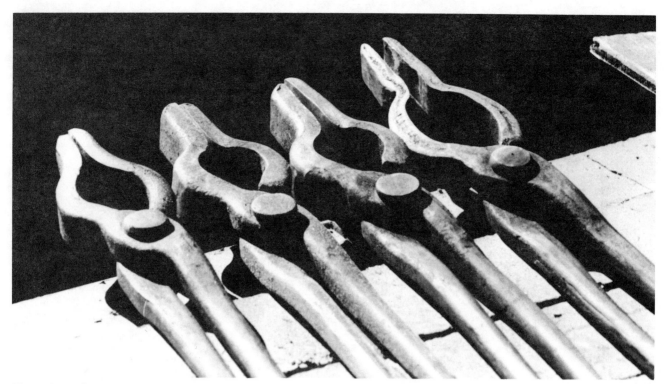

Fig. 14. Various tongs used in forging

blades (say four inches or so) with this torch, if you use the proper sized tip.

Vises

The vises used in forging need three qualities: to be heavy, well-built, and big. They also need to be close to the forge so they can be used more readily. There are countless tasks that these wonderful tools can make easier. You will probably find that you will need two or three of them.

The traditional vise used by the blacksmith was called the *leg,* or *post,* vise. This vise was designed so that the impact from any forging that was done was transferred to the floor, via the leg, instead of being absorbed by the jaw screw. The bigger a vise is, the better. This is especially important with the leg vise.

These vises are getting somewhat scarce today, although they are still being made. If you do come upon one in your travels, and it is in working order, by all means get it.

The *machinist's* or *bench* vise is the most common form of vise in use today. It comes in all sizes and varieties but must be massive. Do not perform heavy forging with this type of vise as you can shear off the jaw screw and ruin the vise. This type of vise is easy to obtain; if you can get hold of a heavy one, all the better.

Regardless of the type of vise you use, it must be sturdy, well-built, and mounted upon a solid and heavy workbench. The best place to mount a vise is on a corner of the bench so you can have three angles of attack to the work.

Drill Press

One of the most useful tools in the shop, the drill press comes in all kinds, shapes, and sizes in all price ranges. It must have an adjustable worktable and adjustable speed. This drill will really save a lot of labor and time. It is also a good idea to have a drill press vise, which will come in handy for holding things that can't be clamped down to the table.

Belt Grinder

The belt grinder, a real gift from the gods to bladesmithing, is the number-one labor-saving tool ever devised. (If you wish to do all of your work by hand, skip over this section and we will wish you well in your toils!)

There are many different models on the market with all sorts of features. Whichever one you choose, make certain that it uses at least a 60-inch-long belt. If the belt is any wider than two inches, you will have a bit of a problem with some work.

The real advantage of having a belt grinder is that it gives you versatility. You have a choice of flat or hollow grinding blades, and can do handles and fittings.

When you are looking around for a belt grinder,

Fig. 15. The leg vise

Fig. 16. The bench, or machinist's, vise

you will be surprised by the price: expensive, but well worth the money. Make sure that the motor is of at least three-fourths horsepower and that the belt has a positive tracking control. This tracking control allows you to move the belt around on the wheels or platen to do whatever sort of work that you wish.

Most of the grinders made today come with a variable voltage motor for 110 or 220 volts. If at all possible, set it up for 220 volts as it will make a big difference as to how fast you will be able to grind.

Abrasive belts will be perhaps the most used item in the shop. The quality of belts will vary greatly from manufacturer to manufacturer. You will want to get the butt-spliced belts. Aluminum oxide is the best abrasive for grinding metals. Stay away from flint or garnet belts.

The backing of most belts will be cloth. X-weight is the heaviest, with J-weight being the lightest. Do not use any of the paper-backed belts of any weight as they will break and split when used for anything heavy.

You will find that the more expensive belts will usually outlast the ones from ''bargain basement'' stores. To give you an idea, I use about four of the quality brand for a full-sized broadsword blade instead of eight to twelve of the lesser quality ones. ''You get what you pay for'' was never truer than with abrasive belts.

You will need at least the following grits:
36 or 50 grit for profiling and rough grinding
120 grit for final grinding
240 grit for prepolish
400 grit for polish prior to buffing
You will use a vastly larger amount of the coarser belts than the finer ones. Get a good selection of all grits.

Buffer

Buffers are what you will be using to put the final finish on your blades and are available in different horsepowers (HP) and various revolutions per minute (RPM). I suggest a minimum of one-half to three-fourths HP at approximately 1,450 RPM. This slower RPM will help to prevent the buffing compound from being sprayed all over you and the room, rather than remaining on the wheel where it's supposed to be.

Floor switches for the buffer and drill press really come in handy. Floor switches activate the machine when depressed by the foot, and therefore stop the machine when the foot lifts from the switch pedal. They are available at most hardware and electrical supply stores for reasonable prices.

Workbench

A sturdy and well-built bench is one requirement of any workshop, but more so with a smithy. Make sure that you have enough room on it to do any kind of task. Keep it cleared of tools and half-started projects, though some clutter can be expected. (It is said that a clean workplace is the sign of a sick mind. If this is truly the case, then I'm very healthy!)

The bench should be the proper height for comfortable work while standing up; about waist high for the average person seems to work out.

If you have the room for two or more benches, put them in; you will be surprised at how much they are used. There are several different designs of benches that I prefer (see Fig.17). I built mine from two-inch by four-inch lumber and three-fourths-inch plywood; it is heavy and solid.

In addition to the tools mentioned above you will also find need of the following items:

dial vernier calipers	steel machinist's rule
assorted needle files	assorted bench files
tap and die set	assorted twist drills
pliers	screwdrivers
pipe wrenches	vise grips
center punches	bolt cutters
hacksaw	coping saw
jeweler's saw*	metal cutting bandsaw*
tin snips	assorted C-clamps
flexible shaft machine*	rawhide mallets

All in all, the tools of the bladesmith's trade are just that, tools. While it is true that good tools will not make a poor craftsman a good craftsman, poor tools will make a good craftsman suffer. Always buy the best tools that you can afford, as it will show in the working of the materials.

A good craftsman can get along without many of the above tools, and in fact you can do some good work without some of the above items. Start your smithing slowly—acquire tools only as you need them. Try to avoid purchasing all manners of gadgets and doodads when first starting out. Rather, add to your tools wisely and thoughtfully; learn to use all of them safely and well. The best tools in the world are no replacements for good workmanship. Do not expect perfection overnight. I have been at this trade

---

*These are really nice items to have around, though you can get along without them.

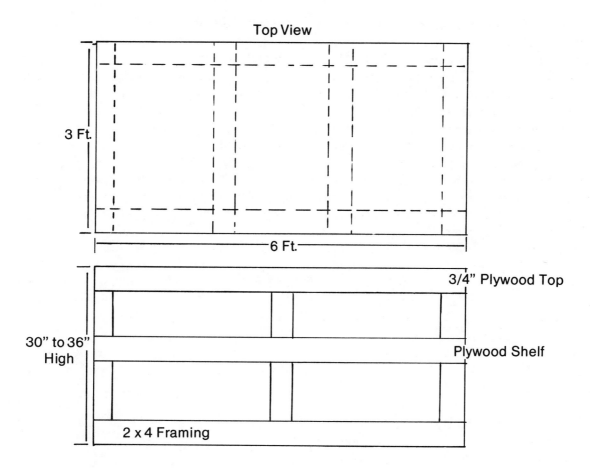

Top View

3 Ft.

6 Ft.

3/4" Plywood Top

30" to 36" High

Plywood Shelf

2 x 4 Framing

Fig. 17. Plans for workbenches

for many years and am still learning.

Tackle the problems you have one at a time, be it in forging, grinding, or fittings. Keep with it and pretty soon you will improve your work to its finest.

CHAPTER 2 —————

Steels to Use

Today's bladesmith, unlike his ancestors, has available to him a vast quantity of high-quality carbon steels which are suitable for forging. It is the steel, in addition to how it is worked, that either makes or breaks the blade.

Every tool has its own specific use. One wouldn't expect a hammer to be used as pliers, or pliers to substitute for a screwdriver. Yet a knife is called upon to not only cut, but to also chop, cleave, and to be occasionally used as a pry bar, as well as serve a variety of other uses.

To make a blade that will be hard enough to take and hold an edge, yet not so brittle as to break, is a very trying task. This is the bladesmith's dilemma.

One-hundred-fifty years ago, when the only steel that the bladesmith had was what he made, he relied upon his own experience and skill in smelting his own iron and making it into steel. But today there are not only consistently high-quality carbon steels, but also alloys about which bladesmiths of the past could have only dreamed.

Notice that I said *carbon* steels. Most stainless steels cannot be forged readily, with the exception of the stainless-steel alloys listed on pages 24 and 25. Most of the stainless alloys available today for the knife-making industry tend toward the *stock removal* method of knife making (in which a steel bar is simply cut, ground, and polished into a blade). The majority of stock-removal makers can use the super state-of-the-art stainless steel alloys as they usually do not do their own heat-treating, but rather get the steel professionally heat-treated in a controlled-atmosphere furnace.

But not all of the modern steels are limited in this way. There are quite a few alloys available that are forgeable into a quality blade. These alloys are available from most tool steel supply sources, and some are quite low in cost when compared to the stainless-steel alloys that the stock-removal knife-makers use.

ELEMENT CONTENT AND HOW IT AFFECTS THE STEEL

The primary ingredient in steel is iron, one of the most common elements found in the earth. It is usually found in the form of iron oxide (iron ore) and is then smelted down into cast iron (*pig iron*). The cast iron is then further refined as other elements are added to its composition to bring about the desired qualities and characteristics in the finished alloy.

The most common element that has an effect on hardness in an alloy is carbon, which not only increases the hardness but can also make the steel quite brittle. Thus using a steel with a high carbon content will result in a hard and brittle blade, while using a steel with a low carbon content will result in a tough blade that will not hold an edge.

The carbon content of an alloy is expressed as a *point* of carbon, with each point signifying 0.01 percent of the alloy. So a 35-point alloy will contain 0.35 percent carbon. The table below displays the points of carbon and the uses for which they are suitable.

Points of carbon	Uses
5-10	Nails, wire. Not hardenable.
10-20	General uses. Not hardenable.
20-30	Screws, some machinery parts.
30-40	Machinery parts. Will harden slightly.
40-50	Gears, axles, hardenable to a degree.
50-60	Crowbars, hammers. Will harden enough to take an edge if properly heat-treated. Will make a very tough and flexible blade.
60-70	Swords, axes, cleavers. Blades for heavy chopping.
70-100	General cutlery uses. Choose a lower carbon content for a tougher blade, and a higher carbon content for a harder and longer-lasting edge.

As you can see by the above chart, a carbon content of at least forty points (0.40 percent) is needed before a steel will harden. A carbon content of at least fifty points (0.50 percent) is required for a cutting edge to be serviceable. Of course, much of the edge-holding capability relies upon how the steel is heat-treated (see Chapter Six). But carbon isn't the only element added to steel. Knowing what you are working with and which alloy is best suited for your intended purpose is an important factor in the choice of a steel. To aid industry in knowing what the content is of a given alloy, the Society of Automotive Engineers (SAE) developed a numerical code for the available steels with certain standards for each alloy.

This code is usually a four-digit number with the first two digits identifying the basic elemental content of the alloy. The second two numbers (here represented by Xs) will usually be the carbon content.

Steel type	Series code number
Plain carbon (non-alloy) steel	1XXX
Manganese steel	13XX
Nickle alloy steels	2XXX
3.5% Ni	23XX
5.0% Ni	25XX
Nickle/Chrome steel	3XXX
Molybdenum steels	4XXX
Carbon/Moly	40XX
Chrome/Moly	41XX
Chrome/Moly/Ni	43XX
Moly/Ni	46XX or 48XX
Chromium alloy steels	5XXX
Low Cr content	51XX
Medium Cr content	52XX
High Cr content	53XX
Chrome Vanadium alloy steels	6XXX
Ni/Cr/Moly alloy steels	86XX or 87XX
Manganese Silicon alloy steels	92XX

For example, alloy 1095 will be a plain carbon (nonalloy) steel with 0.95 percent carbon.

In addition to the SAE numerical code, the American Iron and Steel Institute (AISI) has devised a letter/number code based either upon the alloy's hardening medium(s), content, or use.

Letter code	Steel type
A	Air-hardening steels
D	Die steel alloys
F	Carbon/tungsten alloys
H	Hot work
L	Low alloy
M	Molybdenum alloys
O	Oil-hardening steels
P	Mold steel alloys
S	Shock-resistant alloys
T	Tungsten alloys
W	Water-hardening steels

The numbers that follow the letter codes are standard alloy designation numbers for the industry. This way the alloy content is standardized.

There are quite a few elements used in the manufacturing of the various steel alloys. In addition to the iron and carbon already mentioned, here are listed the more common alloy elements and what they do to the physical properties of the metal.

Manganese (Mn) is normally present in all steel and functions as a deoxidizer. It also imparts strength and responsiveness to heat treatment. It is usually present in quantities of 0.5 to 2.0 percent.

Nickle (Ni) increases strength and toughness but is rather ineffective in increasing hardness. It is generally added in amounts ranging from 1 percent to 4 percent. In some stainless steels it is sometimes as high as 36 percent.

Chromium (Cr) increases the depth penetration of hardening processes and also the responsiveness to heat-treatment. It is usually added with nickle for use in stainless steels. Most of the chromium-bearing alloys contain 0.50 to 1.50 percent chromium; some stainless steels contain as much as 20 percent. It can affect forging, causing a tendency in the steel to crack.

Vanadium (V) retards the grain growth of steel,

even after long exposures at high temperatures, and helps to control grain structures while heat-treating. It is usually present in small quantities of 0.15 to 0.20 percent. Most tool steels which contain this element seem to absorb shock better than those that do not.

Molybdenum (Mo) adds greatly to the penetration of hardness and increases toughness of an alloy. It also causes the steel to resist softening at high temperatures, which defeats the purpose of forging. If you have access to an alloy of below 0.020 percent molybdenum, you should be able to work it without much difficulty.

Silicon (Si) has a beneficial effect upon tensile strength and improves hardenability of an alloy. It has a toughening effect when used in combination with certain other elements. Silicon is often added to improve electrical conductivity of an alloy, and its average concentration is between 1.5 and 2.5 percent.

Tungsten (W), also known as wolfram, is often us- as an alloying element in tool steels as it tends to impart a tight, small, and dense grain structure and keen cutting edge when used in relatively small quantities. It will also cause a steel to retain its hardness at higher temperatures and hence will have a detrimental effect upon the steel's forgeability (red hard).

Sulphur (S) is usually regarded as an impurity in most alloys and its addition to steel is held to a minimum as it is damaging to the hot-forming properties of a steel. It is, however, added to screw stock as it does increase machinability.

Lead (Pb) increases the machinability of steel and has no effect upon the other properties of the metal. It is usually added to an alloy only upon request and then in quantities of 0.15 to 0.30 percent.

Phosphorus (P) is present in all steel. It increases yield strength and reduces ductility at low temperatures. It is also believed to increase resistance to atmospheric corrosion. Phosphorus is, however, treated as an impurity in most alloys.

Though these are not the only elements that are used in the alloying of various steels, they are the most commonly encountered. There are some alloys which are more forgeable than others and are listed in the following pages. These are by no means the only steels that can be used, and you are encouraged to experiment with different steels and heat-treating techniques on your own. There are no hard-and-fast rules governing the metals a bladesmith may use.

CHOOSING THE PROPER STEEL

There are many factors to consider when choosing a steel for use in a certain type of blade. You must ask yourself, is it going to be used only for cutting, or also for utility uses? Does it have to hold an edge for a long, long time or must it be tough or flexible?

All in all, the two types of steel that are best suited for bladesmithing are the water-hardening and oil-hardening steels (though for the advanced smith, the air-hardening steels are more than adequate for forging). Water-hardening steels tend to provide a hard, longer-lasting edge, although they are somewhat brittle; oil-hardening steels do not become quite as hard as water-hardening alloys, but are, on the average, tougher.

The air-hardening steels are tougher than both the water- and air-hardening steels, but they present some problems in forging which will be discussed in a later chapter. The air-hardening steels are not a good choice for the novice smith, but when they are properly forged they make a well-forged blade even better.

The stainless steels are either oil- or air-hardening and are best used in making blades that will be used on or near water. They are forgeable and produce a good sound blade when properly worked.

All of the alloys described below will make good serviceable blades. Different alloys may make certain types of blades better than other types. Choose your steel in accordance with the task the blade is to perform.

Most Commonly Used Bladesmith Steels

In the following pages, we will examine the most commonly used bladesmith steels.

0-1

0-1 is classed as a coldwork die steel and has for a long time been the standard carbon steel for blades, be they forged or ground. 0-1 is somewhat forgiving when it comes to heat-treating and warpage. It is suited for all but the largest blades (such as swords) and those in which flexibility is important.

0-1 contains the following percentages of elements:
carbon, 0.90
chrome, 0.50
manganese, 1.00
tungsten, 0.50

It has the following characteristics:
Wear resistance: medium
Toughness: medium
Red hardness: low
Distortion in heat-treating: very low
Forging: Start at 1,800 to 1,950 °F.
Austenite forging: yes
Quench: oil
Tempering: 350 to 500 °F
Rc hardness: 62 to 57

W-1

AISI W-1 tool steel is an excellent general-purpose steel that has a high degree of hardness to a rather uniform depth. Although it is a water-hardening steel, I strongly suggest that you oil-quench, as this will help to prevent warpage, cracking, and distortion.

W-1 has the following characteristics:
Carbon: 0.60 to 1.40 %
Wear resistance: medium
Toughness: medium
Red hardness: very low
Distortion in heat-treating: low to medium
Forging: Start at 1,800 to 1,900 °F.
Austenite forging: yes
Hardening: 1,400 to 1,550 °F
Quench: water or oil
Tempering: 350 to 650 °F
Rc hardness: 64 to 50

W-2

W-2 is very similar to W-1 and has the same forging and heat-treating requirements. The only real difference between the two is in the content of the alloy, and it is carbon, 0.60 to 1.40%; vanadium, 0.25%.

WHC

WHC tool steel has a slightly lower carbon content than either W-1 or W-2 steels and resists shock and impact better than either of these two steels.

WHC has the following characteristics:
Carbon: 0.75%
Wear resistance: medium
Toughness: high medium

Red hardness: very low
Distortion in heat-treating: low
Forging: Start at 1,850 to 1,900 °F.
Austenite forging: yes
Hardening: 1,400 to 1,550 °F
Quench: water or oil
Tempering: 350 to 650 °F
Rc hardness: 64 to 50

10-SERIES STEELS

The 10-series steels are perhaps the most usable of the available alloys for bladesmithing. They are very stable and quite easy to form under the hammer.

The following alloys contain the following percentages of carbon and manganese:

1050
Carbon: 0.48 to 0.55
Manganese: 0.60 to 0.90

1060
Carbon: 0.55 to 0.65
Manganese: 0.60 to 0.90

1070
Carbon: 0.65 to 0.75
Manganese: 0.60 to 0.90

1080
Carbon: 0.75 to 0.88
Manganese: 0.60 to 0.90

1095
Carbon: 0.90 to 1.03
Manganese: 0.30 to 0.50

Wear resistance: medium
Toughness: high to medium, depending upon carbon content
Red hardness: very low
Distortion in heat-treating: very low
Forging: Start at 1,750 to 1,850 °F.
Austenite forging: yes
Hardening: 1,450 to 1,550 °F
Quench: oil
Tempering: 300 to 500 °F
Rc hardness: 62 to 55, depending upon carbon content

5160

5160 is a medium carbon "spring steel" that has excellent toughness and high durability. It is quite flexible, resists heavy shocks very well, and is well suited for swords, axes, really large bowies and other blades where a larger flexible blade is desired.

5160 has the following characteristics:

Carbon: 0.56 to 0.64%
Chromium: 0.70 to 0.90%
Manganese: 0.75 to 1.00%
Phosphorus: 0.035% maximum
Silicon: 0.15 to 0.35%
Sulphur: 0.04% maximum
Wear resistance: high medium
Toughness: high
Red hardness: low
Distortion in heat-treating: low
Forge: Start at 1,800°F.
Austenite forging: yes
Hardening: 1,450 to 1,550°F
Quench: oil
Tempering: 300 to 450°F
Rc hardness: 62 to 55

L-6

L6 is a low-alloy steel usually used in large saw blades and such. It is a very good steel but is somewhat red-hard due to the vanadium content.

L-6 has the following characteristics:

Carbon: 0.70 to 0.90%
Chromium: 0.03%
Manganese: 0.35 to 0.55%
Nickle: 1.4 to 2.6%
Phosphorus: 0.025%
Silicon: 0.25%
Sulphur: 0.01% maximum
Vanadium: 0.15%
Wear resistance: medium
Toughness: very high
Red hardness: low
Distortion in heat-treating: low
Forge: Start at 1,800 to 2,000°F.
Austenite forging: yes
Hardening: 1,450 to 1,550°F
Quench: oil
Tempering: 300 to 500°F
Rc hardness: 63 to 55

S-1

S-1 is a steel designed to absorb shocks rather than resist abrasion or wear. Its primary use is in hand and pneumatic tools used for chipping and riveting.

S-1 has the following characteristics:

Carbon: 0.50%
Chromium: 1.50%
Tungsten: 2.50%
Wear resistance: medium
Toughness: very high
Distortion in heat-treating: medium
Red hardness: medium
Forging: Start at 1,850 to 2,050°F
Austenite forging: yes
Hardening: 1,650 to 1,750°F
Quench: oil
Tempering: 400 to 450°F
Rc hardness: 58 to 55

S-5

S-5 is used for the same basic tools as S-1, but it is considerably tougher and somewhat harder, due to the molybdenum content. It is a bit red-hard as well.

S-5 has the following characteristics:

Carbon: 0.55%
Manganese: 80%
Molybdenum: 0.40%
Silicon: 2.00%
Wear resistance: medium
Toughness: very high
Distortion in heat-treating: low
Red hardness: medium
Forging: Start at 1,650 to 1,800°F.
Austenite forging: yes
Hardening: 1,600 to 1,700°F
Quench: oil
Tempering: 350 to 450°F
Rc hardness: 60 to 55

Being able to heat up a bar of steel and change its shape depends a great deal upon the type of raw materials with which you are able to start. The industrial standards of steel composition are fairly universal. This is especially evident in the automotive industry, and the following chart indicates the type of steel used for certain products.

Item	Steel
Leaf springs	5160
Plow shares	1060 or 1065
Clock spring steel	1095
Files	W-2 (usually)
Saw blades	L-6

Air jackhammer bits   S-5
Truck coil springs   5160

"Exotic" Forgeable Steels

These steels are not the run-of-the-mill forgeable steels. Some smiths believe that these types cannot be forged no matter what you do to them. This is, of course, nonsense. I have been forging stainless steels, D-2, A-2, and "vasco wear" for years. If you are experienced in forging and have good temperature control, you can forge just about any alloy.

The steels listed below will produce a high-quality blade that will rival the above materials; you also will be working a lot harder to get a blade made from these richer alloys. These alloys lend themselves to the low temperature "Aus-Forging" and will require more time and effort. The results are well worth the extra work.

A-2

A-2 is an air-hardening steel with very desirable properties. It is tough and wear resistant. It is not for the beginning smith, but for the advanced student of the forged blade.

Characteristics of A-2 are:
>   **Carbon:** 1%
>   **Chromium:** 5%
>   **Molybdenum:** 5%
>   **Wear resistance:** high
>   **Toughness:** medium
>   **Distortion in heat-treating:** very low
>   **Red hardness:** high
>   **Forging:** 1,850 to 2,000 °F
>   **Austenite forging:** yes
>   **Hardening:** 1,700 to 1,800 °F
>   **Quench:** air
>   **Tempering:** 350 to 1,000 °F
>   **Rc hardness:** 62 to 57

D-2

D-2 steel is an air-hardening steel and hence may present a problem. On the other hand, it does not warp when quenched. It is very wear-resistant and somewhat red-hard and difficult to forge. I do not recommend it for the beginner, but try it if you wish.

D-2 has the following characteristics:
>   **Carbon:** 1.50%
>   **Chromium:** 12.00%
>   **Molybdenum:** 1.00%
>   **Vanadium:** 1.00%
>   **Wear resistance:** high
>   **Toughness:** high
>   **Red hardness:** high
>   **Distortion in heat-treating:** medium
>   **Forge:** Start at 1,850 to 2,000 °F.
>   **Austenite forging:** yes
>   **Hardening:** 1,800 to 1,875 °F
>   **Quench:** air
>   **Tempering:** 400 to 1,000 °F
>   **Rc hardness:** 61 to 54

440-C

440-C is a high-carbon chromium stainless steel that has become a standard in the knife-making industry. Although it is, in my opinion, unsuitable for large blades and for use where flexibility is required, it will make a very fine blade.

It is forgeable using either a hardwood charcoal or a clean coke fire, as these will not impart any impurities into the steel.

440-C has the following characteristics:
>   **Carbon:** 0.95 to 1.20%
>   **Copper:** 0.50% maximum
>   **Chromium:** 16.00 to 18.00%
>   **Manganese:** 1.00% maximum
>   **Molybdenum:** 0.65% maximum
>   **Nickle:** 0.75% maximum
>   **Phosphorus:** 0.04% maximum
>   **Silicon:** 1.00% maximum
>   **Sulphur:** 0.03% maximum
>   **Wear resistance:** high
>   **Toughness:** medium
>   **Red hardness:** medium
>   **Distortion in heat-treating:** medium
>   **Forging:** Start at 1,900 to 2,100 °F.
>   **Austenite forging:** yes
>   **Hardening:** 1,850 to 1,950 °F
>   **Quench:** oil (and in very small sections, air)
>   **Tempering:** 350 to 500 °F
>   **Rc hardness:** 62 to 57

Note: By the use of a subzero quench after the hardening quench, an extra degree of hardness can be achieved.

154-CM

154-CM is a very good stainless steel that will benefit from the same subzero quench as used for the 440-C. It is one of the most difficult steels to forge as it does not seem to move under that hammer.

154-CM has the following characteristics:

Carbon: 1.05%
Chromium: 14%
Manganese: .50%
Molybdenum: 4%
Silicon: .30%
Wear resistance: high
Toughness: medium
Red hardness: high
Distortion in heat-treating: medium
Forging: 1,800 to 1,950 °F
Austenite forging: yes
Quench: oil
Tempering: 350 to 500 °F
Rc hardness: 62 to 56

M-2

M-2 is a high-speed tool steel, well-suited for blade making. It is quite wear resistant and tough. It is not suitable for the beginning bladesmith as it takes considerable skill to work with. It is prone to cracking during low-temperature forging.

M-2 has the following characteristics:

Carbon: 0.85%
Chromium: 4.15%
Manganese: 0.35%
Molybdenum: 5.00%
Silicon: 0.30%
Tungsten: 6.4%
Vanadium: 1.95%
Wear resistance: high
Toughness: high

Red hardness: high
Distortion in heat-treating: low
Forging: 1,750 to 1,800 °F
Austenite forging: yes
Hardening: 1,700 to 1,750 °F
Quench: oil
Tempering: 350 to 500 °F
Rc hardness: 62 to 58

VASCO WEAR

Vasco wear is another steel for the advanced forger. It is very tough and highly wear resistant. Abrasives barely cut it; once an edge is put on a blade made of it, the blade simply does not get dull. It is easy to forge, and works like L-6. The main difficulty comes after the hardening. At this point vasco wear gets superhard, tough, and difficult to work. Consequently, you must do 90 percent of the work hot, before heat-treating, to be able to work this steel into a blade.

Vasco wear has the following characteristics:

Carbon: 1.12%
Chromium: 7.75%
Manganese: 0.30%
Molybdenum: 1.60%
Silicon: 1.2%
Tungsten: 1.10%
Vanadium: 2.4%
Wear resistance: highest
Toughness: high
Red hardness: medium
Distortion in heat-treating: low
Forging: 1,800 to 1,900 °F
Austenite forging: yes
Hardening: 1,550 to 1,600 °F
Quench: oil
Tempering: 300 to 500 °F
Rc hardness: 62 to 58

CHAPTER 3 ————————

Fire and Forge

Of the four elements, air, earth, water, and fire, man stole only one from the gods. Fire. And with it, man forged his will upon the world.

Anonymous

The bladesmith's fire is the means by which he can heat the steel to its plastic state; therefore, the type of fire, the fuels used, and the tending of the fire is crucial to the smith. It is this fire, its building and maintenance, that should be mastered first.

Many of the problems can be avoided by the use of the proper fuels. Charcoal (not the briquettes you use in the barbecue) was the original blacksmith's fuel. Though it is a good, clean-burning fuel, which works well, it is scarce and expensive. If you can obtain some, by all means use it. (For more information see the section on stainless steel in Chapter 4.)

The fuel most often used by today's bladesmith is blacksmiths' coal (also known as soft or bituminous coal). Soft coal is composed of carbon, 55 to 65%; moisture, 2.5 to 3%; sulfur, 1 to 2%; and volatile matter, balanced.

Coal is usually sold by the hundred weight (generally with a considerable savings if a ton or more is ordered). The majority of coal supplied comes in egg-sized chunks, which will be broken up into thumbnail-sized pieces as the fire is being tended. Don't worry if there are smaller pieces and some dust. These are called "fines" and play an important part in the building of the fire.

As coal burns, the volatile matter and sulphur are released and burn away, leaving what is called a "clean" fire. When this matter is released, a dense amount of smoke and soot accompanies it. Steel forged in a fire such as this can absorb sulphur and other impurities, weaken, and otherwise become damaged.

After the impurities are burned away, the fire is composed primarily of burning carbon. This material is now known as coke or "breeze." A coke fire is a clean-burning fire and is ready to be used in the forging processes. (While some commercially made coke is available, most of it is unsuitable for forge work due to its makeup. It burns far too quickly and requires a larger air blast than does coal, and hence it can cause excess oxidation of the steel.)

You will know when the fire is ready to work in by (1) the lack of the yellowish smoke, and the absence of all the billowing clouds of black smoke; (2) no yellow flames coming from the fire; and (3) the steady reddish-yellow glow of the embers. This is a "clean fire," but it will not impart all of the impurities that a freshly lit or "dirty fire" will.

THE BLADESMITH'S FIRE

It is said that one can learn a lot from how a bladesmith keeps his fire. This is true. If you have a good fire, one that is burning clean with good fuel, you will be able to do better work than you would if your fire were dirty. It is this fire that presents one of the greatest dangers in bladesmithing. An uncontrolled fire is a dangerous fire.

Fire Safety

Remember that you are working with a potentially hazardous fire, so always be cautious when at the forge. Never reach over the fire; always reach around it. Keep plenty of water near at hand, and always wear natural 100 percent cotton or leather clothes when you are working. Always wear eye protection.

Wearing hightop leather safety shoes or boots, with the pant legs outside, will help to prevent any hot iron from slipping down inside your boot. (I had this happen to me once and I really danced around. Boy, did it hurt!)

Also have a fire extinguisher within reach. In actuality, a forge fire is no more dangerous than a home barbecue, but the potential is ever there for a serious mishap. Be prepared for the worst — then if anything does happen, you can keep damage to a minimum.

The best kind of flooring you can have in the shop is old, seasoned concrete. If you do not have a concrete floor, suitable flooring can be made by sturdily framing the area with two-by-six lumber on edge and filling the enclosure with a mixture of clay and salt. If you water the clay/salt mixture and pack it down solid, it will set as hard as a rock. Don't worry about the scale and soot falling on the clay, as it will be ground in and help harden the clay. An occasional watering is all that is needed as maintenance.

Do not try to forge on a linoleum or a carpeted floor. Hardwood flooring is also dangerous as it is highly flammable and prone to scorching if hot metal is dropped.

A safe and effective method of dealing with the hot clinkers and burned-out fuel from the fire is to keep a metal trash can available with approximately six to eight inches of water in it. This water will cool the hot material and will allow its removal to another container (metal with a tight lid) after the day's work is done. Be sure to stir the ashes in the water from time to time just to be sure they are out.

Do *not* place the ashes or clinkers in a plastic container because any hot material can melt or burn through the container.

The Fire

There are two types of fires used in coal forges: the *closed* fire and the *open* fire.

A closed fire is built in an igloo arrangement with a hollow center which is heated from the coals all around. Some smiths use this kind of fire to weld in and for fine work. In the open fire, the coals form a bed and the iron is placed onto the bed to absorb the heat. This type of fire is used for most general forge work. The open fire can also be used to weld in, though it takes more experience to discern when the welding temperatures are reached than with a closed fire.

Starting the fire is easy—keeping it going is another story. To start, clean out any and all debris from the last fire. Take some green (unburned) coal, form a ring of coal around the tuyere, and place a few good-sized lumps on top of the air grate. Crumple some newsprint and place it on top of the lumps in the center of the ring. Put some kindling wood on top of the paper and ignite the paper. After the paper catches fire, start the air blast slowly and steadily until the kindling is aflame. When the wood has a good start, place some additional green coal on top of the fire and turn the blast up a bit until the coal ignites. You will know when the coal has started by the appearance of yellow smoke and the sweet aroma of the burning coal.

If you are making an open fire, add more green coal to the bed until you have a fire that suits your needs. It is a good idea to sprinkle a little water on the fire from time to time as the fire develops to help remove the impurities from the fuel. Do not add too much water as this can extinguish the fire. You can dampen the coal before you add it to the fire, though I recommend that you do this only once the fire is going.

You will need to break up the coal in the forge since it has a tendency to congeal into a solid mass while burning. You can do this by turning the fire over the forge and breaking up the masses into thumb-sized pieces. An open fire is easy to maintain and not difficult to clean and tend.

To make a closed fire, start out the same as you would with an open fire, but sift the fines (fine bits of coal and coal dust) from your coal before you start. I use a screen made from quarter-inch hardware cloth (screen), as any larger pieces of coal will hinder the fire building.

After you have the fines separated, mix them with enough water to make a paste with the consistency of cake frosting. This slurry will harden and form the "igloo" of the closed fire.

When the bed of coal is going well, but not yet to the clean fire stages, place a piece or two of two-by-four lumber on top of the coal bed, in the center of the fire. Then start to heap the slurry over the two-by-four until it is completely covered with a coating about one-and-one-half inch thick, and turn up the blast. The slurry will steam, release impurities (including a lot of sulphur) and harden. And as the wood burns away, it will leave a cavity within which you will be able to forge without difficulty.

I have had good results with using two-by-four pieces six to eight inches long. Do not try to stack any more than two pieces, as an igloo cavity any larger will collapse.

Tending The Fire

The fire will eventually burn down from the green coal into coke, burn at its best for a time, and then slowly get dirtier and go out. You can prolong the process by adding fuel and removing the *clinkers*.

Clinkers are a big pain. They are formed from the ash, iron scale, coal impurities, and flux (if used) residue that are the products of forging. Clinkers cannot be prevented, so they are something that you'll have to learn to deal with.

Clinkers look much like dark glass, and stick to hot metal. They form at the bottom of the fire around the air grate, and can inhibit the air blast. The clinkers must be removed as soon as you suspect that they have formed. If the blast has been cut down, or if glassy globs of stuff are stuck on the metal, then clean the fire.

You can distinguish a clinker by the glossy luster and darker color. Use the poker or fire tongs to remove them. If you choose to leave them in, the clinkers will get imbedded into the surfaces of your work, cause your welds to fail, and cause many other problems. You will be surprised at how big they can get and how easily they are removed once you are adept at finding them.

In the open fire, the only way to get at the clinkers is to dig them out of the fire, rake all of the coke back into a heap, and continue to work. In a closed fire, you will be able to dig them free from the grate and remove them without much difficulty.

To add fuel to an open fire, take wet coal and place it on top of the bed, in the back of the working area of the forge. As it burns clean, rake it into the working area of the fire. Do not add green coal directly into the working area as this will dump all of the impurities of the green coal into the fire that you just burned clean.

To add fuel to a closed fire, add to the bed of coals inside the igloo. To do this, just throw some small pieces into the opening and push them back into the igloo in an even bed, allowing them to burn down into coke. To add the igloo, gently spread more slurry around the outside of the shell. You will need to sprinkle some water on top of the igloo to keep the coal from burning through and caving in.

As the closed fire ages, you will notice that it will have a tendency to cave in slightly. When this occurs, just take a little more slurry and gently add it to the depressed area on the outside shell of the cave, building up the sides if needed.

As long as you keep the fires clean and clinker-free, your work will be easier and the results better.

Do *not*, at any time, throw water into the forge to extinguish the fire, unless there is an emergency. In doing so, you will cause the grate to crack or shatter, produce a vast quantity of scalding steam, cause electrical shorts and the refactory to explode, or cause any number of problems.

To properly shut down a forge fire, turn off the blast, open the ash dump (to prevent any gas buildups that may cause an explosion), and clear away any flammable items. In a few minutes, the fire will be out. It will still be hot enough to burn you if you are foolish enough to poke around in it, but the fire will extinguish itself.

When the forge is shut down, shovel the coal into the water-filled trash can, stir well to make sure that the hot material is extinguished, and cover the can with the lid.

HEATING THE STEEL

There are three different parts of a forge fire. The first is the *oxidizing* layer, which is directly above the tuyere where there is an excess amount of free oxygen. The steel, when placed here, will have a tendency to lose carbon, scale heavily, and burn more readily.

The second layer is the *neutral* layer. This is in the center of the fire and is the best place to position the iron for the majority of forging operations.

The third layer, known as the *carburizing* layer, is on the top one-third of the fire. You can add some carbon to the steel by placing the iron in this section, but this is not a wise thing to do as the steel can absorb impurities as well.

Usually, the hotter you get steel, the more plastic and malleable it becomes. But this is not the case with most of the high-carbon tool steels you will be using. If you get the steel hotter than the red (cherry) color ranges, you will notice that the steel may start to fragment into small pieces that look like cottage cheese. This characteristic is called *red-short* (wrought iron is prone to the red-short effect).

The color ranges that you will be working with will be in the cherry-red range of between 1,500 to

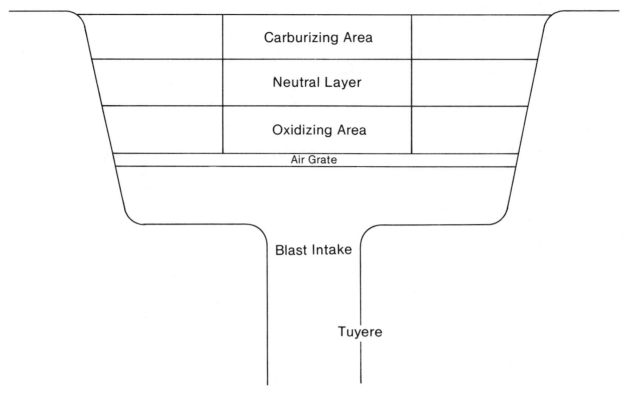

Fig. 18. Forge fire diagram. The characteristics of the fire vary, and depending on where the blade is placed in the fire, carbon can be added or removed from the surface of the steel. The neutral section in the fire's center is the best place for almost all forge work.

1,800 °F. Most of the carbon steels that you will be using have a workable temperature range within these colors. (Note: These colors are as seen in semidarkness, not bright sunlight. Bright light can throw you way off toward the upper end of the ranges by making the heated steel appear less red than it truly is.) No matter what the case, never attempt to forge steel that is below a red heat. You will cause undue stresses and cracks to form within the crystalline structure of the metal. These stresses occur when the steel is in the blue-brittle ranges. This temperature range is within the oxidizing color range of 300 to 700 °F. When in this state, the steel is extremely brittle and easily subject to shock. You can shatter the steel with a hammer impact. (For the oxidizing color/temperature ranges, see Chapter 6.)

It is important that the steel be brought up carefully through the blue/brittle range and into the forging range, as it is easy to cause internal cracking by placing a cold bar into the raging inferno of the forge. After the steel is to the proper temperature, it is ready to work. Always heat the steel in the center of the fire while the heat is gradually increasing. Remove the steel from the forge while the blast is still on, and the steel is still heating. In so doing, you are helping to prevent some grain growth.

It is a simple matter to become accustomed to the color ranges you will be working with; nevertheless, check the temperature tables in Chapter 2 just to be sure.

Iridescent Color Ranges

°F	Color/Comments
1200	dull red
1400	red
1500	cherry red
1600	full cherry red
1800	orange (cutoff point for forging most tool steels)
1900	orange yellow
2000	yellow
2100	(top temperature range for 440-C stainless steel)
2200	full yellow
2400	light yellow

You should never forge carbon steels above the cherry-red/orange color ranges unless specified by the steel's specifications. (It is a good idea when in doubt to experiment on a scrap piece of steel to test the color ranges that you can work in.)

BASIC FORGING PROCESSES

The basic forging processes are pretty much the same for all blades. The *drawing-out, tapering, shaping, packing* and *annealling* techniques are used for every blade that you will forge.

I strongly urge the beginner to start out using low-carbon mild steel to learn the basics. By doing so, you will prevent problems that may arise while you are learning the proper color ranges. It really is an easy task to forge a blade, and I feel that forging gives the steel a life of its own.

In my opinion, stock removal is just taking a bar of steel that is as thick as you want and wide enough to accommodate any curve that is in the blade, and grinding the blade out of that bar. Sounds rather boring, doesn't it?

Forging a blade is altogether different. You take a plain bar of ''lifeless'' metal and create in it a ''soul'' through the fires of the forge. You hammer it to your will, shaping and refining it to the way you feel that it should be. In other words, *you* are actually creating a tool unique unto itself, through your labor, sweat, and will, instead of a dead bar of ground-away metal. It's true, you will be grinding away some metal from the blade, but you will only be refining the shape and bevels you will be hammering in. I feel that through this labor not only is a superior blade made, but its own individuality is assured. Through forging you are freed from the limits that the size of the steel seem to impose upon you, as you will see for yourself.

You must approach forging with an attitude of creating not only a blade, but working a little bit of yourself into each blade that you make. (Believe me, each one will cut you.) Smithing is hard sweaty work, but it can be a highly enjoyable and educational experience.

Getting Started

With the fire burning clean and the steel at the proper forging temperature, you are ready to start. The first step is drawing-out, or lengthening a piece — keeping it the same width while reducing the thickness and making it longer.

To draw out a piece of steel, first place the flat of the steel on the anvil. With a cross peen hammer, strike a series of blows with the peen across the bar, creating a groove. Form an array of such grooves down the length of the bar. Make sure that the grooves run perpendicularly to the direction in which you wish to lengthen the bar. Hammer these grooves close together, reheating the steel as many times as required.

After you are finished, flip the hammer over and use the face to hammer the now-grooved surface smooth. In doing this, you have spread out the surface area with the peen and are leveling the surface smooth with the face. You will be surprised at how much the metal has stretched.

This process is used in forming tangs, lengthening steel that is too thick, widening stock, and just about anything else that you wish to do. It can be done on the flat or the edge surfaces of a bar. You will have some slight spreading on the width, but this is easily controlled by hammering with the face of the hammer on the piece being held edgewise on the anvil.

Since you are actually stretching the steel, you can cause a curve in it by only peening along one side of the bar and flattening the peens. The steel will curve away from the edge being worked. (This is a good way to forge heavily curved blades.)

You can also draw out by placing a bottom fuller into the hardy hole and driving the steel down into it, and flattening. Both work, but it is easier to just use the peen.

To widen a bar, use the drawing-out technique, but align the peen grooves parallel to the length of the bar.

Upsetting a piece is simply increasing the thickness or width of a bar. This seldom has to be done, but it's convenient to know how to do if the need arises.

Heat the very end of the bar and place it vertically (hot end down) onto the face of the anvil. Strike medium-heavy blows on the cold end. If the piece starts to bend, straighten it immediately. Before returning the bar to the fire for the next heat, it is a good idea to hammer a very slight taper into the upset end as this will help to center the steel and prevent bending. After three or four heats, you should have a considerable amount of steel at the end. You will, of course, shorten the bar a bit by doing this, so this must be taken into consideration when working.

To taper a bar, start at the very end and strike at an angle toward the end. On flat stock, hold the bar edge up and strike the bar with medium blows. You will have to alternate striking on the edge and flat to keep the bar from folding over. You will notice that the cross section of the tip is thickening, so you will need to draw this section down with the cross peen to keep the thickness uniform.

Tapering is used in forming points, tangs, and anything else that needs to be tapered.

A *right-angle bend* is rather easy to accomplish and

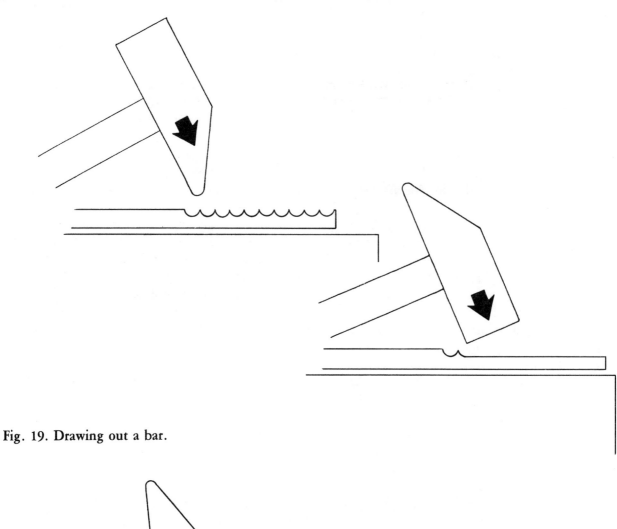

Fig. 19. Drawing out a bar.

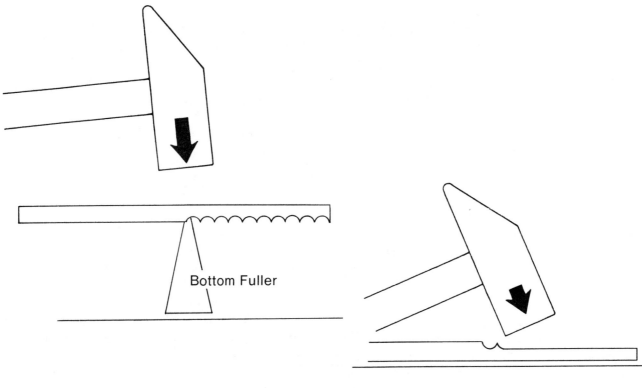

Bottom Fuller

Fig. 20. Drawing out a bar using a fuller.

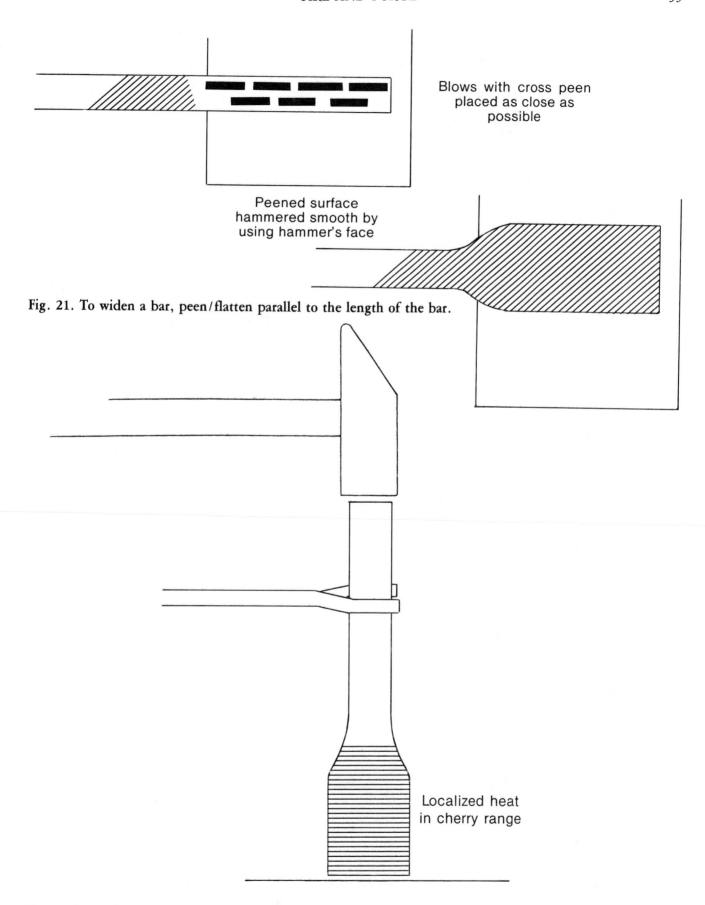

Blows with cross peen placed as close as possible

Peened surface hammered smooth by using hammer's face

Fig. 21. To widen a bar, peen/flatten parallel to the length of the bar.

Localized heat in cherry range

Fig. 22. Upsetting a bar (increasing its width or thickness)

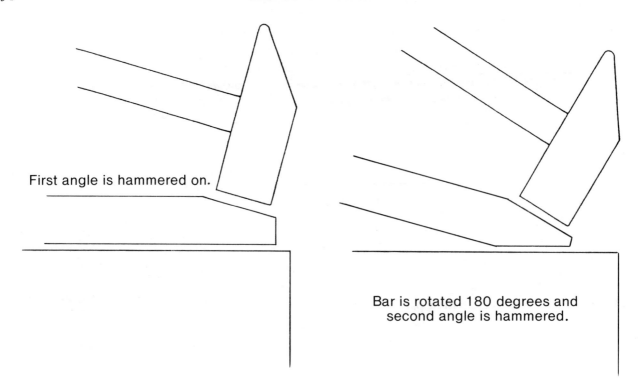

First angle is hammered on.

Bar is rotated 180 degrees and
second angle is hammered.

Fig. 23. Tapering, or pointing, a bar

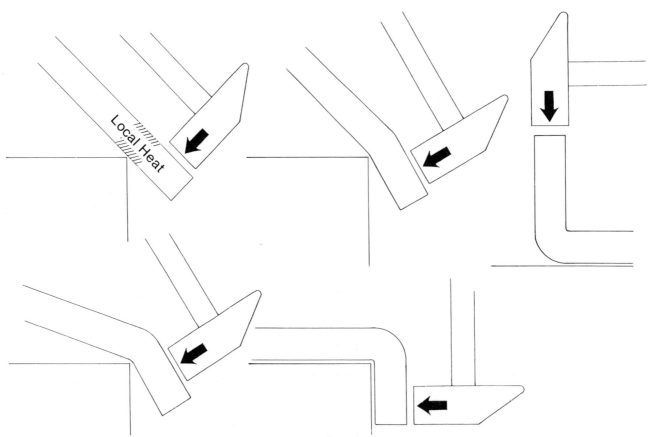

Local Heat

Fig. 24. Ninety-degree bends: Work the bar over the edge of the anvil until the bend is well formed. To tighten
the bend, place the bar on the anvil surface as shown and strike the upright ''leg'' until the bend is tight. Do not
strike too hard, or the bend will fold in upon itself, ruining the piece.

quickly done in one or two heats. Make a local heat in the area of the bar you wish to bend and place the center of the bend over the (rounded) edge of the anvil. Using a light hammer, start striking the bar down to the side of the anvil until you are swinging the hammer like a pendulum. When this is completed, strike the bar on the hammer face to ''tighten'' the bend into a sharp 90-degree angle.

Sometimes the stock that is available only comes in round bars. But you can flatten a round bar into a rectangle by forging. First take a heat (heat the steel) and hammer the round into a flattened oval (cross section). Do this for the entire length of the bar. When finished, you will have flat and parallel surfaces on the bar. Next, you will be working on squaring the rounded edges by striking the bar edgewise on the anvil with the flat face of the hammer. Alternate between striking on both edges and on the flat of the piece.

You can now draw out the piece to the required length or width by using the cross peen and hammer face. You will be surprised how large a piece a round bar will forge out.

From time to time, you may need to cut a piece off a bar, using a technique known as *hot cutting*. This is easily done by using either a hot chisel or a cutoff hardy.

Using a hot chisel is an easy task. You simply mark where you need to cut the piece (a piece of soapstone does well, and the mark will not burn off) and return it to the fire. At a light-cherry heat, cut through the metal with the hot chisel. Care must be taken to cool the chisel often (in water, after every few hammer blows) to prevent it from becoming overly hot and

losing its hardness. Also, as you are getting closer to cutting through, it is wise to lighten the blows to prevent the cutoff piece from flying, or damaging the edge of the chisel.

It should be mentioned again that all chisel/cutting operations should either be done on the anvil pad or on a scrap piece of soft iron plate resting on the anvil's face. Never use a chisel (or any sharp-edged object) on the unprotected surface of the anvil's face. Any scars, nicks, or dings you put into this surface will be transferred to the surface of the piece on which you are working.

Using the cutoff hardy is also easy; in fact, in many ways, it is easier than chiseling. Mark the piece on the opposite side than the surface you wish to cut. Place the cutoff hardy in the hardy hole in the anvil face. Return the piece to the fire and remove it at a light-cherry heat. Place the piece that is marked side-up on top of the cutoff hardy with the mark directly over the edge of the hardy and strike the piece down on top of the hardy until you are almost completely through. Now take a brass hammer (to prevent damage to the hardy) and finish cutting through the piece using ''shearing'' blows to one side of the hardy's edge. I suggest that you strike these shear blows on the loose end of the piece (the end being cut off) as this will prevent the piece from flying off and about.

These are the basic procedures used in forging a blade. They are not difficult, but they do require practice. You will use these techniques quite often for most of the blades you will make. This is especially true with the tapering and drawing-out processes.

CHAPTER 4 ————

Forging Blades

Before you start to forge a blade, you must have an idea as to what type of blade you are going to make. The types of knives that are in use today are basically grouped into the following categories:

Hunting/skinning knives are usually single-edged, with a point or trailing point. Blade lengths run from three to five inches or more. The edges are somewhat curved convexly (sometimes referred to as the belly) to allow the maximum effect to the slice with the minimum of effort. The best edge is fine and narrow, but not delicate or flimsy. The primary job here is for the edge to remain very sharp, and to slice and cut, not chop. A hollow or very fine flat grind will be the best for this type of blade.

Utility knives are also called "camp knives" and are very similar to the hunting/skinning blades. They are usually single-edged, sometimes with a swagged-back edge, and tend to be a bit thick and heavy due to the type of cutting required. Utility knives are not as curved as the skinners. These are multipurpose blades and should be ground a bit thicker than the skinning/hunting knives.

Fighting knives run the line of single, double or single/false-edged blades. Blade lengths run from four to nine inches (or longer) in any number of shapes and designs. Included in this heading are bowies, daggers, shortswords, and other nonsporting designs (including the so-called "survival knives"). Most of the fighting knives made today are hollow or flat-ground and can be quite heavy. They are rugged in their construction and are built to take heavy use and abuse.

Art knives are some of the finest blades ever crafted. This group of knives includes some of the most wierd, poorly designed, and downright useless knives one can imagine. The extremes that are represented under this heading are quite evident. Usually the art-type of knife is not ever meant to be used and is a collectible. The art knife is an opportunity for the maker to go all-out in design, finish, and embellishment, to see exactly what he can accomplish on one given blade.

Swords. Exactly where the term knife leaves off and the term sword takes over has been pretty vague. It seems to me that any blade over eighteen to twenty inches is a sword. Be it a simple broadsword, claymore, or rapier, the making of a sword is quite different from the making of a knife, and presents its own problems. Every bladesmith should at one time in his life undertake the task of forging a sword. It can be a very enriching and humbling experience.

In evaluating the design of a knife, you must not look at just the blade, but the overall function of the entire knife. Will the blade use all of its cutting edge when slicing? Will it be easy to control for delicate jobs or is it only for rough cleaving/chopping work? Will the handle be comfortable to hold? There is no replacement for good design. A wood model is a good way to test your designs before they are made in steel. The time you spend refining your designs will be well spent and can prevent design errors that cannot easily be corrected on a finished knife.

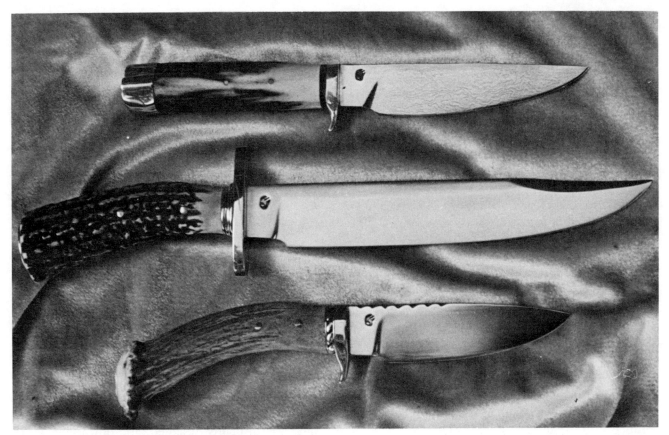

Fig. 25. Three knives by Sean McWilliams: a utility/cam knife (top), a traditional bowie (middle), and a drop-point hunter (bottom) — all with stag antler grips.

Besides the overall design of the blade, you must also consider the type of grip construction which you are going to use. There are three ways of attaching the grip on a blade and each has its good points as well as its bad.

The *full-tang* handle is perhaps the strongest of the three. This handle has the blade material forming the center of the grip for the entire length and width. It is sandwiched between two (or more) pieces of wood, horn, or other material with all the pieces pinned and glued together in such a way that the steel is visible. The majority of custom blades made today are of full-tang construction. The full-tang is also the easiest and quickest to forge since the only heavy forging and shaping to be done is to the blade.

The *hidden-tang* grip is structured in such a way that the tang is smaller than the blade and passes completely through the grip material (it is completely covered by the grip). It is a good alternative to the full-tang construction, as when properly constructed it is a very strong grip that shows off the beauty of the handle material on all four sides.

The *partial-tang* handle is the weakest of the three and has a very poor reputation in knife circles. This handle has a small stub tang riveted (or cemented) into an opening in the end of the handle material. Most of the commercially available kitchen cutlery is made this way. When properly constructed, with quality materials, the partial-tang knife can be quite a rugged design. A case in point are the Japanese samurai swords and Indo-Persian shamshirs (scimitars), which have grips made after this fashion.

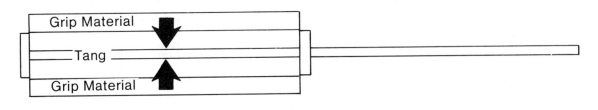

Fig. 26. Full-tang construction

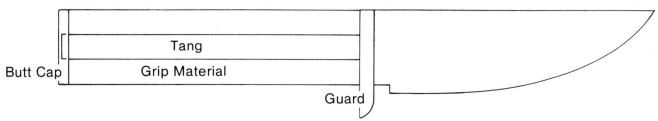

Fig. 27. Hidden-tang construction

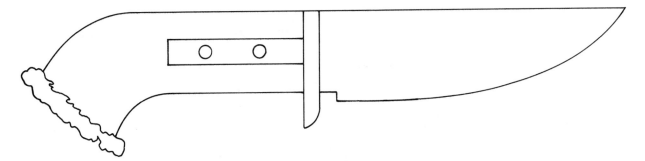

Fig. 28. Partial-tang construction

This method is best of the three for use with stag antler and other naturally curved handle materials.

As you can see, keys to a strong handle are proper materials, good workmanship, and design. All three grip attachments can be used to their fullest and produce some very beautiful and rugged grips.

EXECUTION OF THE DESIGN

One great advantage that a bladesmith has over a stock removal maker — unlimited design capabilities. You are not limited to working within the boundaries imposed by the sizes of the steel bars. You can shape and form blades that cannot be ground from a bar either in cross section or profile. The bladesmith can give a progressive temper and have the edges of the blade cutting hard and the back soft. It will be you, and not some steel mill, that will decide as to what shape you will be able to give your creation.

Let your imagination run wild and experiment with different designs and types of blades. Try some of the older designs as well as the new. Keep yourself informed as to what is being done by others and feel free to ask questions of other bladesmiths.

Forging To Shape

The question arises as to how far down to forge the edge on a blade. Usually a reduction in thickness of 50 to 80 percent is sufficient to fracture the crystalline structure into a tighter pattern and enhance cutting ability. The more you thin the blade through forging the better, and the less you will have to grind away.

On the other hand, the more you forge down the thickness, the less cross section you will have to play with when you start grinding out the decarburization, hammer marks, and pits. As you get better at forging, the thinner you will be able to forge a blade. I usually heat-treat after forging and profiling as I can take the edges down to about a sixteenth of an inch or so of thickness.

THE SINGLE-EDGED BLADE: HIDDEN TANG

To forge the single-edged blade with a hidden tang, start out with a piece of high-carbon steel nine-by-one by one-fourth inch or so. This should make a knife with a six-inch blade and a four-to five-inch handle.

Heat the first two inches or so to a full cherry-red in a clean fire, place the hot steel on edge on top of the anvil, and draw out the tang. You will need to alternate between sides and flats to keep the thickness uniform. Make the tang about one-half inch wide at the blade end and taper to one-fourth inch at the end.

If you are using a partial-tang design, such as a stag antler grip, you will do the same basic techniques as with the full-hidden tang but you will not be making the tang as long. You should make it as long as possible so you will be able to have a secure grip attachment.

When finished with the tang, draw out the point of the blade by using the hammer face. You will notice that the edge held down upon the anvil will be straighter than the edge struck by the hammer. Use

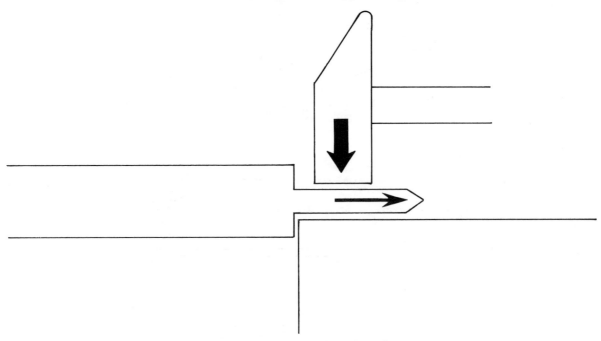

Fig. 29. Reduce the width of the tang by striking the steel on its edge.

the hammer strikes to give the blade a "belly" curve to the point. The straight edge will become the back of the blade. Alternate striking on the edge and flat as required to keep the cross-section thickness uniform. Also alternate use of the cross peen and hammer face as needed. When you are satisfied with the blade shape, reheat the entire length and go on to the next step.

If you wish to make the blade wider, now is the time to do so as you can readily refine the shape of the blade. In order to widen the blade, strike with the cross peen in line (parallel to) with the length of the blade. Strike from the blade edge and work back toward the spine. You will be accomplishing two steps at once. You will be widening the blade and starting the edge bevels in one step. (This is the same basic operation as drawing out except that you will be widening the piece instead of lengthening it.)

After the profile shape is completed, place the blade edge down on the anvil horn and bend it

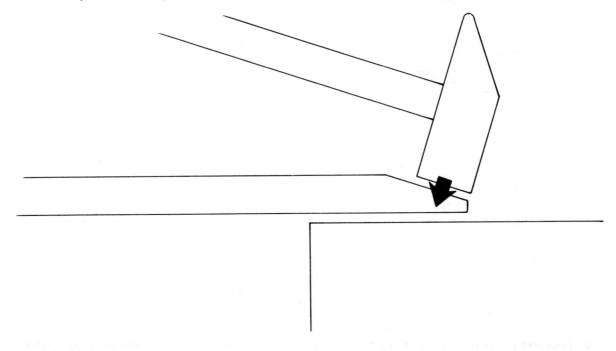

Fig. 30. Pointing and profiling

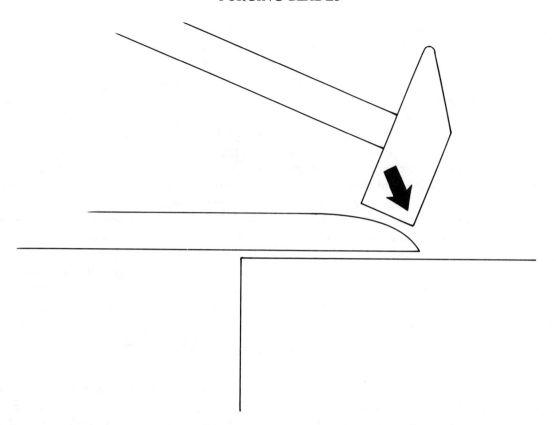

Fig. 31. Use slightly forward/down-glancing blows to work the belly curve into the blade.

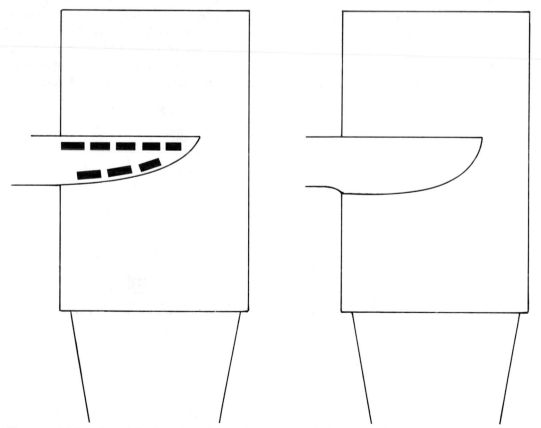

Fig. 32. Hammer blows for widening the blade: Strike with the cross peen so that the peen runs parallel to the edges of the blade. Flatten the peened area with the hammer face.

widthwise into a curve (so the edge is on the *inside* of the curve). The reason for this is that when the bevels are hammered onto the blade, the hammered edge will stretch and cause the blade to straighten out. Just how much of a curve is up to you, and experience will make this step easier to judge. Right now it's hit or miss.

You are now ready to bevel the blade and *pack* the edges. Place the heated blade with the cutting edge on the outside of the anvil's edge. Hold the blade flat and, using the cross peen, strike along the *inside* of the curve in an even pattern the length of the blade. Keep count on the number of blows you strike. Flip the blade over and repeat the process using the *same* number of blows. (Note: By using the same number of blows, you can help to minimize warpage and refine the grain structure.) When finished, flatten the surface with the hammer face. The blade should have straightened considerably.

It is this edge packing that gives a forged blade its superiority over a ground piece of steel. This packing should be done at a lower heat than the rest of the forging, below the critical temperature of the steel that you are using. This low-temperature packing will fracture the crystalline structure more, giving a tougher and sharper blade.

Try to keep the blade as straight and as flat as possible. A good way to test for straightness is to place the blade onto the anvil's face and look for gaps between the anvil and the blade. Looking down the edge is another way to detect waves and bends. If required, you can reheat and straighten almost any problem bend that you have.

After you are through with the forging and are satisfied with the blade's shape and straightness, heat the entire blade to an even dull-red heat and let cool slowly in a pile of sand or ashes. This annealling will help relieve any stresses that may be built up within

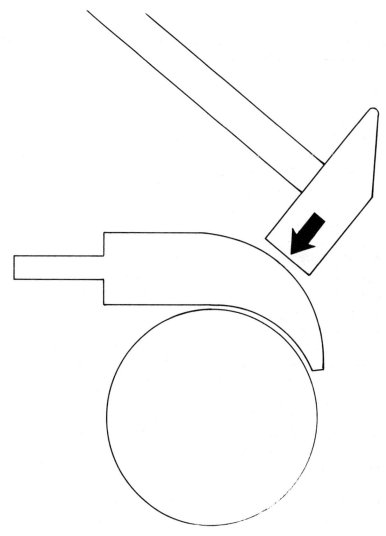

Fig. 33. The blade must be curved *into* the cutting edge so the steel, when compressed, will straighten the blade out to its original shape.

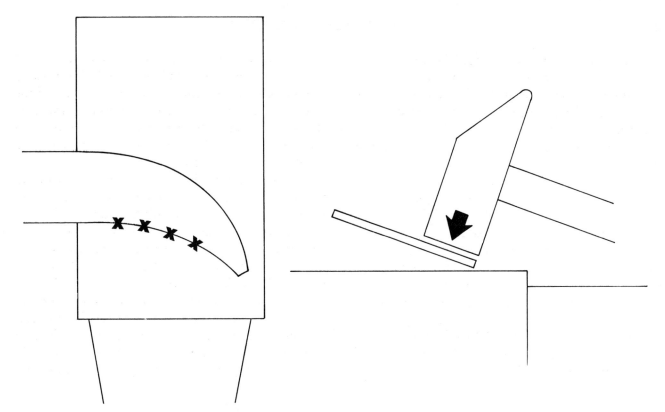

Fig. 34. Place hammer blows along the inside edge of the curve while holding the blade at an angle to the anvil surface. Alternate sides so each side gets the same number of blows.

the steel. It also allows for easy filing and refining of the shape.

When the blade is cooled, it is ready to be ground to final shape and the rough grinding started.

THE DOUBLE-EDGED BLADE: HIDDEN TANG

Forging a double-edged blade with a hidden tang is somewhat more difficult than a single-edged one. Start by drawing out the tang and pointing the bar.

When this is accomplished, do not curve the piece as in the single-edged blade; instead, go directly to forging the bevels. Place your blows on alternate sides of the center of the bar and use the same number of blows on both sides. Be sure to overlap and place your blows evenly so a center ridge is formed as you work the blade. If you do not create the center ridge, you will cause the blade to curve and wave. When you are finished on one complete side, flip the blade over and do the other side. On a double-edged blade, you will need to cant the blade at a small angle to allow the hammer to do its work. Make sure that the forged side is flat on the anvil surface so that the flats will be forged in properly on the side on which you are working.

It is extremely important that the number and placement of your blows are identical on both sides of the spine and on each side of the blade. This will help to keep the internal stresses within the blade even and prevent warpage and stress buildup during heat treatment.

After the edges are beveled, straighten and anneal the blade in the same manner as a single-edged blade.

FORGING THE FULL-TANG BLADE

A full-tang blade is easier to forge than the hidden-tang design since you will spend far less time on forging out the tang. All you have to do on a full-tang blade is profile the tang to the shape you wish; otherwise, the techniques are exactly the same for the forging of the blade. As for the handle area, this is a different story. You will want to forge the profile of the grip a little on the large side. In this way, you will have some excess steel to remove on the grinder in case you make a slight error in your forging. Remember that once the steel has been removed, it can't be put back, so be sure to leave more material on the tang than you think you'll need.

If you would like a tapered tang, you can do the tapering with a hammer using the cross peen hammer face, or you can file or grind the taper in. However, it would probably be faster if you simply grind the

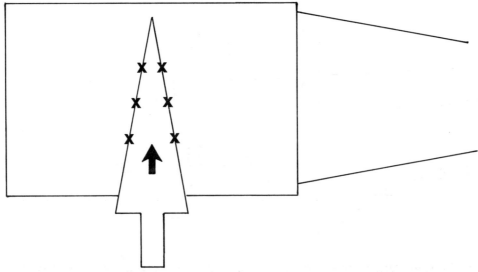

Fig. 35. Work from the ricasso area . . .

Fig. 36. . . . and pack both sides by alternating edges on the anvil surface as you work the blade to the tip.

taper into the tang. Also take into account that if you do forge the taper into the tang, any other curve you put into the grip area will affect the thickness of the steel in the area of the bend. This effect will be a thickening on the inside of the curve and a thinning on the outside of the curve. Of course, you can remove any excess, evening the thickness on the grinder.

After you are through with the forging of the blade, no matter which design you use, you will need to anneal the blade to normalize the stresses that have accumulated within the blade during the forging processes.

To anneal, simply place the blade *on top* of the fire and let it heat to a dull blood-red. This temperature is below the critical temperature of the steel. Let cool slowly and then continue to work on the blade.

As you can see, you will be able to expand your present ideas into more elaborate and difficult designs as you get more adept at the forge.

FORGING A SUPERIOR BLADE

There is a process that is seldom used nowadays in forging called austenite forging or ''aus-forging.'' In this process, you are working the steel under its critical temperature, in the narrow temperature range between the hardening temperatures and the blue-brittle ranges. In doing this, you will be fracturing the crystalline structure without any of the grain-enlarging that the next heat would produce if you were doing the standard higher-temperature forging.

This low-temperature forging is a lot of hard, time-consuming work, but it will make a superior blade. Aus-forging works well with almost all of the steels you will be using, especially air-hardening steels like A-2 or D-2. See the section at the end of this chapter for further details on forging air-hardening steels.

You will need to know what the critical temperature is for the steel you are using and its upper limit in the blue-brittle range. Most of the working color ranges for this type of work is dark to dull cherry-red. Hence, your working time is limited and the metal will not move as readily as when it is worked at the hotter temperatures. Do not be surprised if you have time for only three or four hammer blows with each heat before the metal cools. You will also have to strike harder than normal to move the same amount of steel, as it will not want to move

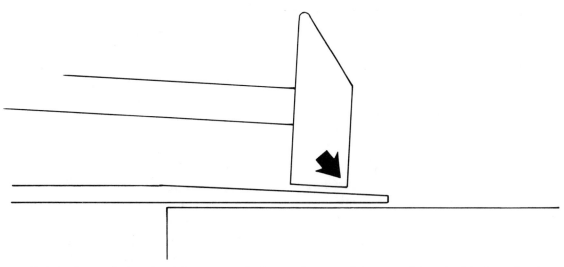

Fig. 37. Use slightly forward glancing blows to push the steel out and away, making the blade end thinner. Start tapering from the end and work toward the ricasso.

under the hammer.

As long as you are working in the low temperatures, you have to be careful that the steel does not drop below the dull-red range. If it does and you strike the steel, you can crack it.

If you do not wish to forge the entire blade at this lower temperature, you can get similar results by edge-packing with this technique.

I was told about aus-forging by an old blacksmith from Germany years ago. This man forged cutlery for the German Army and has had fifty years of experience in forging blades in the Solingen factories. At first, I was a bit skeptical, as his English was limited and I speak no German, but then I tried aus-forging on my own and found that it worked.

Forging Air-Hardening Steels

The air-hardening steel alloys are forgeable in two temperature ranges: the low range *under* the critical temperature and the upper range above the critical temperatures.

When forging these alloys, remember that at no time when you are working in the higher ranges should you let the steel cool below the critical temperature as it will harden and crack as you are working it. Keep the steel glowing in the bright-cherry range (above the critical temperature) as you are working, and remove it from the fire while the heat of the blade still increases. This way, you can be somewhat certain that you are not working the steel as it is going through the hardening processes.

During the austenite forging process, never let the steel get to the critical temperature (or above), or you will have the same hardening problem as with the high-temperature forging.

Work in the dull cherry-red ranges to complete the low temperature forging, and do not let the steel cool into the blue-brittle ranges while you are working. If you do get into the hardening temperature ranges, do not work the steel. Instead, return it to the fire and turn the blast down to anneal the steel; start forging over again.

You will find that the aus-forging process works especially well with D-2 tool steel, which is a very good steel, overlooked by a vast majority of bladesmiths. When properly forged, this steel will out-perform almost all other alloys (save vasco wear) in terms of cutting ability and edge-holding.

Hard-To-Forge Steels

Though they respond differently under the hammer and do not seem to want to move as well, M-2, vasco wear, D-2, A-2, 154-CM, and 440-C are all forgeable. The key to successful forging of these materials lies in the temperature ranges, which are in the fully cherry-red range. These steels work best when not forced into submission, but worked slowly.

The major problem of these high-alloy steels is that they are prone to cracking and grain separation. This cracking and separation problem is brought about more from poor forging than the alloy itself. Do not force the steel to shape by using heavy blows. These alloys are not in the least bit forgiving and will take three to five times the amount of time, effort, and skill to forge into a blade.

The best way to work these resilient steels is slowly and carefully. Keep the steel within the cherry-red ranges when working, or you will ruin the steel.

Any misplaced hammer blows can result in disaster, with the steel cracking or breaking up. The weight of the hammer is another important factor. Use a five-pound hammer if possible as it will do the same amount of work on these alloys as a three-pounder will do on high-carbon steel.

Care must also be taken in forging the bevels and packing the edges as these are the areas most likely to fracture and crack with such steel. Work them slowly and with well-placed blows.

You can, of course, use the low-temperature forging on these steels as well, but the labor involved will be considerably more than that spent on most other blades. These alloys will make a very good blade when austenite-forged.

These hard-to-forge steels will give a very durable and long-lasting edge, though they will be a bit on the brittle side. Due to this brittleness, they are best used for blades under ten to twelve inches.

Forging Stainless Steel

Forging the various stainless steels presents different problems than forging the other high-carbon steels, namely the working temperatures and the fuels used.

While you can use coal/coke as a fuel, you can easily poison these steels as they have a tendency to quickly absorb any impurities that are present in the fire. You can circumvent this by using a clean-burning fuel, such as hardwood charcoal, the original fuel used by the blacksmiths of antiquity. It is a very clean fuel that burns hot and quickly. It is not as widely available as coal, but it can be found.

Charcoal is the partially burned remainder of wood, usually maple, oak, or ash, that has had the majority of the volatile material (resins and tars) burned out, leaving a burnable carbon. This material should not be confused with the barbecue briquettes used for cooking, which burn away far too quickly and produce vast amounts of fine gray ash.

As charcoal burns, it consumes the carbon, leaving a light ash that in no way harms the metal. This ash can, in fact, aid in welding as it will form a flux and help to remove any impurities in the weld. Since the fire burns quickly, the ash produced is in no way harmful and there are none of the impurities of coal to deal with. You can add fresh fuel as needed to the fire without any time delay.

Start a charcoal fire in the same manner as a coal/coke fire. Get the kindling lit and add the charcoal on top of the fire. As the charcoal catches, add additional fuel until the volume is great enough with which to work.

As for fire maintenance, you will need to remove some of the ashes from time to time, dump the ash trap, and add additional fuel as needed. With charcoal, there are no clinkers to worry about clogging the grate, sticking to the work, or dirtying the weld. If you are unable to locate any charcoal and you do not have the facilities, time, or inclination to make your own, a *clean*-burning coal fire will suffice.

Forging A Stainless Blade

Stainless steel doesn't move under the hammer as well as high-carbon steel, as it has a tendency to feel harder when it is in the working temperature ranges. This characteristic is called "red hard." This red-hardness is brought about by the alloy's contents and its intended use in industry.

Since the red-hard characteristic is something you have to learn to deal with, work slowly and with well-placed hammer blows. The crystal structures of stainless steel are much the same as high-carbon steel, and many of the techniques used for high-carbon steel will work for stainless steel.

Another effect of the red-hardness is the higher forging temperatures that are typical of stainless steels. I strongly suggest that you do the majority of the forging at the higher full-cherry red temperatures and do the final forging/edge-packing at the lower aus-forging temperatures.

There is also a strong tendency for cracking to occur while forging the stainless-steel alloys at the recommended forging level specifications. 440-C is especially prone to this cracking due to its chromium (16 to 20 percent) content. Work this 440-C at a bright cherry-red, and do not try to stretch this steel beyond its limits.

As far as 154-CM (ATS-34) is concerned, the cracking problem is not as severe, though it can still occur at the higher temperatures. This alloy is also a little more forgiving in heat-treating as it doesn't seem to warp as much as 440-C. These two alloys (440-C and 154-CM) are the standard steels of the stock-removal knife makers, but they are good forgeable steels.

The mill specs suggest that you forge these steels at 1,950 to 2,100°F. However, I have found that the steel at these temperatures will have a tendency to crack and have grain separation occur at an alarming rate. Work these alloys slowly at a full cherry-red and you will have fewer problems than if you worked at a higher temperature.

The more you work high-carbon steels, the better. Not so with some stainless alloys. Though they can be very prone to grain enlargement during heating, they do respond well to forging (so well, in fact, that a properly forged and packed stainless blade, such as alloy 440-C and 154-CM, will perform like a high-carbon blade in the cutting and edge-holding ability).

MAKING CHARCOAL

If you cannot find hardwood charcoal for forging your stainless steel, you can make your own without much difficulty. You will need a supply of hardwood, the best of which is maple, ash, or oak (though any other readily available hardwood will do).

Once you have the wood, it should be cut into one-by-one inch strips, six to ten inches long. You will also need a heavy metal container with a tightly fitting cover.

Start a fire with the hardwood in the container and add fuel until the fire is going well. After the fire has burned the wood to a solid black color throughout, cover the container to put the fire out. You can tell when the wood is reduced by removing a piece or two, extinguishing it, and breaking it in two or three pieces. Be sure to do this out in the open and away from any flammable materals.

Let the container stand covered for two to four hours thereafter to be certain that the charcoal is no longer burning. Remove the charcoal to another metal container and wet it down. Let the charcoal dry and you are ready to use it as fuel.

You will need at least twice the charcoal to accomplish the same amount of work that you would do with a coal/coke fire. This can be a disadvantage to those who cannot find ready-made charcoal and have to make their own. It is not difficult to do, but it does take practice, patience, and experience.

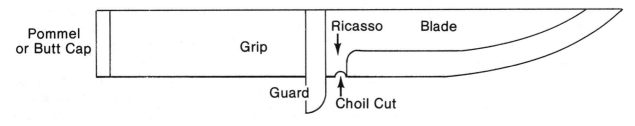

Fig. 38. Diagram of a knife

CHAPTER 5 ———————

Rough Grinding

One of the more important steps in the production of a blade is refining the profile and grinding the edge bevels. A properly ground blade is one with a continuous, uninterrupted edge to the end of the bevel without flaws or breaks in the grind angle. This proper technique is acquired through patience, practice, and a steady hand.

Rough grinding serves to remove the unwanted hammer marks from the visible portion of the blade. Most of the unwanted steel will be removed in the rough grind. The blade blank must be fully annealled before starting to grind to allow for easier grinding and less stress buildup within the steel.

There are four generally accepted types of ground edges that are used in blade making today. Each type has its own strength and weaknesses. They all will serve to make a good blade, but it is the maker's decision as to which one to use.

THE HOLLOW GROUND EDGE

The *hollow ground* blade (concave edge) is perhaps the best choice for "slicing only" blades such as skinners, hunters, filet knives, etc., as the edge is very thin and will take to sharpening quite easily. It is somewhat fragile when compared to the other three grinds, and it is not a very good idea to deeply hollow-grind a blade that will be used to chop through bone, wood, or armor. The majority of blades made today are hollow ground.

This grind style is an old style, dating back to circa 1200 A.D., or so. The hollow ground produces a light

and strong blade that takes a very sharp edge easily. It was used for some of the European broadsword blades, but the grind was very slight, almost flat in the concaves on the edge bevels.

Fig. 39. Cross section of a hollow, or concave, ground blade.

THE CANNEL GROUND EDGE

The *cannel* edge (the convex or "apple seed" edge) is an excellent choice for heavy-chopping blades such as swords, axes, cleavers, and anything else that will be used to hack through various and sundry items such as bones, wood, and backyard jungles.

The cannel ground makes a decent edge, and will hold it for a long time. It is rugged since the edge is backed by a heavy cross section, and will tend to be heavy when finished. This is a very old grind, as it was the edge used on the European broadsword for centuries. It is not a very difficult grind to master once you understand the idea that the whole blade will have a nice rounded surface.

This grind will not sharpen to the super edge that a hollow ground blade will, but it will take an edge and hold that edge practically forever.

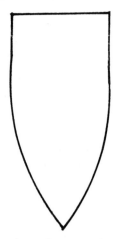

Fig. 40. Cross section of a cannel, or convex, edge.

THE FLAT GRIND

The *flat* grind is the "happy medium" between the hollow grind and the cannel grind. This grind is what I use for most of my blades. It will take an excellent edge that will withstand chopping and still retain its cutting ability. It produces a medium-weight blade that will sharpen easily. The only real drawback is that this is a rather tricky grind as the edge bevel has a tendency to be "flaw prone."

The flat grind has been used by most of the iron-working cultures from the early years of knife making. This is perhaps the best general-purpose grind as it gives strength to the edge without adding too much weight to the blade.

You can also achieve a flat-ground blade by hand filing the bevels instead of using a grinder. The Japanese used a tool similar to a draw knife (a wood-working plane) to scrape away the unwanted material while they worked on their sword blades, with great results.

THE CHISEL EDGE

This edge has been used to edge swords and knives in some parts of the world. It is used today for carpenter's axes and wood chisels. It is a very specialized type of edge, as it will leave a dead-straight cut on one side of the cut surface. It can be a very sturdy and usable edge when properly made. It doesn't take a superb edge, but the blade will be serviceable. The chisel edge is best suited to tools and utensils.

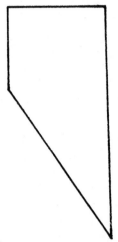

Fig. 42. Cross section of a chisel-edged blade.

PROFILING THE FORGING

Profiling is refining the shape of rough forging until it meets your satisfaction. The amount of material removed will vary, but it is usually quite small when compared to the amount of steel being wasted if you were using the stock-removal method of knife making. If you are removing a good amount of material, then you haven't fully forged the blade to shape. Be mindful of the fact that ten minutes in a forge equals half an hour on the grinder.

Use a coarse belt on the grinder or a file to do the final shaping. The lines should be exactly the way the blade is supposed to be in its final form at this point (except for the edge bevels being ground and finished), and no additional work should be expected on the shaping of the blade.

Since the blade has been annealed, there is no reason to worry about overheating the steel and ruining the temper.

When you have forged the final shape of the blade, you are ready to proceed to the rough grinding.

Fig. 41. Cross section of a flat ground blade.

The Flat Grind

You will be using the flat platen on the belt grinder to remove the hammer marks on the blade bevels until a very smooth and even surface is obtained on the blade.

First refine the shape of the rough forging and remove all of the forge scale from the blank. Use a sharp, coarse (fifty grit or so) belt. Mark the center of the edge with a scratch-awl so you can tell when to stop grinding. You should stop grinding when you are approximately one thirty-second of an inch from this line, on both sides of the blade.

Second, start the belt tracking slightly to the left edge of the platen and start to grind the blade with the cutting edge up, left to right (from choil to point). You will need to start at the same place for each pass on the grinder. As you make each pass, the area nearest the handle will have a tendency to grind away quicker than the rest of the blade. To correct this, let up on the pressure a bit when you are working this area.

It is important when you first start a bevel to maintain the same angle on the blade for the first few passes so a flat surface is formed from the grinding. This is not difficult to do as the bevels that you have hammered in will help you "feel" the flat surface as you are grinding. Do not rock the blade while focusing on the bevel or you may start a different bevel and throw off the grind.

When starting out, there will be a tendency for the blade to "dig into" the off-edge of the platen. This can cause a deep line to be ground across the blade at the point of contact. To prevent this from happening, make sure the pressure is even and steady across the entire surface of the belt.

If you need to bring the edge thickness down, place the blade flat against the belt and add slightly more pressure along the edge of the blade, keeping the flat in contact against the belt.

If you need to bring the grind back toward the center or spine of the blade, place the bevel flat against the belt and slightly add pressure along the back part of the bevel.

Continue with the even passes until the bevel is flat, smooth, and as high as you wish on the blade. You can vary the angle of the bevel by positioning the blade against the belt.

You will need to cool the blade every now and then. Get in the habit of periodically quenching it while grinding it so you will not have to worry about overheating the blade after you have heat-treated it.

When you are satisfied with the bevel and are for all intents and purposes finished, reverse the process and do the other side. You will, of course, be working from the right side of the grinder with the belt tracking along the right edge of the platen. You will be working edge up, right to left, from choil to point.

If, by chance, you are doing a double-edged blade, it is better to do both bevels of each edge (different sides of the blade) than to try to get both bevels on the same side done. (If you choose to do both bevels on the same side, be advised that this can cause warpage of the blade while you are grinding.)

You will want to mark both choils for the plunge cut so they will be even and oriented straight across the edges.

Continue to grind until both sides of the blade are ground. Be careful around the choil as it is very easy to grind away too much metal. This will cause a little wave in the grind line which looks terrible in the finished product.

I strongly suggest that you leave this area thicker than the rest of the blade, just getting them close, and then going back over them to line them up and even them off after the rest of the blade is finished being rough-ground.

After the blade is rough-ground, take the blade and run it along the flat of the grinder point-down so the grinder marks run parallel to the edge (not across it). This will help to prevent any stress cracks from developing along the edge.

A flat-ground blade is far more difficult to obtain than a hollow-ground one, for the hollow will guide the grinder along the blade.

Hollow-Ground Blade

The hollow-ground blade is the most commonly ground blade style in use today. It is the standard grind used by the majority of commercial and custom cutlery manufacturers. When properly done, it will leave a blade cross section that will lend itself to taking a very keen and easy-to-maintain edge. This edge is the most delicate of all the edges and lends itself more to slicing and cutting than to chopping and heavy cleaving.

To start the hollow-ground blade, you will need a wheel that is at least six inches in diameter on your belt grinder, though an eight- to ten-inch wheel is better. A larger wheel makes a larger hollow across the blade that is wider and a bit shallower than that effected by a smaller wheel. This wide hollow is easier to control, and you will not have a tendency to grind the center of the hollow too thin as in a smaller wheel.

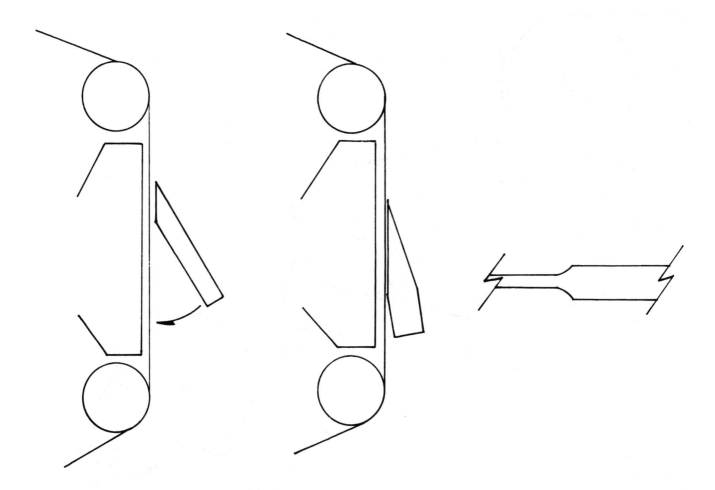

Fig. 43. Flat grind: (Left) Rotate blade edge up into the platen to form the edge bevel. This will also widen the bevel as you decrease the angle against the belt. (Center) Repeat the process on the opposite side, holding the same angle as on the first bevel, until the two bevels are identical. (Right) Edge view of plunge cuts and ricasso/choil area. These cuts must be even and matching for best results.

Start the grinder with the belt tracking to the left and start with the edge up, from choil to point. Make sure that you have already marked out the center of the edge.

Place the center of the blade into the wheel and "hog" out a center groove the entire length of the blade, from choil to point.

You will then start back at the choil and rock the edge into the wheel a bit. Keeping the wheel in the previously cut groove, take another pass. Repeat this process over again until you come into the inscribed line. You must be careful not to grind into the blade too deeply as it is quite easy to make the center cross section far too thin or to even grind right through the blade. This sounds difficult to do all at once, but it is easier than it sounds.

When you are finished with this side, flip the blade over. With the belt tracking slightly to the

right, start to grind the new side. As you get the feel of grinding, you will be able to tell by touch that you are holding the blade at the same angle for each pass on the grinder. When the blade is finished, even up the choils and grind the edge in order that the lines are parallel to the blade.

Cannel Grind

This is the easiest grind to do on a blade. There are no grind lines to worry about, and no real flaws can be made. This type of grind has been referred to as a "poor" flat grind and is in no way similar to a flat grind.

The idea behind doing a cannel-ground edge is to have two gentle arcs, one on each side of the blade, coming together at their ends, forming the cutting edges. This is easy to do, especially if your belt grinder has a slack area of the belt.

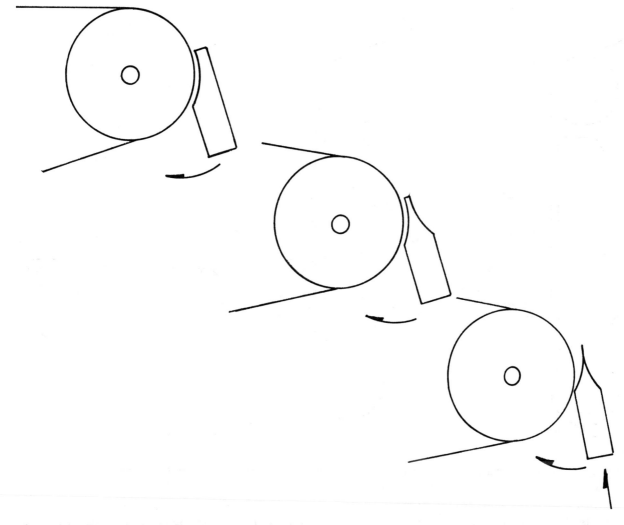

Fig. 44. Hollow grind: (Left) Rotate blade into the contact wheel edge up to form start of the hollow. (Center) Repeat the process on the opposite side of the blade until the bevels are even. (Right) To widen the edge bevel, simply move the blade up and into the wheel, causing a new radius to be cut on the back part of the original bevel.

Start the grind by marking the center of the edge and then, starting form the choil working edge up, grind a bevel to the point. You will want to make a series of "steps" in the grind, each one a little shallower and farther in toward the center of the blade. You should be using the flat platen or one of the contact wheels. When you are done, do the remaining edges so the blade will appear to be faceted and flawed.

When both sides of the blade are completed, start on the slack section of the belt, taking the entire length of the blade across the belt in one pass, the idea being to round the straight areas of the previous ground areas into an even arc. This is not as difficult as it sounds and is quite quick to do.

As you can see, there isn't that much difficulty in grinding. Everyone has some problems when they first start out, but all it takes to get through the steps is practice. Remember to keep the grind lines straight and the choils/plunge-cuts even and straight.

Chisel Edge Grind

The chisel grind is simply a flat-grind bevel from the center or back of the blade, ground only on one side to an edge. This is done exactly the same way as the flat grind except that there is only one bevel ground to the edge instead of the usual two.

Hand Filing the Bevels

You can also form flat or convex bevels by filing them in by hand. This is time-consuming and involves a lot of hand labor to accomplish. You will need to use a good quality single- or double-cut file and a lot of room to clamp the blade down to the table.

Start the filing with full-length strokes on the

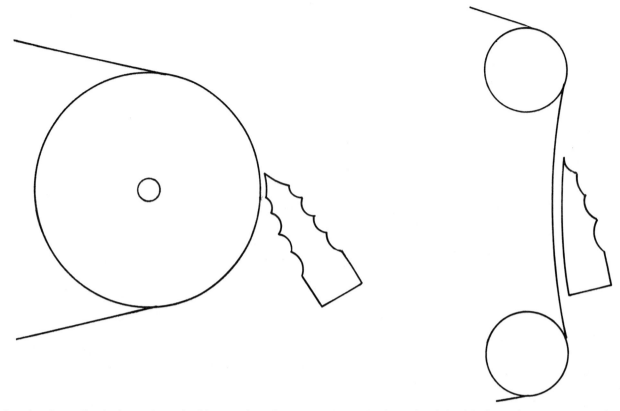

Fig. 45. Cannel grind: (Left) Grind in a series of grooves along the length of the blade, using a contact wheel to rough form the cross section. (Right) Using a slack belt, smooth out the surface and finish the cross sectional shaping.

blade, trying to maintain the angle that was originally forged into the blade. If the file isn't cutting, then anneal the blade and try again. It is important that the steel be dead soft, as a file will not cut hardened steel, but will quickly dull to the point of uselessness.

The full-length strokes can remove a lot of material quickly as long as the file is kept clear of debris. A file brush will remove any clogged steel from the file teeth. If allowed to remain in the file teeth, the steel shavings from the blade can dig in and gouge deep scratches into the surface of the blade that are difficult to remove by hand.

Use the same number and length of strokes on each side of the blade to keep the edge spine centered on the cutting edge. Also be careful not to impale your hand on the point, which can easily happen if you slip while filing.

Using a file is the "old way" of grinding, and it does take considerable time to do. The more work you can do in the forge, the less you need to file away. Regardless, be prepared to spend a long time at

this, and expect sore muscles as well.

No matter which grind you choose to do, the majority of the shaping of the bevels can be done while forging. Forging the bevels not only cuts down on the amount of grinding, but also on the volume of metal that is to be removed, so you will be saving materials and time.

A flat-, chisel-, or cannel-ground blade can almost be finished on the anvil as the bevels are 90 percent formed if properly forged. A hollow-ground blade is a different matter. With the "hollow" edge, you will need to remove a bit more steel (30 percent or so) than on a flat-ground blade. Each grind has its own strengths and weaknesses which should be taken into account when deciding on what type of edge will be made on what blade.

All in all, once the blade is profiled and rough-ground (whether it's by hand-filing or machine-grinding), it is ready for heat-treating and tempering.

CHAPTER 6————

Heat-Treating

Once a blade has been forged, annealed, and rough-ground, the next logical step is the proper heat-treatment and tempering of the steel.

There are many myths about secret processes, ingredients, and such involved in forming a blade in the lore handed down from times long past. Maybe they are based on fact; maybe not. Regardless, a blade must be hardened and then tempered properly to be able to perform its intended function.

The processes involved in the heat-treating of a blade are very simple: you heat the blade to the proper temperature, quench it in the proper medium, and temper the hardness back to where it is not too brittle, but still hard enough to hold the edge. Sound easy?

Before you attempt to harden the steel, remember the type of steel of which the blade is made and what its hardening temperature range is. For most carbon steels, these temperatures are in the red-color range. Check the tables for which steel you are using. Knowing your alloy's hardening and tempering temperatures is the most important part of the hardening/tempering process (if you are going to use a piece of steel of which all you know is that it's a high-carbon steel, use pieces of scrap to experiment with first).

What causes the hardening of steel?

The basic ingredients in steel are iron and carbon in the form of carbide crystals. It is this carbide content that plays the most important factor in the hardness and edge-holding abilities of the steel.

In the annealed state, the carbides (often called cementite) are enveloped within the iron matrix. When heated to the proper temperature, the carbides start to melt and dissolve into this matrix. This state is referred to as *austenite* (it is sometimes referred to as the *critical* temperature as well). Once the steel reaches the austenite stage, it is ready to be quenched. This sudden cooling causes the carbides to form needle-like structures in the crystals called *martensite*.

In the martensite state, the steel is its hardest, as it is under a great deal of internal stress and quite brittle. In order for the steel to be usable as a blade, it must be softened to reduce the brittleness to a workable degree. This process is called tempering

The tempering processes will remove some of the stress by breaking down the martensite into *troosite*. This removes some of the hardness as well (tempering is actually a controlled form of annealling). Knowing the proper tempering colors for a given alloy is an important factor in the heat-treating of a blade.

THE HARDENING PROCESS

To harden the blade, bring it through the oxidizing colors slowly and into the iridescent range. This prevents the steel from becoming "shocked" and possibly cracking. This heating should be done in a very clean fire with a slow and steady blast. It is best to place the blade in the fire edgewise, not on the flat, as this will help to prevent warpage. Turn the blade over every now and then to prevent a curve from being warped-in by the expansion of the metal.

The proper color to harden most carbon steels is a full cherry-red (check the alloy specs). The color/temperature should be even along the entire cutting edge(s). As soon as it is, remove the blade from the fire and quench it point-first (vertically) into the quenching bath. This should be done quickly and carefully so as not to cause any warpage, twisting, or cracking.

There is another way to tell if the steel is hot enough to harden properly, and that is by using a magnet on the surface. If a magnet doesn't stick to the steel, it is at the proper hardening temperature. This has something to do with the iron matrix and carbide crystals. It works and is relatively foolproof.

After the blade has cooled, remove it from the bath and wipe it clean. Most of the fire scale will have fallen off from the hardened portion of the steel. It should be a nice steely gray color.

You will be able to tell when the blade is cool enough to remove from the bath by watching the oil. After the flame-up is out, the oil will be moving in and around the area of the blade. This convection is caused by the heat from the blade and appears in the form of little ripples and eddies on the oil surface. When the convection ceases, count to thirty seconds, and remove the blade from the oil. It will be cool enough to remove from the oil without damaging the hardening process, but use caution, as it may still be too hot to handle bare-handed.

If you are using an oil-hardening steel, there will be a flash fire when the steel is first immersed in the quenching bath. If you totally submerge the blade below the surface of the oil, this fire will usually self-extinguish. If it fails to do so, simply cover the oil and the fire will burn out. Some bladesmiths have a CO_2 fire extinguisher that they spray into the quench tank to displace any oxygen and hence prevent a flame-up.

A word about the quenching medium: If you are using a water-hardening steel, it may harden satisfactorily in a light oil bath. Experiment with scrap pieces before you attempt to harden a blade. Never attempt to harden an oil-hardening steel in water unless it is pattern-welded; otherwise, the steel will crack or shatter upon quenching. Be certain the container the medium is in is nonflammable, heat-resistant, and deep enough to totally cover the entire length of the blades to be hardened, plus six inches.

To check the blade's hardness properly, apply the file test, trying to cut into the blade with a steel file. If the blade has been properly hardened, the file should just skate off the surface with no cutting effect.

After hardening, the steel is very hard and brittle. If it is dropped, it may shatter upon impact. In this state, the blade will hold an edge for a very long time, but it won't be tough or serviceable as a knife.

Note that care must be taken so that the blade does not remain at the critical temperature any longer than required to get the temperature even about the cutting edges as the following problems may result:

Decarburization: When the blade is heated to the iridescent colors, the carbon on the surface of the blade will quite often combine with the free oxygen in the fire and burn off. The longer the blade is hot, the more carbon is lost. The result is easily seen on the surface. A blade that has started to decarburize will have a somewhat "marbled" appearance on the surface. (This is not a problem as this surface is ground away in the final grind.)

Grain Growth: Another problem caused by heat and time is the grain or crystal growth of the steel. While forging, the crystalline structure of the metal is fractured and the grain growth is retarded by the impact of the hammer (causing the grains to fracture into smaller crystals). Once the heat-treating process is started, there are no retarding impacts and crystal growth resumes unhindered.

The larger the crystal structure, the weaker the steel becomes. The sooner the blade is quenched after the proper temperature is reached, the better. The grain growth occurs very quickly; after only a few moments, the enlargement of the crystals starts. To prevent any problems, quench as soon as possible after the heat is even.

These problems are lessened if you keep the time the metal is at the critical temperature to a minimum.

THE TEMPERING PROCESS

With the blade now at full at-quench hardness, you are ready to remove the brittleness (along with some hardness), by *drawing-back* or tempering. There is a trade-off with hardness as the tempering can draw the hardness down to a point where the blade will be super tough but far too soft to hold even a semblance of an edge. Knowing where to stop with the temper is very important.

The blade is first cleaned to a bright and shiny surface using a 80- or 120-grit belt.

Hold the cleaned side of the blade up *above* the fire, and watch. You will notice that it remains a clean and shiny bright steel color for a period of time. It will then progress through the oxidizing color range as below:

Color	°F
No color change	200
Pale yellow	300
Bright yellow	350
Straw yellow	400
Dark straw yellow	425
Brown	450
Purple	475
Violet	500
Dark blue	525
Bright blue	550
Blue-gray	575

The above colors are only a general guide since the temperatures given are approximate. These colors will work on the "simpler" alloys of sixty to 100 points carbon.

The color at which you quench depends upon the type of steel you are using and for what purpose the blade is to be used. I suggest the following tempering colors:

Most cutting blades: bright-yellow range. This will allow some flex in the blade with good edge-holding. Good for hunters, fighters, and general-duty blades.

Chopping blades: dark straw/brown range. This will allow some additional flex with a good edge. Good for fighters, bowies, and general-duty blades.

Swords and heavy chopping blades: brown range. This temper will allow considerable flex with the proper alloy of approximately sixty points carbon. Use it for the really big blades where flexibility and shock resistance is most important. Good for swords, really big bowies, meat cleavers, and axes.

Spring steel: blue range. This is used for super tough springy needs such as rapiers and lock-back springs.

When the desired color is reached, quench the blade to stop the tempering process and, if the blade is single-edged, clean the blade once more and draw an additional temper to a dark blue only along the back of the blade by holding the blade spine down to the fire. (In properly doing this, the toughness of the blade will be greatly increased without sacrificing any hardness along the edge.) If everything is done correctly, the spine should be dark blue and the edge should still be the same color as when you started.

It is a good idea to practice the hardening, especially the tempering process, on a piece of scrap of low-carbon steel. It does take a bit of time to learn the colors and temperatures, and any time given to this will be well spent indeed. Remember to check the tables as to hardening and tempering temperatures.

Another technique is used for single-edged blades that involves the heating of a piece of cast-iron pipe placed on the surface of the forge, with the curve of the pipe forming a hollow. The pipe is allowed to heat up, and the blade is then drawn across the pipe, along the blade's spine until the desired edge color is reached. The thermal conduction of the steel will place a progressive temper in the blade with the spine being softer than the edge. This will work only with a single-edged blade.

If you wish, you can temper in your kitchen oven (be sure to let the blades bake for at least two hours) and do the drawing-back on the spine with the oxyacetylene torch. I strongly urge this when stainless steels are used for the blade as they do not always oxidize properly and can cause problems.

After the blades are done baking, run the oxyacetylene torch along the back of the blade to draw the hardness out. This works especially well when the edge is held down into a cold-water bath while the torch is being used.

Feel free to experiment thoroughly with the heat-treating and tempering processes as you may hit onto something that really works well for you.

Air-Hardening Steels

Air-hardening steels like D-2 and A-2 are not difficult to heat-treat. When the blades reach their critical temperature, remove them from the fire and let them air-cool. You can get better results if you hit them with a blast of compressed air. Warpage will be minimal due to the fact that the steel will not be shocked and placed under all of the stresses that an oil-or water-quenched blade may suffer.

After hardening, draw a temper using the same steps as an oil- or water-quenched steel.

Correcting Warpage

Prevention is the best possible cure for a warped blade. Warpage can be prevented (or lessened) by leaving a thick edge of 0.063 inches or so, annealling properly before the hardening quench, forging evenly, and properly heating and quenching during heat-treating.

As your skill increases in forging, you will no longer need to rough-grind the blade and will be able to heat-treat from the forging. This should help prevent warpage.

From time to time, no matter how careful you have been, blades will warp. Usually the warp is correctable, but sometimes a blade is so twisted that nothing can be done to correct it.

If you have a blade that has a "kink" or two, do not worry about it. After the blade has been tempered, grind both sides shiny, and place the blade in the vise with the "kink" sticking out of it about an inch or so. Use the oxyacetylene torch with a medium-sized tip, and heat a very small section of the center or the spine of blade to the straw/brown range. Torque it in straight. Remove the blade from the vise and quench the blade in the appropriate medium. You may have some heat "bleed" into the cutting area, but as long as it remains the same color as the original tempering color, no damage has been done.

If properly done, you will not affect the cutting-edge, but will have softened a portion of the cross section (that is not all bad as it will toughen up the blade a bit).

You can do this as needed for any blade as long as it is not twisted. A twisted blade (corkscrew) is not easily corrected. The best way to deal with a twist is to reheat the blade to a medium-red color, restraighten, and reheat-treat. This can be done once, and once only, as severe grain-growth can weaken the structure of the blade.

Under no circumstances should you hammer on a heat-treated blade. To do so could crack the steel and shatter it as well. There is no reason to do this, and it will only lead to disaster if you do.

Heat-treating is one of the important differences that forging has over stock-removal methods of blade-making, allowing for a variable temper in a blade. This is where the non-cutting areas are softer and tougher than the cutting edges. This variation on the hardnesses will make a tougher and more resilient blade than one that is hardened all the way through. It is an important step that should be perfected.

HEAT-TREATING STAINLESS

The majority of stainless steels harden in oil. Some, like 440-C, benefit from a subzero quench. All in all, treat stainless like high-carbon and you should not have any difficulty in hardening and tempering.

Heat the steel to a bright-cherry color and oil-quench. Take care that you do not heat the tang/ricasso area as stainless does have a tendency to have

stress cracks in areas of square-cornered joints. If you are not getting good results in the oil, go to a lighter oil in the quench. *Never* quench stainless steel with water. Sometimes the stainless will need a lighter oil than high-carbon steel to harden properly.

Stainless Steels and The Subzero Quench

Some stainless steels require a subzero quench in order to be used to best advantage. While this sounds difficult, it isn't. All that it really requires is a container long enough for the blade to be submerged, enough acetone to fill the container to cover the blade, and about one pound of dry ice.

Break up the dry ice into small pieces and crush (be careful as it is very cold and can cause instantaneous frostbite). Place the dry ice into the bucket and slowly pour in the acetone. Do *not* throw dry ice into a bucket of acetone. It can detonate.

Due to the amount of acetone used and the fumes that will be produced, perform all of the subzero hardening out-of-doors, well away from sources of ignition.

After the ice and acetone are in the container, wait a little while for the dry ice to cool down the temperature.

When the blade is hardened, but not tempered, it is placed into the cold acetone. The blade must be at room temperature and free from the quenching oil. Failure to do so will probably result in cracks or warpage (along with the air turning blue with expressions of dissatisfaction and disgust).

After about thirty seconds, remove the blade. Be sure to use tongs — you do not want to put your hand into the liquid (it will bring new meaning to the word cold). Let the blade warm to room temperature, and temper as usual.

Temper in your kitchen oven. This way you will not be misled by the tempering colors as they can be off due to the contents of the stainless alloy. Oven tempering will temper the blade without relying on a color change as a temperature indicator.

By using this subzero quench with 440-C, you will obtain a few extra Rc points of hardness without any sacrifice of toughness. I have used this a few times and found that there is a difference between a blade that was subzero-quenched and one that wasn't. It does work.

CHAPTER 7

Final Grinding

The final grind is perhaps one of the most important cosmetic steps in the making of a blade, and should be done slowly and carefully.

Actually, there is no great difference between the final grind and the rough grind. The steps are the same, with the only difference being in the amount of steel to be removed and the grit of the belts being used.

The idea behind the final grind is to bring the cutting edge down to a sharpenable thickness and remove the coarser grit scratches with the progressively finer ones until you are ready for polishing either by hand or buffer.

How far down do you take the edge? I suggest that you take the edge down to around ten-thousandths of an inch or so for a slicing/cutting edge. For a heavy-duty blade, about fifteen-thousandths. For a sword on which you will need a lot of edge-backing, I strongly urge at least twenty-five thousandths of an inch. A blade this thick will not take a super edge, but then again a sword really doesn't need to be razor-sharp.

Of course, all depends on the foreseen use of the blade. If you want a really sharp edge, grind the edge thinner; if you want a more rugged edge, grind it less, or thicker.

After the blade is fully heat-treated and tempered, start the final grind. Take it very slowly and cool the blade often. If the blade starts to change colors, you are damaging the temper. You can actually anneal the blade to the point of uselessness if you allow it to

get too hot. The point and the ricasso areas are quite prone to this occurrence. A good rule to follow, to avoid this, is if the blade is too hot to handle, then it's too hot. You can cut down on the amount of heat buildup by using new, sharp belts for the final grinding.

All that you are doing in the final grinding is repeating the rough grind process, cleaning up the grind lines, and making certain that all of the unwanted hammer marks are removed. You can do some minor profile changes as long as the steel doesn't get overheated while you are doing so.

If you grind and prepolish the flat areas of the blade first (riccasso, spine, flats, etc.), then do the same for the bevels. You will find it easier to keep the grind lines sharp and clean.

You should start out with a sharp 50- or 120-grit belt, depending on the amount of material to be removed. Use the coarser belt for heavier removal, and the finer belt if the amount of metal to be taken off is slight.

You will notice that there are few, if any, differences between rough grinding and final grinding. If you are doing a hollow-ground blade, make certain that you are using the same size of contact wheel that you used for the rough grinding or you will ruin all of the work you have so far accomplished.

After the blade is final-ground to the proper edge thickness, the grind lines and all of the surface decarburization are removed, and the final grinding is completed. You are ready to start the prepolish with the 120-grit belt.

After the blade is ground to 120-grit and all of the coarser marks are removed, coat the blade with "Naval Jelly" until it turns gray and then rinse it off.

By etching the blade with Naval Jelly between each grit application, it will be easier to see if you are removing *all* of the deeper marks.

After the 120-grit step, apply a 240-grit and remove all of the 120-grit marks. A word of caution: As the grits get finer, it will become increasingly difficult to maintain the correct bevels; take it slowly and carefully.

When the 240-grit is completed, etch the blade with the Naval Jelly, and go on to a 400-grit until all of the 240-grit marks are removed. There is no need to etch after the 400-grit step.

After the final grinding is complete, the next step is to anneal the ricasso/tang area so it will allow filing of the choil and ricasso/tang.

Use the oxyacetylene torch to heat the ricasso/tang until it turns blue. Be careful around the edge plunge-cuts as there will be a tendency for the heat to "bleed" up the blade, thereby softening it.

After the annealling is done and while the tang is still hot, check to be sure the tang/blade alignment is straight. If not, this is easily corrected, as the steel is rather easy to straighten because it is no longer hardened.

If you are making a hidden- or half-tang blade, cut the shoulders of the tang so they are square and even. Clamp the knife in a vise by the tang and file the shoulders square with a file. Make certain that only the very end of the shoulders are even, as a totally square junction here is very weak and prone to

breakage. A rounded transition is best for these blades.

Next, with a hidden-tang knife, thread the end of the tang. Make sure that when you grind the threaded area that you remove any sharp corners or you will not be able to start to thread the tang, and the die will bind and break off some of the teeth. The diameter of the threaded area will rely upon the thread size you use. The thread size is pretty much up to the individual. I suggest using one-fourth by twenty (see Appendix B) for most knives; five-sixteenths by eighteen for bigger blades and three-eighths by sixteen for swords. Put a slight taper on the starting end to break the corner and to allow for an easier start of the thread-cutting.

When starting the thread, a steady downward pressure must be maintained, and some cutting oil is to be applied to both the tang and the die. When started, do not move the die stock level, and keep the pressure constant as you cut the thread. Let the die do the cutting.

There is no reason to thread an area any longer than one-half to three-fourths of an inch. Daggers and knives really don't need a great deal of threads. Swords, on the other hand, require stronger threads and a little more threaded area as the pommels tend to weigh a bit more because they are quite massive when compared to dagger fittings.

When this is done, move onto cutting the choil(s) out of the blade's edge at the plunge cut. This cutout will be a great aid in sharpening the blade and will prevent the blade from coming to an abrupt halt against the stone when it hits the end of the edge.

If you are making a full-tang blade, all that re-

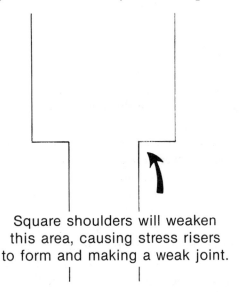

Square shoulders will weaken
this area, causing stress risers
to form and making a weak joint.

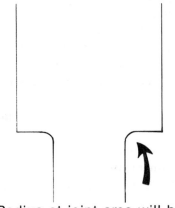

Radius at joint area will help
prevent stress risers from
forming, making a stronger
blade/hilt attachment.

Fig. 46. An example of the differences in tang shapes

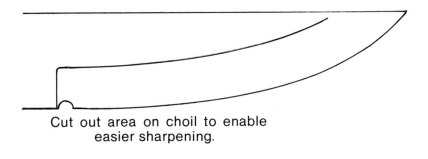

Cut out area on choil to enable
easier sharpening.

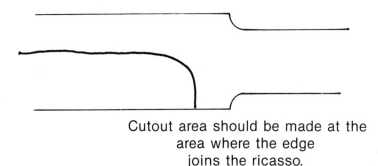

Cutout area should be made at the
area where the edge
joins the ricasso.

Fig. 47. Choil cutout placement

mains is to cut out the choil(s). To do so, use a small round file (one-eighth to one-fourth inch diameter) and cut to a depth of one-half the diameter of the file.

If you are using hand files to do the work, use a sharp single-cut file to do the filing and then go to wet/dry sandpaper in 120-grit wrapped around a hardwood or micarta block to finish the grind out. Use plenty of water while filing as this will float out the gritty material, making the whole operation somewhat easier.

After the 120-grit step is completed, etch the blade with Naval Jelly, and then return to sanding with 240-grit paper on the block. To aid in seeing whether all of the 120-grit scratches are being removed, work the 240-grit at an angle to the 120-grit marks. This will allow you to see the new surface being exposed, and will enable you to know where any additional work (if any) is required.

When the 240-grit is completed, re-etch and start with the 400-grit wet/dry paper until the surface of the blade is shiny and clean. This fine of grit will wear out very quickly and will need to be replaced frequently in order to get the best results. Patience and time are all that's required to do this hand labor. Keep at it.

With the above procedures completed, you are ready to put the finishing touches on the blade.

CHAPTER 8–
Fittings

With the blade final-ground, tang-threaded, etc., you are ready to start on the fittings (hand-guard/bolster and buttcap/pommel).

There are several ways to go about making the fittings. You can either make them from a bar, sheet, or rod of material, or the fittings can be cast, filed, or forged into shape. The final decision is up to the maker. Then again, there are some knives that really don't require a bolster or other fittings, such as some of the full-tang blades like boot knives and hunters.

For a hidden-tang knife, it is best to fit the grip material to the tang before you start to make the fittings, as this way you will be able to burn the grip on-to the tang without softening the joint between the guard and the blade (see Chapter 10 for further information).

In making the fitting for a hidden-tang design, start out with a piece of stock that is a little wider and longer than what you want to end up with. The guard can be brass, bronze, copper, German silver, stainless steel, or just about anything you have on hand and want to use. Just be certain that the material isn't too hard to drill through and/or file or you will not be able to achieve a good fit on the blade.

You will need to measure the tang both in width and thickness. Once you have these dimensions, you are ready to start making the guard.

First you will need to slightly taper the tang behind the blade. This will allow the bolster to be slid up the tang without too much difficulty. (A difference of

five- to ten-thousandths of an inch is about all that is needed.)

The next step is to select the guard/bolster stock and mark a center line along the entire length of the piece. Then mark the length of the slot along the center line of the stock so you know where to start to drill the pilot holes.

After this is done, select a drill that is slightly smaller in diameter than the tang's thickness for the pilot holes. Center-punch two pilot holes (one at each end of the line you drew on center line of the stock) and drill through the material. You will then want to punch and drill the next series of holes between the first two in a way that will slightly overlap the first two pilot holes.

You will need to open the slot by using a small round or square file (a chain saw file works very well for this). When you are able to get a small flat file in-to the opening, you are ready to start squaring up the slot and fit it to the blade. An automotive points file is very good for getting into such a narrow slot.

There will be a tendency for the side opposite the one you are working to be narrower than the one facing you. To correct this, turn the piece around every few file draws. Take it easy and do not remove great amounts of metal or you may remove too much and have to start anew.

Once the slot is squared up, try to slip it on over the tang and see how far up it will go. If it doesn't go all the way up to the ricasso, remove the fitting and continue filing away the sides of the slot and trying to

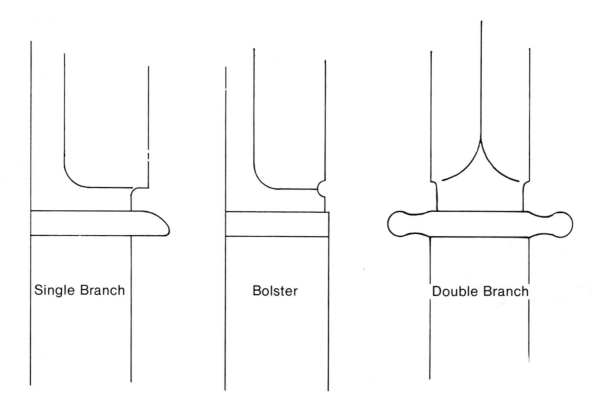

Fig. 48. Various handguards

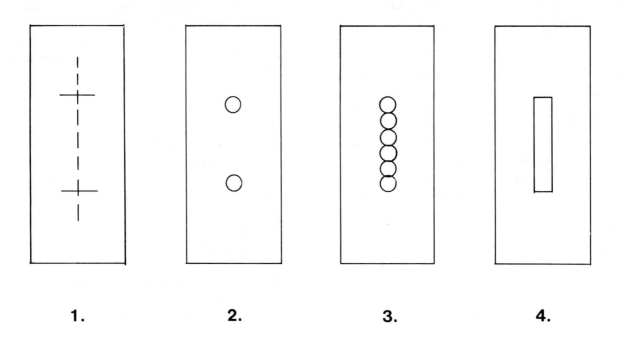

Fig. 49. Slotting the guard: 1. Center line drawn, and tang slot width determined.   2. First two holes drilled.
3. Hole drilling completed. 4. Slot opened up with files.

fit the piece after every few strokes of the file. Be careful that you keep the slot even and as square as possible.

As you get closer to the final fit, you may notice that the tang/ricasso junction is not truly square. This is easily corrected by filing the corners of the junction with a bastard or mill file. Since this area is already annealled, filing it should pose no problem. If by chance you do run across a hard spot, anneal the area again with the torch and let the blade cool slowly.

It is very important that only the area that is in actual contact with the guard fitting be square. A slightly rounded taper from the blade's ricasso to the tang is best. A totally square joint will cause stresses during use of the finished knife to be localized and the blade can easily snap off at this point.

When the final fit of the guard is made, it should be snug, but not too tight. Care should be taken in the fitting so there are no gaps between the two meeting surfaces. A close fit not only looks better than a sloppy one, but it will make it easier to solder and clean up.

Note: A closer fit of the guard can be achieved if you first fit the piece until it almost (but not fully) slides up to the tang shoulders, and then heat the piece to expand the slot so the piece will slide the rest of the way. This sweating-on of the piece will result in a tight "press fit" and will allow for a very small and clean solder joint.

After the guard stock is fitted to the blade, you can either remove it and shape it to your desires, or you can silver-solder it to the blade first and then do the shaping.

Some blades require preshaping work of the guard/bolster while others do not. If the guard does not require preshaping work, polish the blade side of the guard before you attach it in place, then the guard will be easier to clean up and accept the final polish later.

If the design requires a preshaped guard, fully shape and polish it before final attachment.

ATTACHING THE GUARD

If you are going to slide the guard over the tang, you can either silver-solder it, braze it, pin it, or just simply press-fit it on. If you are careful and the fit is extremely close, you may be able to forego the soldering or brazing entirely. If not, you will have to decide which attachment process you will perform.

A low-temperature silver solder has a couple of advantages over brazing. The first advantage is the

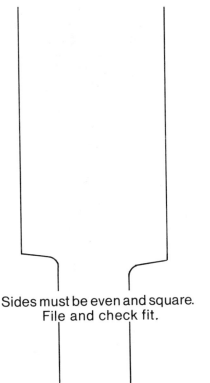

Sides must be even and square. File and check fit.

Check squareness by sliding slotted barstock up to ricasso and levelling the blade in a vise. Remove material as required with files.

Fig. 50. How to correct an unsquare ricasso

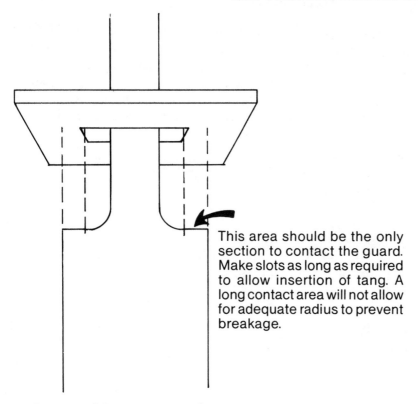

This area should be the only section to contact the guard. Make slots as long as required to allow insertion of tang. A long contact area will not allow for adequate radius to prevent breakage.

Fig. 51. Proper and improper tang/ricasso

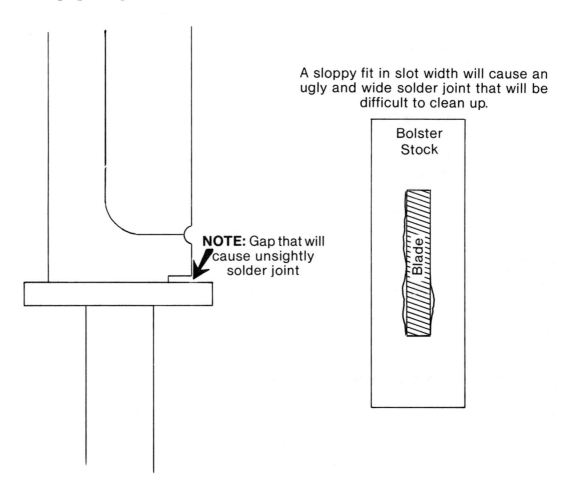

A sloppy fit in slot width will cause an ugly and wide solder joint that will be difficult to clean up.

NOTE: Gap that will cause unsightly solder joint

Bolster Stock

Blade

Fig. 52. A good fit versus a poor fit

lower temperature the solder flows at (430°F vs. 1,600°F for the brazing). This means you will not remove much of the temper in the blade area next to the solder joints.

Second, the solder is easier to do and to clean up afterward.

With brazing, though it will enable you to attach a stronger joint, you risk the removal of the temper of a larger portion of the blade by heat conduction. It is also considerably more difficult to clean up afterward than is the solder.

Of course, you can rivet on the guard by drilling a hole clean through both the guard and blade, then riveting a small brass pin through to secure the two together. I don't like this idea, though some makers prefer this method of attachment over the first two. It seems that the area of the riveting is already the weakest part of the blade, and drilling a hole or two through the blade just makes it weaker.

Low-Temperature Silver Soldering

Low-temperature silver soldering should not be confused with the silver soldering used in jewelry work. In all practicality, the silver solder used in jewelry construction is more along the lines of brazing than soldering. These jewlery solders flow at 1,100°F. Although I imagine that you could use these solders, you will need considerable skill in soldering in doing so.

The low-temperature silver baring solder is available from most knife-makers' supply firms, along with the required flux.

Now that we have said the word on solders, we can get back to the work at hand.

With all of the presoldering shaping of the guard completed, and the guard polished, you are ready to solder the guard into place. First clean the areas to be soldered with acetone. This will remove any oils and compounds from the joint area. Next position the guard on the blade and apply the flux. Use an acid brush to apply the flux, and do not be skimpy with flux. Make certain that the entire area to be soldered is well coated with flux.

Fluxes are basically an acidic solution, so make certain that you are wearing eye protection and have some baking soda handy (to throw on any spilled flux) in case of an accident.

After the fluxing, you will want to heat the area to be soldered with a propane torch. A helpful hint: Most of the low-temperature silver solders come in a wire-like coil. You will get better results if you flatten the solder with a hammer into a ribbon. You will be able to apply less solder with less resultant cleanup if it is flattened first.

Make sure the entire joint is evenly heated. As you are heating the area, try the solder on the joint area. When the solder starts to flow, you should start to lay the solder into the joint. Apply the solder a little at a time. The solder will flow into the joint if the joint is clean. The solder will run into the hotter areas of the joint and will have a tendency to even itself out.

If the solder is beading up on the surface of the joint, then you didn't apply enough flux, or the joint is too hot. Do not apply any more solder as this will cause cleanup problems. Apply more flux to the joint area, and the solder should start to flow into the joint. Use the least amount of solder possible to do the job. The more solder you have on the surface of the joint, the more you will have to remove later on.

After the solder joint is made, let it cool to solidification. Then cool the guard and blade in water, wipe them clean with a clean, dry rag, and oil the blade.

Note: An alternative method of applying solder is to place small clippings of solder along the joint after fluxing, but before heating. This technique is commonly used in jewelry work and it works, though the technique takes considerable practice to perform it properly without blowing the clippings all around with the torch blast. This technique will result in a cleaner joint than the first technique, and will be easier to clean up afterward.

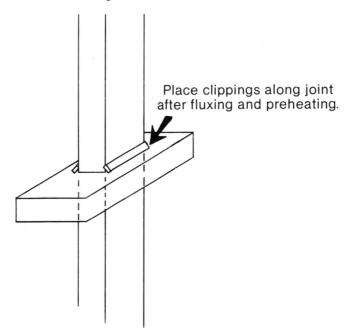

Place clippings along joint after fluxing and preheating.

Fig. 53. Solder clippings along joint

To clean up the joint, use the buffer. If there is a great deal of solder build-up on top of the joint, use a flexible shaft machine with a fine knife-edged wheel (if you have access to one) or a piece of flat-sided, knife-edged micarta as a sanding stick. Use a 240-grit (or finer) wet/dry paper to clean up the joint, and then buff.

If you have globs of solder all over the joint area, you can scrape the solder away by using a small sharp wood chisel, and then do the final cleanup with the sandpaper/buffer. If you have a flexible shaft machine, solder cleanup is easy — simply use a tapered edge cratex wheel on an arbir to clean up the joint area.

A good solder joint is one on which there is no solder anywhere else on the blade/guard except along the joining surfaces, and which is free of voids and bubbles.

Brazing

To braze, you will have to use nonleaded brass or other brazeable material for the guard. You will have to use an oxyacetylene torch and the proper flux for the materials you will be brazing.

If there is a long ricasso area of the blade, you will be better off than if you had a small one. You will be heating the joint area to approximately 1,500°F to join the two pieces, and a larger ricasso area means less of a chance of the heat bleeding into, and softening, the cutting edges.

It is best that the surfaces of the guard and blade be closely fitted. Brazing works best if the guard is of a ferrous alloy. Steel, iron, or stainless steels lend themselves well to brazing.

With the two pieces fitted together, you will need to get them hot enough for the braze rod to flow. For most joints, a one-sixteenth- or a three-thirty-second inch-diameter bronze rod is best.

With the oxyacetylene torch, heat the braze rod until some of the flux sticks to the rod. (There is no need to buy special flux. The borax used in forge welding will work well.) When the rod is coated, start to heat the joint area until both joining surfaces are a medium-red color. Apply the rod while playing the torch over the joint surface and the rod until the rod melts and flows into the joint. Use as little of the braze rod as possible. It should flow evenly and follow the heat along the joint line. The less of the braze rod you use, the less excess you will have to clean up. After the braze is made, let the blade cool slowly.

If you are using a ferric metal for the guard, you

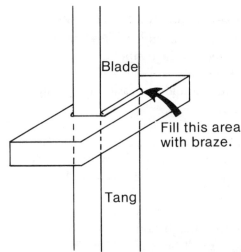

Fig. 54. The braze should be done on the *blade* side of the bolster, as this will allow for easier cleanup. If the tang side is brazed, it will be nearly impossible to clean up and still have squared corners for grip fittings.

may want to braze it to the blade before heat-treating and tempering. If you are careful in the forge and your fire is fresh and clean, you should be able to heat-treat the blade without damage to the blade or the guard.

I personally do not recommend brazing for attaching guards, but it does provide a secure fit, and is considerably stronger than the low-temperature silver soldering.

Pinning

Pinning a bolster/guard is another method used to secure the fittings. It does require a great deal of close tolerance work, as there will be no solder or braze to fill any gaps that may develop during the fitting.

Carefully fit the guard on the blade, and then drill one or more holes completely through the guard and blade to allow a pin to be inserted. The pin will secure the two pieces together.

Most pinnings will use a three-thirty-second-diameter hole to utilize the same size of braze rod. If you are using a stainless steel or German silver guard, use either a stainless steel or nickle silver pin — unless you wish to be able to see the contrasting color of the rod when you are finished.

Be certain that the holes you drill intersect into the blade's tang, or else you will have wasted a hole. After the holes are drilled, insert the pin. The pin should extend about one-sixteenth to three-thirty-seconds of an inch beyond each side of the blade. The ends of the pin should be smooth and square before you start to peen the ends.

With the pin inserted into the hole, place this

Hole drilled completely through guard and blade

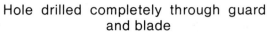
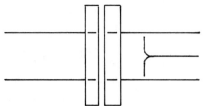

Pin inserted into hole

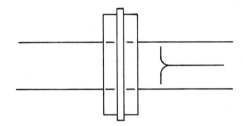

Fig. 55. Pins are inserted in the brazing guard and blade prior to peening.

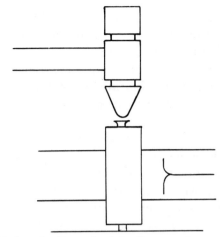

Using ball end of ball-peen hammer, tap lightly to mushroom pin over. After 2 or 3 blows, flip over and start to mushroom the other end.

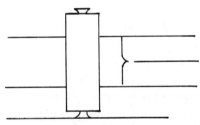

Alternate ends every few blows until they are well peened over and flattened.

Fig. 56. Peening of the pins

assembly on the anvil. Using the peen end of a small ball peen hammer, start to peen the end over on one of the pins. After you have formed a head on one side (this will take only a few light blows), flip the assembly over and peen the other end until a head is formed. You will then need to alternate the sides every few blows until the pin is completely peened over and the joint is tight. When you are finished with one pin, do the remaining pins.

When the pinning is finished, you should carefully file or grind down the pins until they are flush with the surface. Polish as usual. If you were careful and did everything correctly, you should not see the pins in the guard.

Lost-Wax Casting

In addition to the above methods of making the various fittings, there is another technique that lends itself quite admirably to affixing a guard to the blade: the lost-wax process. This technique is most often used for the making of jewelry, using gold, silver, and various bronzes as the casting medium.

The process involved is rather simple. First carve from wax the item to be cast. Then encase the wax in plaster or a similar substance. Finally, burn out the wax at a high temperature and, while the mold is still hot, pour in the molten metal.

The object cast will look exactly like the wax original, save for a slight difference in size (two to three percent smaller due to metal shrinkage). The

shape, surface textures, and configurations of the cast piece will be identical to the wax model.

The best wax to use is either the expensive jeweler's carving wax or the more reasonably priced machinist's wax. Jeweler's wax is available in three hardnesses — soft, medium, and hard. The different hardnesses are differentiated into colors which vary from manufacturer to manufacturer, as for some reason the color of jeweler's wax is not standardized.

The machinist's wax is a medium-hard wax that was developed to be used as a program check for CAD-CAM/Numerical Control machines in the aerospace industries. Machinist's wax has one great advantage over the jeweler's waxes: if it is re-melted, it retains the same hardness. Machinist's wax is available from many tool and die and aerospace suppliers.

Machinist's wax cuts and tools easily, holds its shape very well, and can be polished to a very smooth surface with far less effort than can jeweler's wax.

Machinist's wax is, however, a bit more difficult to locate than jeweler's wax, which is sold through most jewelry supply shops.

Regardless of the type of wax you are using, you will need carving tools of one kind or another. These can either be purchased or made from just about anything.

The majority of the waxes are best worked cold, without using heated tools. Wax usually cuts into small chips while being carved. The texture you leave on the original will be transferred to the metal, so work slowly to achieve the desired result.

There will also be some shrinkage of the metal as it cools from its molten state into the object. Though this shrinkage will be very slight and usually is not of much consequence, it can present some problems in certain designs.

As you are working, you will find that the wax may start to soften from the heat of your hands. If this happens, simply place the wax into a pan of cold water or a freezer for five to ten minutes until it is once again cool and hard.

Almost any design imaginable can be made in wax and cast into bronze, silver, gold, or any other castable material. This is a skill best learned by doing. Everyone works differently, and the tools used vary from person to person.

The actual carving is easy to do. If an error is made, the removed material can simply be built up again by applying melted wax to the affected area and letting it cool before reworking. (The techniques involved are far too numerous to be included in this book, as I have only intended to give an overview of the processes employed. There are numerous books on the techniques which are listed in the bibliography.)

When the piece is finished, the surface can be smoothed out by rubbing it with a nylon stocking and a little lighter fluid. A point to remember is that the surface texture of the wax will be transferred from the wax into the finished casting, so the better the finish on the wax the better will be the finish on the casting, and the easier the cleanup.

You do not need to have a fully equipped jewelry-making operation to use the lost-wax method. There are numerous jewelry and artist's foundries which specialize in pouring one-of-a-kind designs, statues, jewelry items, and the like, and they will do the spruing, investing, and rough cleanup as well. Foundry prices are very competitive, and you will be better off if you get several quotes. Obtain some samples of the items that various foundries have cast in the past.

Also, if you plan on doing more than one copy of an item, most foundries can make injection wax molds from the original casting. This process allows multiple reproductions of the original carving.

Lost-wax casting can dress up a plain blade and turn it into a true art form. It should be delved into further to develop the skills needed to their fullest.

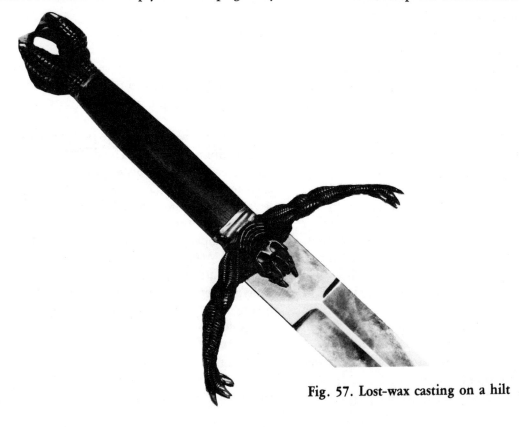

Fig. 57. Lost-wax casting on a hilt

CHAPTER 9 —————

Grip Materials

There are numerous grip materials available to the knife maker today, but to list each one individually would be quite a task. All of the materials can be grouped into two major groups: natural materials (various woods, bone, ivory, horn, stag, shell, stone and anything else obtained from nature) and man-made materials (materials made of plastic and resin products including *micarta, pakka-wood,* and *diamond wood).*

The natural materials are, for the most part, prettier and more desirable to the eye than the artificial materials, which in turn tend to be more stable and less susceptible to the effects of time and the elements.

Regardless of the materials you choose to employ, there are certain facts of which you must be aware when you are working with these materials on a grinder.

The major concern is the dust that is caused. Wear a respirator/filter when you are grinding handle material, regardless of the type of material. No one can be too safe, and the vast majority of handle materials, both wood and plastic, are either irritants or just plain toxic.

Breathing all of the dust produced by grinding just isn't safe. Who knows what effect it could have on your health ten years or so down the line? This is especially true of ivory, bone, and horn. The dust from these materials can injure your lungs and literally kill you.

NATURAL MATERIALS

The natural materials are rather easy to obtain — almost every custom knife-makers' supply house will have them. The more popular materials are the tropical hardwoods such as cocobolo, bocote, wenge, and various rosewoods. Most of these hardwoods are quite stable when properly seasoned and are attractive to behold. The hardwoods are usually available in a scale or block form and are reasonably priced. The form you acquire depends on the style of knife you are making.

The cut hardwood scales are more suited for full-tang blades. The grip material on full-tang blades is pinned through the grip material and the tang. The blocked-out material can be used for the partial tang or the full-hidden tang (where the tang runs through the center of the grip with only the material showing around the four sides). You can always split the block into scales. The cost of the blocks is usually less than that of the scales, so I suggest that you buy material by the block.

If you can find the exotic wood in the form of board lumber, the savings are considerable over the costs of the precut blocks and scales. Many of the more exotic hardwoods are available in precut "standard" lumber sizes. You will need to do some thorough searching in your area for the exotic hardwood dealers, but the search is well worth the effort in the long run.

With ivory and stag antler, as well, you have a

choice of the form in which you may receive it. You can get either slabs, cut sections, or the rough tusk/antler. Prices are considerably less for the rough pieces, as when you buy the specially cut pieces you are paying for the sawdust as well as the received material. Ivory is usually sold by the pound. A pound of decent, solid tusk should be able to yield three or four good-sized block grips or six or more pairs of slab grips per pound.

At the time of this writing, African elephant ivory obtained from the Botswana government is legal, as is any fossil ivory or ivory taken by an Alaskan native (Eskimo) with the Alaskan Fish and Game Seal attached. All other "fresh" ivory is illegal. This goes for walrus tusks, narwhal horns, Indian elephant tusks, and sperm whale teeth. To purchase illegal ivory is a U.S. federal crime, and carries heavy penalties and long prison sentences to boot. Deal with only established reputable dealers, and do not purchase any ivory that isn't from the African elephant.

Exotic Hardwoods

The most beautiful woods in terms of variety of color and contrast are not indigenous to North America; most come from the world's tropical areas. The varieties of these woods seem endless and the spectrum of colorations and figures run from wood of solid colors with little or no figure to dazzling, vivid color with glorious figure. Described below are some of the more common hardwoods available to the bladesmith today.

African blackwood is dense wood with charcoal-gray background and black figure. This wood is hard and stable, takes an excellent finish, and does not need to be sealed.

Amazon rosewood is dense and heavy. Its color varies from a golden brown to a reddish brown with very strong figure. Amazon rosewood is easily worked, but it should be sealed.

Angico is hard wood with a distinctly wavy grain. The color of this wood ranges from tan to brown and will darken over time. Finish with oil.

Ash is domestic wood with a light creamy color and a dark-brown grain figure. It has an occasionally curly grain. Ash is an often overlooked wood that is actually very tough and stable in service. Finish with oil.

Bocote (cordia, Mexican rosewood) is light colored, golden-brown wood with strong black figure. This is hard and heavy wood that needs sealing in order to fully bring out the figure. Finish with oil.

Cocobolo is very hard, dense, and oily wood, with a reddish background and orange and black figure. This is very beautiful wood that darkens and acquires a patina-like finish with age. Cocobolo is very stable and easy to work, but is oily and toxic, so wear a mask to guard against dust.

Desert ironwood is one of the hardest woods available. It varies in color from a creamy yellow to a dark brown with darker brown to black figure. This wood needs no sealer and is very stable in service.

Ebony is totally black wood, is hard, and takes a beautiful finish. Because ebony is prone to cracking if not properly cared for, it should be well seasoned before using and needs to be sealed.

Goncalo alves is reddish brown to golden-hued wood with dark brown figure, which is very hard and dense.

Hickory is light cream to white-colored, straight-grained domestic wood that is very tough and flexible. Hickory is dense and hard, and responds well to flame graining. Finish with oil.

Lignum vitae is the hardest known wood available. Called "ironwood," the grain can be anything from straight and plain to jumbled and interwoven. A fresh-cut piece will be yellow and gold, oxidizing to shades of green and dark yellow. Lignum vitae responds well to an oil finish and will sand very smooth due to its tight grain. It will check if not properly cared for.

Maple is tan domestic wood with various types of grain (running from straight, curly, and fiddleback to burled). It responds well to aquafortis, heat, and an oil finish and is a beautiful wood that is often overlooked in favor of the more exotic woods.

Oak is a wood of many varieties, all of which are quite beautiful. Most varieties of oak have an open grain and require a good sealer and oil finish. Colors range from light tan to dark reddish brown. This is a good wood for the simple, sturdy knife, or as a base for a wrapped grip.

Padauk is dense open-grained wood, which is red-orange when first cut, but seasons to a brownish red over time. Because padauk has little figure, it is mostly used for its coloration. Padauk should be sealed and finished with oil.

Purpleheart is dense close-grained wood, which is light purple in color when first cut, but oxidizes to a rich dark purple in a few hours. Finish with oil. Note: Purpleheart wood is toxic and should be worked while wearing a mask at all times.

Rosewood is a family of wood which is usually very dense and heavy. It contains a large amount of resin which can cause problems in finishing (especially East

Indian rosewood). A light oil finish is best for rosewood, and no sealer is required.

Walnut is a domestic wood of many varieties, all of which benefit applications of sealer and an oil finish. Walnut is a bit soft for a hardwood, but it is very stable and can have a great variety of figure and grains. An oil finish and waxing bring out the most beauty.

Wenge is a strange wood that has a unique grain, especially when quarter-sawn. It has a dark brown base color with a tan figure. A very pretty wood, wenge has an open grain requiring a sealer, and an oil finish brings out the best of the wood.

Most hardwoods benefit from an oil finish, followed by two or three coats of a good paste wax. The secret behind a beautiful finish is the surface preparation. A smooth surface will enhance the figure more than will a rough surface. Sandpaper of 180- or 220-grit will bring out the most figure from all woods.

Use a sealer on the open-grained woods (walnut, wenge, cocobolo, and the like), followed by a light sanding. Then apply the finish.

The best finish to use is a hardening oil finish like tung oil or Danish oil. These oils will penetrate the wood and harden, forming a moisture-resistant barrier. Do not use mineral oil or other nonhardening oils, as these will only evaporate and do nothing to protect the wood.

It is also a good idea to apply one or two coats of a paste floor wax. Any paste wax that contains carnauba wax will suffice. Wax will protect the finish as well as provide a polish.

If you are using an oily wood like East Indian rosewood and would like to lighten the color and remove the excess oils, soak the block of rosewood in acetone for three to nine days, changing the acetone every day. The oils will leech out of the wood, causing the acetone to become purplish in color. After several days, the acetone will remain lighter in color. Remove the wood and let it season for at least two months before use. The coloring will be a considerably lighter reddish purple, with a brownish red figure.

Horn

Horn has been used as blade grip material for countless centuries. But how does one obtain flat pieces from a round horn?

There are suppliers of this material who either sell precut scales or a flattened rough sheet. Most of the commercially available horn is from the water buffalo of India. (The Indians seem to be exclusive suppliers of the horn and stag antler market.) Buffalo horn is basically a black material with some lighter streaks of white and occasionally brown. You can, however, use domestic cattle horn if you know what to look for in a rough horn and how to flatten it.

In order to press your own horn, you will first need to find a source of raw horn. Animal rendering plants and slaughterhouses are the best local sources. After you have found a supply, obtain horns that have thick and solid tip sections and relatively thick walls. The surface scale will come off and reveal variations of color within the horn.

The thick tip sections of the horn can be made into hidden-tang knife handles, while the thick wall sections make fine scales for a slab-handle blade.

Now comes the fun part. You will need to make a pressing plate. I made mine from two pieces of three-eighths-inch stainless-steel plate, eight by ten inches with a three-eighths-inch pin-and-hole arrangement in each corner to help hold the plates in position while I tighten them together.

The pressing plates are put in a vise which is tightened together after the rough horn sections are placed between the plates; placement is similar to a sandwich arrangement.

You will need to smooth the horn either by hand or on the belt grinder, trim off the thinner sections, and cut off the solid tip. A coping saw or a bandsaw works best for cutting horn. Remember to wear a respirator/dust filter since horn dust is bad for your lungs.

After you have the horn trimmed, cut strips off the horn as wide and long as you want them, or within the limits of the horn's size.

Place the horn sections into a pot of boiling water — boiling the horn will make it soft. The period of time required to soften the horn depends on the horn's thickness. It can take anywhere from five minutes to half an hour or more. Experience will enable you to tell how long a piece of horn must boil before it is soft enough to press flat. As a safe start, try twenty minutes.

After the horn has boiled, remove it from the water (while the water is still boiling) and place two or three pieces of horn between the pressing plates. Then tighten the vise until the plates are flat. You must press the horn rapidly so it doesn't start to harden before it's pressed.

You will know if the horn is too hard when you hear it crack in the press. If you hear a small crack, no real harm may have been done, and you usually can save the piece. Just place the piece(s) back into the

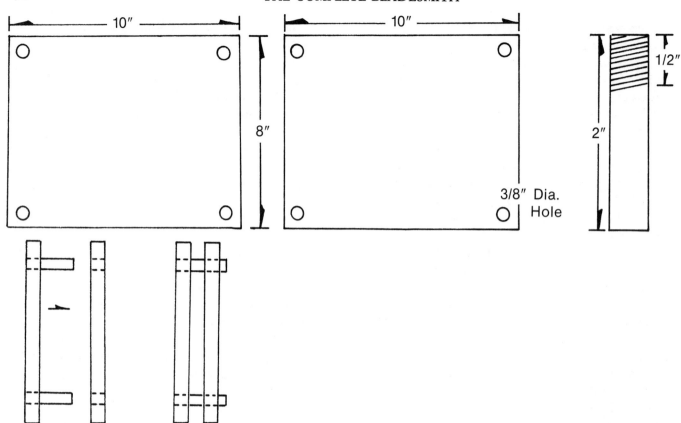

Fig. 58. The horn-pressing plates are made from two pieces of mild steel, with a hole in each corner of the plates. The holes on one of the plates are threaded 3/8 by 16. Four two-inch long and three-eighths of an inch in diameter pins are threaded with the 3/8 by 16 thread down a half inch on one end, and are polished on the other end to prevent binding in the holes. The pins are tightened into the threaded holes, and the plates fitted together, being careful not to mar the inner surface of the plates.

boiling water for a few more minutes.

If the pieces are soft enough, continue to tighten the pressing plates until the pieces are flat, and then tighten a little more until the plates and horn pieces are snug and tight. Leave the whole assembly to cool in the press overnight.

The next morning you can release the press and remove the horn sections. You should have several flat pieces of horn ready to be made into handles.

You can refine the shape of the flat horn on a belt grinder using the flat platen to make certain that you have a flat surface from which to work.

You can use the same techniques for horn grip making as with wood, except that horn is temperature sensitive and has a tendency to chip and crack a little. Keep the horn cool while working it. If the horn is allowed to heat up, it will start to return to its original round shape.

To finish horn grips, you must sand the grip finer and finer with grades of abrasive until you reach about a 400-grit. Then buff the horn until it takes on the luster of polished steel. You can buff the horn to a high polish — the better polish you achieve, the

more figure you will be able to see in the horn itself. This material should not be overlooked.

Ivory

Ivory is a beautiful material, but it exhibits several peculiarities in its working. African elephant ivory is made of dentin. Basically, elephants' teeth ivory is susceptible to cracking, burning, decay, and other problems associated with the natural grip materials. But, many of these problems can be avoided by properly working the piece and taking good care of it.

When working with ivory, wear a respirator. The dust can have harmful effects on your lungs. Even if you are hand-sanding, the ivory dust can get to you.

The number one problem with ivory is that it has to be worked slowly and without any heating of the workpiece. If the ivory gets too hot, the surface of the piece will start to burn, craze with small brownish cracks, and flake. To prevent this from occurring, use only sharp, new belts on the grinder from start to finish, or file, shape, and sand entirely by hand.

Also, since ivory is heat-sensitive, you do not want to drill through the tang while the ivory is affixed.

Use a wood chisel, file, or rasp to cut out the opening after the primary hole is drilled.

Ivory carves beautifully and is readily shaped. It also takes a wonderful finish, and the color and grain variations really stand out when properly polished.

You can shape ivory to any design or style. You can carve, checker, scrimshaw, color, and just about anything else you can imagine with this material. The only limit is the size of the basic material. When done, polishing the piece to fully bring out its beauty is simple.

I will go into the polishing of ivory after I deal with the second greatest problem encountered when working with ivory: cracking. Cracking can be a great frustration if the ivory in question is already on a finished knife.

The cracking of ivory is caused by the loss of moisture in structure of the dentin. If a piece is slowly dried over a period of several years with the cut ends sealed with wax or white glue, then the cracking will be held to a minimum. If a fresh piece is rapidly dried, it will usually crack up to the point of being useless. I learned a rather expensive lesson when I left a small tusk section resting in direct sunlight for only ten minutes and then retrieved a tusk full of cracks.

Keep the ivory cool and out of direct sunlight until it is absolutely dry.

I usually keep my ivory for six months to a year after I obtain it before I even cut into it — just to be sure. Even then, I seal the cut surfaces with glue.

If you must use fresh, unseasoned ivory, you can prevent problems by "stabilizing" it after you are finished working and shaping the grip. Stabilization, which will actually seal the ivory, involves the use of a vacuum chamber. If you plan to use a lot of ivory, you would be wise to own a vacuum chamber. Vacuum chambers are expensive to buy, but are easy to build out of an old auto air-conditioner pump and an electric motor.

The plans I have provided will be quite helpful in constructing a vacuum chamber.

If you have neither the time nor the inclination to build a full-sized vacuum chamber, you can make do with a hand-operated vacuum pump (available from tool shop supplies) and a mason jar. Hook up the pump to the mason jar, seal the ivory within the jar and start to work the pump. It takes a little longer than the conventional vacuum pump, and you will not get the same amount of vacuum, but this pump will work.

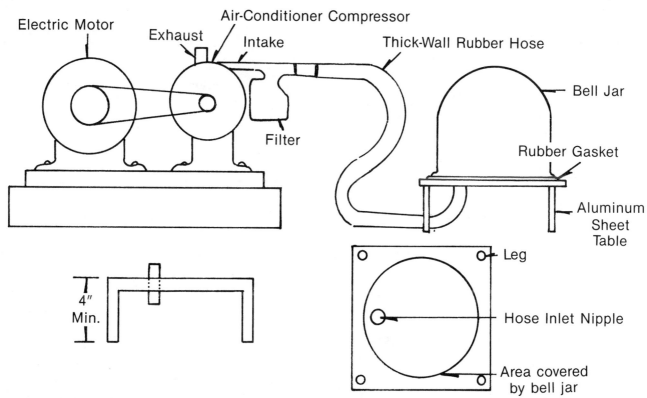

Fig. 59. To construct the bell jar vacuum chamber, mount the motor and compressor on three-quarters of an inch thick plywood, connecting the two with a pully and V-belt assembly to drive the compressor. Make the bell jar table from heavy gauge aluminum sheet. The legs of the bell jar table should be no shorter than four inches to prevent kinking in the vacuum tubing.

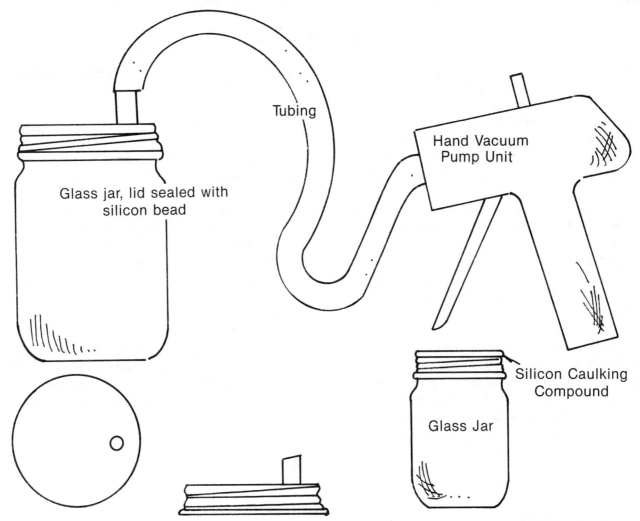

Fig. 60. The hand vacuum pump unit consists of a bell jar with a modified lid, attached via a thick-walled rubber tube to a hand vacuum pump. Solder a nipple connector into a tight-fitting hole in the lid and attach the tubing. To form an airtight seal, place a bead of silicon caulking around the jar's mouth. When the caulking is tacky, use an oiled glass plate to press the bead down, forming an even surface for the lid to contact, forming the seal.

Regardless of which type of vacuum chamber you use, you are now ready to proceed in stabilizing the ivory. Once your grip is finished, but not polished, you can stabilize it. The rough shaping should be completed. The ivory grip can either be separate from the knife or already mounted on the blade. It makes cleanup easier if the ivory is not attached to the blade, and you can get to all of the grip area without difficulty.

In order to commence the stabilization of the ivory, you need to coat the piece with any cyano-based adhesive such as Krazy Glue, Super Glue, or Locktite 440. You will be coating the entire surface of the ivory. You can work in sections. Be certain to keep some acetone at hand in a squeeze bottle in case you glue yourself to the ivory. These glues set in a heartbeat, and do a good job of bonding skin to just about anything around. Also, wear safety glasses in case the glue sprays a bit.

Coat the ivory with the glue. Put an even coat on

the ivory, but don't go overboard as a small amount of glue will do the job.

When the ivory is coated, place the piece in the vacuum chamber on a piece of waxed paper. Seal the chamber and start the vacuum. You will need to pull at least fifteen inches of mercury to do a good job. The more vacuum you pull, the better penetration you will get into the ivory.

As the glue gets pulled into the ivory grain, the glue will start to harden and fill in the pores and small cracks that are not visible to the naked eye, sealing them and preventing any new ones. You will need to maintain the vacuum for a period of time — from a few minutes to half an hour or more depending on the amount of glue used.

After the glue has hardened, you may remove the ivory from the chamber and finish the grip, if you had coated the entire piece, or do the next section in the same fashion as the first.

You will, of course, have to sand away the excess

glue when you have finished the stabilization process, but the presence of the glue will in no way hinder the polishing or detract from the beauty of the ivory.

I strongly suggest that all of the ivory you use be stabilized, regardless of its age or how well seasoned it is. By doing so, you can only prevent problems. Some of the denser stag antler will benefit from the stabilization process, for this antler is quite prone to checking under certain conditions as well.

Stag Antler

Stag antler is one of the most underrated knife materials available today. There is much variation from piece to piece. The color ranges from white, to beige, to brown, and into red. The surface can be smooth or gnarled, and any combination of colors and textures.

The majority of the stag antler available today comes from India. It is taken from the Sambar or the Sika deer. The Indian stag has denser and harder antlers than do native North American stag, and is legal to use or sell in all fifty states. Though some states prohibit the sale of any part of any game animal, this does not apply to the Indian stag. These antlers are obtained yearly from the dropped antlers of the Sambar stag or the Sika deer, which are raised for their antlers and are in no way harmed when the antlers drop off. These shed antlers are then processed and sold to knife-maker suppliers and various world cutlery manufacturers.

There are several distinct differences between Indian stag and domestic American antlers, the most important being the color ranges (from brown to red to black). Another difference is that Indian antler is denser and less porous than the American antler.

No matter which antler you use, it must be worked in a slow and careful manner, along the same lines as ivory. Use new grinder belts, and do not overheat the piece. Wear a respirator since antler dust is just as harmful as ivory or horn dust.

You may wish to stabilize the antler to prevent cracking while working. Work the stag basically as you would ivory, but be careful while you are cutting the antler so you do not cut too deeply into the core. The core of the antler is quite porous, grainy, and slightly off-color.

Working Ivory and Stag Antler

Ivory and stag antler handle in pretty much the same way. Use only new sharp belts and cool the material frequently. Ivory is carvable only with sharp

tools. Be careful of the grain, and re-sharpen the tools frequently to keep the cutting edge from sticking and starting a crack.

Polish the surface with finer and finer grits of abrasive. Stop at 400-grit and buff with finer buffing compounds. *Do not use the same buffing wheels that you use for metal.* Use fresh, clean wheels, and keep them only for ivory and stag antler work. Make certain that you thoroughly clean the buffing compound from the piece before you go to the next finer compound. The sheen and polish of the ivory will be smooth, glassy, and brilliant. Stag will be somewhat less brilliant, but far more colorful. Polishing will bring out the grain and color of the ivory, as well as those of the stag. Do not rush the polish as you can burn the surface just as easily as when sanding.

If you do burn the surface of the ivory or stag, save the piece by slowly abrading away the burned surface until you get down to the unburned areas.

You will need no sealer or finish if you stabilized the material before you started to final sand and polish. A little wiping down from time to time is all that is needed.

The beauty of these materials should not be overlooked.

Working With Horn

Horn was the plastic of medieval man. It can be heated in boiling water, as previously mentioned, and formed into a variety of shapes. It is also a very hard-to-glue material. As a matter of fact, for many years chemists' and pharmacists' spoons were made of horn because nothing would stick to its polished surface.

Horn is made of hair, the same material as fingernails. Like wood, horn is workable and will take a beautiful finish.

The key to a beautiful finish on this material is patience and fine sanding. Treat it like ivory, using progressively finer polishing compounds on a clean buffing wheel.

MAN-MADE MATERIALS

The artificial materials are, as a rule, more stable and a lot plainer than the natural materials.

The most common man-made material used in the custom-knife industry today is *micarta*, a laminated material compressed under thousands of pounds of pressure per square inch and held together with a phenolic resin.

Micarta is available in different laminated

materials such as paper, linen, and wood. The paper and linen bases are made in several colors, ranging from white to black.

Paper micarta has been a replacement for natural ivory for a long time, as it takes a finish that is somewhat similar to that of ivory, and can be scrimshawed.

Micarta is a very stable material that will not rot, crack, or corrode. It works well with tools, but you should not attempt to burn the grip through, as you will destroy the material.

Micarta takes a satin finish. The linen-based material will even show the weave of the linen layers when finished.

Micarta is impervious to moisture and is a good grip choice for blades such as the survival knives.

Another artificial material is known as *pakka-wood*. This is actually wood that has been compressed to 25 percent of its thickness and laminated with resins in a fashion similar to that of micarta. It is available in various colors and grains and is very stable and hard. Pakka-wood works well with tools and takes a high polish.

Do not attempt to burn the grip in with pakka-wood or you can delaminate the wood.

You can work these artificial materials just like wood, except that you will need to sand the grips a bit finer, as there is no grain to hide the sanding marks. You can either buff the material or create a satin finish. No sealers or oil finishes are needed.

The man-made materials are a good choice for use on blades that will be used in or around water or in very humid or moist environments. They are very stable and do not swell or shrink.

If these materials weren't so artificial looking, I would use them more often, but I personally prefer the natural wood, ivory, and other organic materials for my grips.

No matter which material you choose to make use of, the key in bringing out its best figure and beauty is careful working, sanding, and the finish. Work slowly and keep all the materials cool.

CHAPTER 10 ———

Grip Making

The various handle and hilt designs of various construction present their own unique problems. A full-tang blade needs scale grips to sandwich the tang from either side, whereas the hidden- and partial-tang blades require a solid block of material to form the grip. The techniques used in the making of the handles will vary as well. As this is the part of the knife that you hold on to, it should be smooth, comfortable, and well done.

FULL-TANG BLADE GRIPS

The full-tang grip is made of two, three, or more pieces of material that are stacked so the blade tang is between the layers of grip material.

The full-tang blade grip is a strong and simple design, and, when well done, is quite comfortable to hold. To begin forming this grip, drill a series of three-thirty-second-inch holes through the grip, either around the edges, down the center, or both. These holes are for the pins which will hold the grip together. Since the tang has already been annealled, there should be no difficulty in making the pin holes. If there is, use a cobalt or carbide drill.

When the holes are drilled, select the grip material, which should be long and wide enough to cover the tang, as well as about one-quarter-inch to three-eighths-inch thick. Fit them to the tang.

If the blade has a guard, fit the grip material snugly up against the guard so there are no gaps seen either against the guard or between the grip material and the tang. If there is no guard, fit the grip material to the tang surfaces only. Then shape and final-sand the front side (blade end) of the grip material.

Clean the tang with acetone to aid the epoxy bond between the grip material and tang. Epoxy one side of the grip into place, being careful not to allow any epoxy on the top surface of the tang. Clamp and let harden.

When the epoxy is hard, unclamp the grip and drill completely through the handle using the holes in the tang as a guide. Use the same-sized drill you used for the tang holes. When the drilling is completed, clean the bare tang surface with acetone, epoxy the second grip piece onto the tang, clamp, and let harden.

Finish the drilling, using the holes in the first side as a guide. This sounds like a simple way to do this process, and it is. This way there are no errors in hole placement or alignment.

Shape the grip on the belt grinder (or use a file or rasp) until the grip is 90 percent complete. Pin the grip to the tang by using a matching size of welding or brazing rod. Make the pins approximately one-sixteenth-inch too long on each side of the grip. Peen the pin into a mushroom shape, alternating between sides, striking one pin at a time. When finished peening the pins, complete the final shaping of the handle.

You can do almost all of the grip shaping and

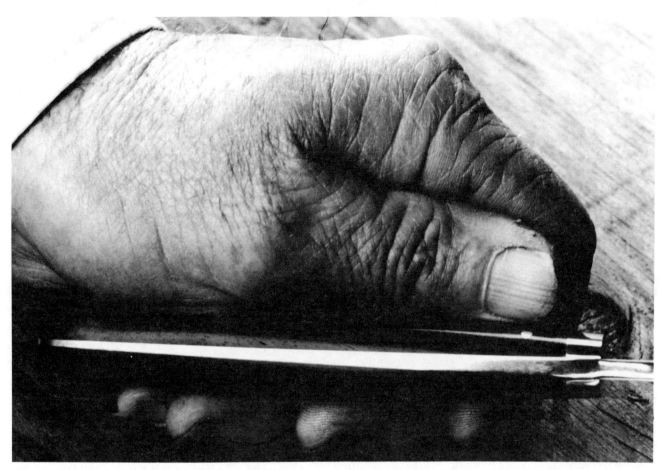

Fig. 61. A full-tang knife with the tang tapered to aid in balance

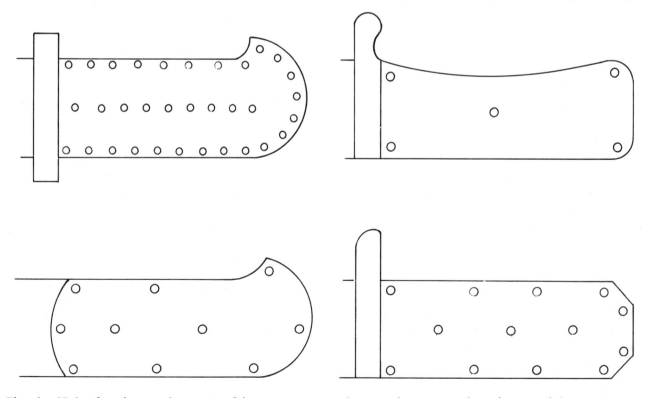

Fig. 62. Holes for pins can be arranged in any pattern as long as they secure the grip material.

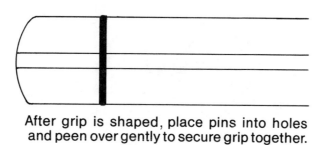

Tang

Grip Scale

Epoxy together & drill holes when cured.

Epoxy other side and drill holes using first set as guide.

After grip is shaped, place pins into holes and peen over gently to secure grip together.

Fig. 63. Pin process

polishing on a belt grinder. If you are using power machinery, care must be taken not to scorch the grip material. The edges of the steel wear out belts and can dull the grit belts quickly to the point where, instead of abrading, the grip belts are rubbing and building up heat. Be very aware of this and avoid any heat buildup. This is especially true if you are using stag antler or ivory since these materials are very heat-sensitive.

Care must also be taken so that the bond of the epoxy isn't broken and the pieces come apart. If this does happen, start the pinning immediately so that you can save the grip. As long as you do not remove too much of the pinning material while you are working the grip, you will not cause any damage to the grip's construction.

After the final shaping and polishing of the grip is completed, apply the finish or buff as required by the grip material.

HIDDEN- AND PARTIAL-TANG KNIVES

These two designs are similar in their fitting except that the fitting is done up against the guard in the partial tang, while the guard and pommel/buttcap are to fit in the full-hidden tang.

These two designs use solid blocks of material as the basis of their handles. First, drill a hole (the same diameter as the thickness of the tang) completely

through each block lengthwise. Then open up one end of the hole until it is as wide as the top of the tang, using a wood chisel or rasp. If you wish, you can rough out a slot in the grip material by drilling several holes in a line and then carefully removing the web between the holes.

I suggest that you do the following before you permanently attach the guard. In this way, any heat that bleeds up toward the blade will not cause the solder to run and ruin the attachment.

Wrap a piece of wet leather around the blade and clamp it in a vise. Heat the end of the tang until it is a blue-black color, and push it into the slotted end of the grip block. The heated tang will start to burn its way into the hole, allowing the block to slide up the tang toward the guard. When the grip material won't go up any farther, remove the block and reheat the tang. Repeat the burning in until it is all the way up to the ricasso. Expect a great deal of smoke with this process; if possible, do this outside, as the smoke of some of the more exotic hardwoods can be irritating to the eyes. Also make certain that you are wearing eye/face protection and a respirator at all times when you are burning in the grip.

Do *not* do this process with ivory, stag antler, or horn. You will destroy these materials if you try to burn the tang into them. You will have to fit the grip to the tang by using chisels and rasps only, since any

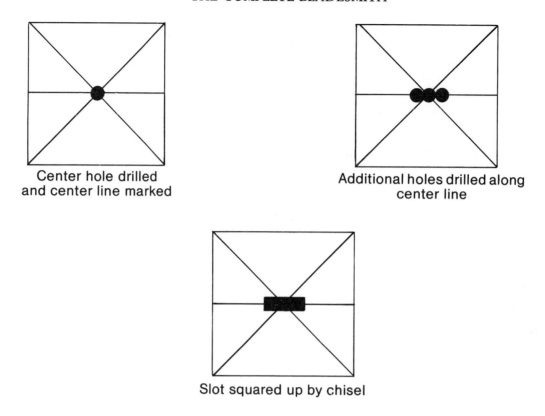

Center hole drilled
and center line marked

Additional holes drilled along
center line

Slot squared up by chisel

Fig. 64. Slotting the grip material on one end

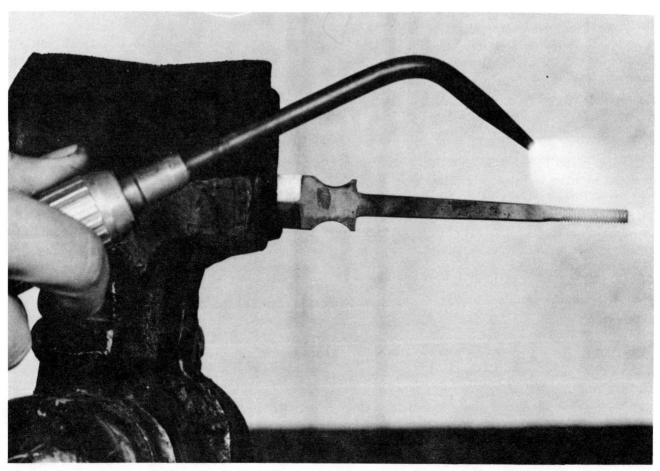

Fig. 65. In preparation for burning in the grip, the tang is heated with the oxyacetylene torch.

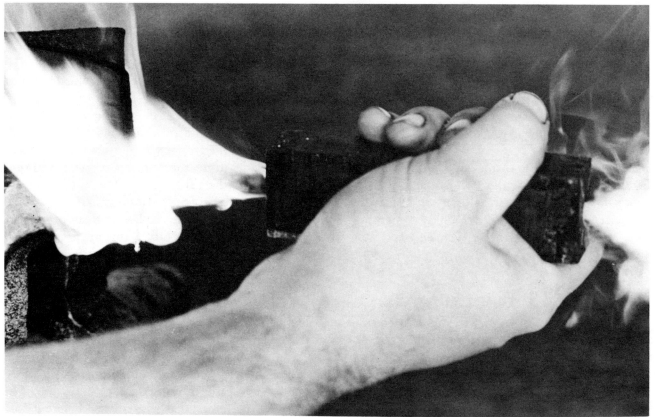

Fig. 66. To burn in the grip, the block is slid up onto the hot tang, burning it into place. (Note: A heavy leather glove should be worn for safety; glove is omitted here for photo clarity.)

Fig. 67. Completing the process of burning in the grip, the block is slid up to the ricasso, then removed and doused in water to prevent further burning. Let the tang air-cool slowly.

heat will cause cracking, crazing, and destruction of the material.

After the wood is fitted to the tang, attach the guard so you may proceed with the handle.

Check the fit of the grip against the guard. You want a tight close fit with no gaps or spaces.

If you are working on a partial-tang design, draw a center line on the grip so you know where the tang is underneath the grip. This way, you can drill the pin holes accordingly. After that is done, epoxy the grip, allow the epoxy to harden, drill holes, and pin.

Two pin holes are usually all that are needed for the partial-tang design. When finished pinning, carve or otherwise form the final shape, sand, and finish.

FITTING THE POMMEL/BUTTCAP

On the full-tang design, with the block fitted snug and square against the guard, trim the block so approximately one-quarter inch on the threaded section protrudes beyond the end of the block. Screw on the pommel/buttcap and check the fit. There should be no gaps or spaces between the grip, guard, and pommel. If there are gaps, remove the high spots with sandpaper or a file. Work slowly so as not to remove too much material. Check for alignment and gaps. When the pommel is fitted, remove the block and shape the grip.

Check the grip's fitting from time to time as you are working to be certain that you are not removing too much material. Sand and finish the grip prior to the hard assembly. The more time and care you take in the fitting, the better the knife will look. The major difference between a factory-made blade and a handcrafted one is the fit and finish of the knife.

The custom-knife maker usually can afford the extra time it takes to do a superb job on the final fit and finish, whereas the factory has to make literally hundreds of blades in the shortest time possible, and the fit is one place where time-saving shortcuts are taken. Work slowly and do not try to rush the job.

When the grip is finished, let it sit overnight before you epoxy it into place. This way, if the grip cracks from too much heat during the fitting, you will not have the trouble of breaking the epoxy bond to replace it.

Now is the time to do the final polish on all of the metal parts of the blade. You will not want to polish after the grip is attached, as you can soil the material with the buffing compounds and ruin its appearance.

After the grip has set overnight, epoxy it permanently into place, making certain the alignment is correct and the excess epoxy is removed before it has hardened. A bit of light oil on a paper towel works surprisingly well for removing the unwanted epoxy before it is hard. After the excess is removed, let the knife grip harden and cure.

Besides the various epoxies on the market, there is another compound that works very well for final

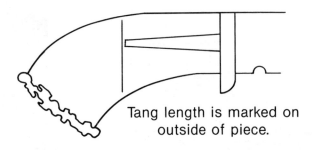
Tang length is marked on outside of piece.

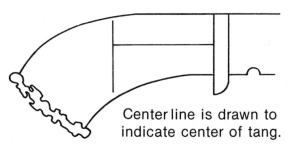
Center line is drawn to indicate center of tang.

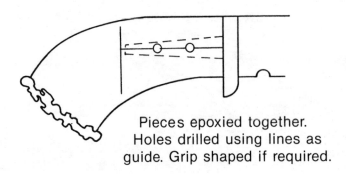
Pieces epoxied together. Holes drilled using lines as guide. Grip shaped if required.

Fig. 68. Partial tang fitting, drawing line, drilling and pinning.

Fig. 69. The pommel is fitted tightly up against the handle material and aligned to the blade.

assembly: rifle bedding compound. This material is a mixture of fiberglass fibers suspended in a resin that hardens into a very stable and durable material. It is available from most gunsmith suppliers. Rifle bedding compound does have one drawback, though. It is very dark in color, and this can present a slight problem if used in conjunction with light colored, translucent grip materials like ivory or mother-of-pearl. It does, however, serve quite well with almost any wood, even the heavily resinous woods like cocobolo or lignum vitae, which can actually "repel" epoxy, preventing a good bond. Bedding compound will adhere to resinous woods as well as the nonresin

bearing, with equal strength.

With the final polish done, the grip fitted and complete, the blade is finished except for the sheath and sharpening.

WIRE-WRAPPED GRIP

The wire-wrapped grip is one of the traditional grips used on medieval swords and daggers. It is a pretty grip which provides a good gripping surface and lends itself well to the "old" patterns of blades. It is not difficult to make, though it does take considerable preparation to do properly.

You will need to acquire enough round wire to

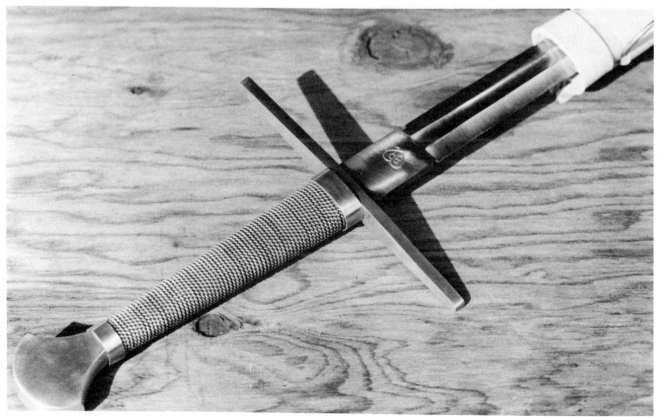

Fig. 70. A bastard sword with brass wire-wrapped grip made by the author.

make enough twisted wire to wrap the grip from end to end. I have found that 0.063-inch-diameter (14 gauge) wire in either brass or stainless steel works well for most sword hilts. For daggers and smaller hilts, 18-gauge wire looks better. Make certain that the wire is fully annealled, or you will run into difficulty in twisting the wire. Annealled wire is available from most wire suppliers and is quite inexpensive. (If it is not available in your area, you can use half-hard wire as well, with good results.)

To twist the wire, you will have to stretch it taut and twist it together. I make lengths of about sixty feet or so by running the wire from one end of my shop to the other. This gives me enough twisted wire to wrap several grips.

When the wire is uncoiled, make certain that there are no kinks or tight bends in the wire, and run the wire so the center forms one end and you have both loose ends at the opposite end. Use an electric hand drill to do the actual twisting. I have found that if you use a ring in the drill's chuck, you will get good results.

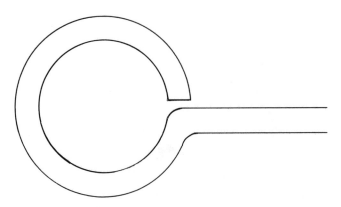

Fig. 71. A wire wrap tool made from 1/4 round stock to fit drill chuck

Securely wrap the loose ends of the wire through the ring and pull the wire taut so that when twisting you will not have any untwisted sections or kinked areas.

Start the drill, slowly, and the wire will twist itself into a spiral. Wear a full face shield *and* eye protection, as a sudden break in the wire could cause the wire to double back, cutting anything that gets in its way.

Continue the twisting until the wire is a tight spiral — keeping a constant tension on the wire. The wire will gradually shorten due to the twisting. A tighter twist will be easier to wrap than a looser one, and it will make a more comfortable grip as well, so keep a tight hold on the drill.

After the twisting is complete, the wire will need to be annealled to soften it so that it can be tightly wrapped around the grip core. Use a torch to heat the twisted wire until it is a soft red color, and let cool slowly.

If you have access to a lost-wax-jewelry-burn-out-kiln, you can use it, as it makes for a better annealling. Simply coil the wire, place it into the kiln, and set the kiln for 1,100°F. Let the wire bake for two to three hours.

Fit the wood grip core as usual, but make it undersized so the wire will not protrude beyond the fittings. Though I have had good results using hickory, ash, and oak as the core material, you can use most any material, as long as it is tough and resilient. The undersizing will be dependent upon the diameter of the finished twist. This undersized core will promote a neater looking grip when finished.

When the core is shaped and the wire annealled, drill a three-thirty-second-inch diameter hole through the grip at the bottom of the handle next to the edge. Use this hole to anchor the wire when the wrap is started. (If you are using smaller diameter twists, use a correspondingly smaller drill diameter for the anchor hole.)

Secure the end of the wire in the hole and start to wrap the wire around the grip. Keep a constant tension on the wire and wrap it close, spiraling up the grip.

The tighter you are able to wrap the wire, the better the grip will look and feel in the hand. When the grip is completely wrapped, cut off any excess wire and clamp the end of the wire to keep it from unraveling.

Soft-solder the end of the wire to the next row to secure the wire while you are working on the collars (you can use plumber's solder and a propane torch). Do not worry if you toast the undercore with the torch a bit, as this will not present any real problem as long as you don't destroy it. One or two little drops are all the solder you need. Be careful not to use too much, or the solder will flow along the twisted wire and ruin the appearance of the grip. This area will be covered by the collar, so you will not be able to see the solder joint.

With wires soldered, make two collars for the grip. Brass, copper, stainless steel, or German silver will do nicely. Use 14- or 16-gauge sheet metal. Anneal it before making the collar.

For the top collar, one-quarter-inch to three-eighths-inch strips will work. Bend the strip around the grip tightly, forming it to the shape and taper of

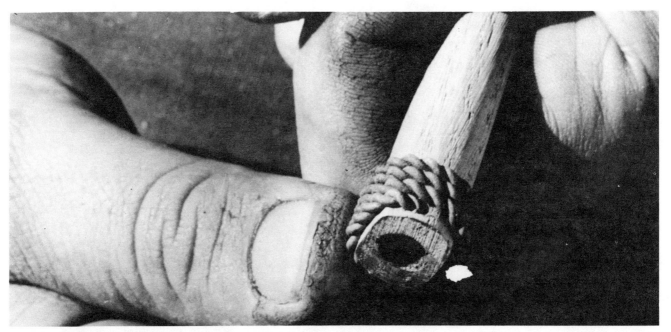

Fig. 72. Start wire wrap by securing one end in a hole and wrap tightly around the cone, keeping constant, even tension on the wire as you wrap.

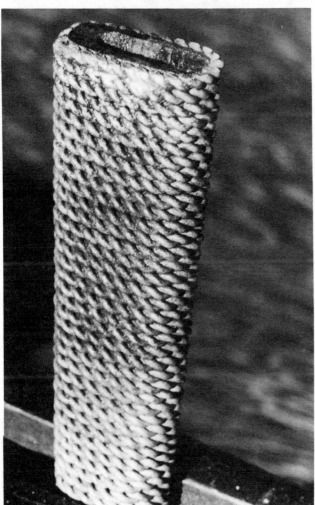

Fig. 73. Wrap completed and end soft-soldered and trimmed flush

the grip.

After the collar strip is to size, trim or file away a small amount (one-sixty-fourth inch to one-thirty-second inch) to make the collar fit tighter on the grip. This slight undersizing will cause the collar to stretch slightly when it is slid onto the grip, making for a tight, gap-free fit on the wire.

Make certain that the two ends of the collar meet squarely and that there are no gaps or misalignments before you solder.

Hard solders are jewelry solders. The alloys used in these vary. The solders that are best for use are silver-bearing solders, which flow between 1,140 and 1,350 °F. Use the lower-temperature solders for the joints.

Hard-solder the ends together to form the ring. To do the actual soldering, use a self-pickling hard jeweler's soldering flux (available from most jewelry supply firms) and the oxyacetylene torch with a small tip. Set the torch flame to be slightly rich on the acetylene, apply the flux, and heat the joint until the solder flows evenly along the joint. Use the smallest amount of solder that will do the job. The less excess solder you use, the less you will have to clean up. Let the solder solidify. Then quench in warm water.

When the soldering is completed, trim off any excess materials, and square up the width of the collar so it forms an even band. Clean and polish the entire collar and buff the outside surface before you proceed further. You should not be able to see the joint on the surface of the collar.

Fig. 74. Hard solder collar closed to make the bands on the grip

With the collar cleaned, position it on the grip. If the grip is tapered, start the collar from the smaller end and slide it up to the larger end until it is in position.

Place the grip onto the blade and secure it in place before you start to tighten the collar. In so doing, you will prevent the wire from sliding off the grip core. The hand guard will keep the wire in place as the collar is being worked up tight against the guard. If the collar is too tight to tighten by hand, use a pure copper punch and a very light hammer to drive the collar up to the cross. You will need to alternate sides as you drive the punch, so the collar will not bind on the way up.

When this is done, remove the grip with the collar still in position and soft-solder the collar in place. Repeat the entire process with the bottom collar, and secure it in place as well.

With the collars soldered onto the grip, clean and polish the entire grip. Buff the wire as well as the collars, and rinse the grip area with a light oil to remove any buffing compounds that may be embedded in the wire twist. When the compounds are removed, clean off the oil with acetone to prepare the surface for the lacquer.

Lacquering the grip will help to fix the wire and prevent it from shifting in the hand. Use one or two coats of a clear lacquer; brush on and let dry. Remember that two lighter coats are better than one heavy coat. Let dry overnight.

After the lacquer is dry, buff the surface of the grip to remove the surface lacquer, leaving some lacquer

Fig. 75. First band soldered into place

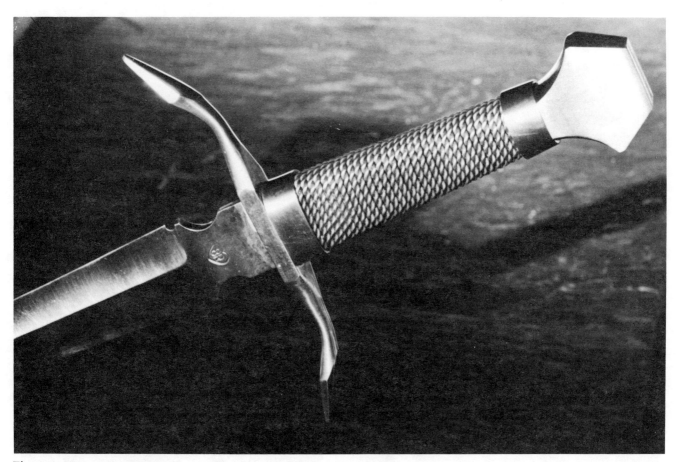

Fig. 76. The completed grip

between the wires as a cement to fill the gaps. You should not be able to see the lacquer between the wire.

Clean away the buffing compounds (do not use acetone or other solvents as such substances will affect the lacquer) and assemble the blade. The wire grip will make the blade feel a bit more ''solid,'' and it can have an effect on the overall balance of the weapon as well.

With the grip completed, it is ready to assemble onto the blade using the usual methods of assembly.

CHAPTER 11

Polish and Finish

With the blade all but completed, we come to the subject of the final finish/polish.

I personally do not see any need for a mirror polish on a blade that will see use. The first time the blade is used, the polish becomes scratched, and all of the work put into the polish is wasted. A good polish though, *will,* help to prevent rust and corrosion. Besides, it looks good.

Polishing is an abrasion process. Finer grits are used to remove the coarser grit marks left by previous compounds. That's it in a nutshell.

The setup to a good polish is made in the final grinding. All of the coarse grit marks must be removed by the next finer grit, or they will show up in the final polish and prove quite stubborn to remove.

The first polishing grit is 240. You can buff after the 240-grit and achieve a smooth, satiny finish. Most custom knife makers prefer to take the prebuffing grits up to 360 or 400 (some even finer to 600).

The finer the grit you can use on the grinder, the sharper the grind lines should be. A buffed-over grind line looks terrible and is a sign of haste and making the buffer do more work than it should. To keep these lines sharp, use the finest grit belt that you can before you start to buff.

The type of wheels and buffing compound will affect the final polish. Sisal wheels, when charged with a coarser (black grease based) compound, will remove a lot of grit marks, but they will also buff over the grind lines just as easily. Only use sisal wheels for set-

ting up the surface for the final polish, making certain that all of the grit marks from the abrasive belts are removed.

After the sisal wheels, use either a hard-sewn muslin (cloth) buff or a medium felt wheel with a fine buffing compound. *Do not* use more than one grade of compound on one wheel. If you are using a coarse compound on a certain wheel, then use *only* that compound on that wheel. If you use a finer compound on top of a coarser one, then you will have coarser compound streaking throughout the buffed surface that is caused by the mixing of the two different grades. The result looks terrible.

As you are using the finer compound, the shine should come up and really start to gleam. You will be able to see if there are any coarser grit marks in the surface as well. If there are, you have two choices: either live with the grit marks, or return to the last grade of abrasive belts and start the buffing process over. Also, if you apply a generous amount of light oil to the blade while you are buffing, it will aid in the cutting action of the compound.

A word about safety: Buffing the blade is perhaps the most hazardous step in knife making. The buffer can snag the blade, tear it out of your hands, and hurl it at a very high speed in any direction. I have seen blades stick into concrete walls and floors, driven by the high velocity the buffer imparts. This can be prevented by properly using the buffer. Do not at any time buff the blade with the edge leading into the wheel. *Always buff from the back or spine of the blade* since the chances of the blade becoming snagged in the wheel are greatly reduced. Never buff on the top of the wheel. Always use the bottom third of the wheel that is facing you. If a blade does snag out of your hands at this point, it goes down and back, away from your vitals.

Buffing can be dangerous, but only if you do something foolish and thoughtless.

Nevertheless, the key to a good polish is patience. It is easy to spend the same amount of time on the final polish as you did making the whole rest of the blade.

If you are making a hidden-tang blade and it hasn't been assembled permanently yet, the time to assemble it is between the medium and fine buff.

FINISHING DAMASCUS STEEL

The finishing process of the pattern welded blade (see Chapters 16, 17, and 18) is different from the nonlaminated blade. Namely, you will need to etch the laminated blade to bring out the pattern to its fullest.

The best time to etch the blade is after the final buff and before you assemble the blade. This way there will be a smooth surface on which the acid may bite.

This etching process is especially important if any nickle or chrome alloys were used in the laminations as the acid will have little (if any) effect on these metals. Pure nickle will remain bright and shiny, retaining its luster, while the steel layers will etch out to be dull and gray.

To etch, use any of the various etches listed in Appendix A, and apply them carefully to both sides of the blade. Be certain that you are wearing eye and face protection and rubber gloves.

Before application of the acid, the surface of the blade must be 100 percent clean of all grease, oils, and other compounds. Acetone works well as a degreasing agent and dries quickly, leaving no residue. Use a generous amount and wipe the blade

dry with a clean cotton cloth. Once the blade surface is cleaned in this manner, do not handle it with bare hands or contaminate it in any other way. A clean surface is the most important factor in etching the blade to get the best results.

Apply the etch with an acid brush, keeping the surface wet with the acid. The length of time of the actual etch will vary, depending on the strength of the acid and the materials used in the blade. Use baking soda (sodium bicarbonate) after the etch to neutralize the acids. Rinse the blade well, clean it, and dry it. Finally, apply a heavy coat of a good quality oil, after the etching, to prevent rust.

A nickle/tool steel blade will etch very quickly as the nickle will not be affected. Most of the chromium/nickle alloys that you will use will respond well to aqua regia, diluted nitric, or hydrochloric acids. Thirty to sixty seconds is about all the time that is needed for a good etch. A slight "topography" will develop as the tool steel is eaten away and the nickle is left unaffected.

To bring out the best nickle/tool steel patterns, clean the surface of the blade well with acetone, and warm the blade slightly with a blow drier. With the blade warmed, apply an even coat of cold bluing solution. This will blacken the entire blade. Rinse the bluing off with clean, cold water, dry the blade, and polish it with a quality paste metal polish and a soft cloth. Use a little oil to aid in the cleaning. The polish will remove the blue from the nickle and leave the steel a darker gun metal gray. The contrast will be considerably enhanced.

A carbon steel/mild steel lamination will be a different matter. Etching based solely on carbon differences will be very subtle. The etch compound used should not be very aggressive, and it should be applied over a greater period of time (ten to thirty minutes, or longer as needed). The color variations will be in the silvery-gray ranges, and will rely mostly on the topography and the slight differences in coloration.

Once the acid etch is done and the blade is cleaned, dried, and oiled, it is ready for assembly.

CHAPTER 12
Sharpening

Sharpening is the last step of knife making. Putting a good edge on a blade is perhaps the one area in which everyone has problems.

There are numerous ways to achieve a sharp edge. The first edge put on a custom knife should be done on a machine, with the remaining sharpening done on a stone and a leather strop.

The number one priority is to keep the cutting edge running down the exact center of the blade's edge. This is referred to as the *spine* or the *backbone* of the edge. If this is off, it will be very difficult to get a superfine edge on the blade.

To start, use a fresh, sharp 120-grit belt on the largest contact wheel you have. Set the edge bevel by holding the blade edge up into the wheel at the desired angle, anywhere from 20 to 45 degrees (depending on the desired use of the blade).

Take a full pass on the edge without stopping. Turn the blade over and do the other edge. Alternate edges until the blade has a burr edge.

After the burr edge is raised, repeat the process using a 240-grit belt to put a finer burr on the edge. The burr, also referred to as a *feather,* will now be finer and the bevel set for work on the stone.

The subject of sharpening stones has stirred great controversy — natural stones vs. man-made, ceramic stones vs. the various sharpening steels. They all work to a degree, but I feel that natural stones are best.

The soft Arkansas, the hard Arkansas, and the extra-hard black Arkansas stones are the best media on which to sharpen the blade. Unfortunately, as of a few years ago, the supersoft Washita stone is no longer available. The Washita was a good starting stone for setting up the edge and getting the feather finer and finer.

With the edge set up for the stones on the 240-grit, start the honing with the soft Arkansas stone. Make certain that the entire stone is well saturated and awash with a light oil. The oil will keep the stone's pores open, reducing its abrasiveness. *Do not* use water on an oil stone. There are water stones that are available for this purpose, and using water on *these* stones has the same effect as oil on an oil stone. If you use water on an oil stone, you will clog the pores and ruin the stone.

With the oil covering the stone, start to hone the edge by holding the blade edge-down at the exact same angle you set on the wheel. Make the stone cut into the edge as if you were shaving off thin slices from the stone's surface. Alternate sides of the blade with each pass on the stone.

Keep a constant pressure on the blade so the stone grinds evenly. This doesn't have to be a heavy downward pressure, just an even pressure. Too much pressure can cause the feather to be bent over and difficult to remove. Too little pressure, and the stone will not cut as it should.

As you are honing, you will find that if the blade has a "belly" curve, the curve may be sharpened before the rest of the blade. If this happens, lighten up a bit on the pressure as you come around the curve to even up the edge condition.

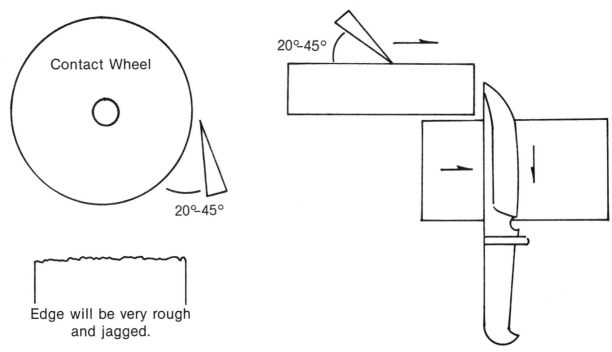

Edge will be very rough
and jagged.

Fig. 77. Hold the blade to be sharpened edge-up onto the contact wheel and take one long, even pass,
maintaining a starting angle of 20 to 45 degrees.
Repeat on opposite sides until a burred edge is
formed.

Fig. 78. Holding the same edge angle as on the belt
grinder, start to hone on the sharpening stone, cutting into the stone as if shaving the stone away, while
pulling the blade across the stone's surface. Maintain
an equal number of strokes on both sides of the blade
so that the sharpening angle remains constant.

As you are working on the soft stone, you are
removing the coarse feather due to the abrasive action
of the stone and replacing it with the finer feather
left by this action of the stone against the blade.

When the edge is finer than the wheel's edge (you
can feel the difference), go on to the harder stones,
using the oil to lubricate the stone and sharpening
angle with which you started.

The hard Arkansas will knock the feather down
even further, causing the microscopic serrations to be
finer and the cutting edge thinner. After a few
minutes on the hard Arkansas, proceed to the black
surgical stone.

Use a lighter pressure than you used previously, as
well as plenty of oil. The black surgical stone will just
about eliminate the feather, making it several
microns thick and smoother than the previous two
stones.

After the black surgical stone, the blade is sharp,
though it can be improved even further by stropping.

Stropping removes the feather and leaves the
blade's edge polished smooth and very sharp. A
stropped edge will not feel as sharp as an unstropped
edge, as what you are feeling with the unstropped
edge is the feather, not the actual edge. Some makers
strop the edge off on a buffer. To do so takes a great

deal of practice so that the edge is not ruined, but it
does make for a mean and thirsty edge if properly
executed. I suggest you use the traditional method of
a leather strap and rouge compounds.

In preparing the stropping strap, use a long leather
strap (thirty-six inches long or so), two to three
inches wide, and charge the smooth surface of the
leather with jeweler's red rouge and oil. To do this,
moisten the rouge with the oil, and apply the mixture evenly to the leather, working the mixture into
the surface of the leather with more oil. Saturate the
leather with the oil/rouge mixture. Now the strop is
ready to use.

This slurry of oil and rouge will actually remove
more of the burr and leave a smoother edge than the
rouge alone. Keep the strop moist with oil, as this
will make it easier to strop.

To actually strop the edge, secure one end of the
strap to a table, and work the blade over the charged
leather surface with the edge being pulled across the
surface backward (in the opposite direction of the
sharpening). Use a gentle pressure, keeping the
pressure constant and alternating sides of the blade.
The stropping will eliminate almost all of the feather,
making the edge very smooth and sharper than most
other blades.

The first edge will usually take the longest, with the later touch-ups hardly taking any time at all (if there hasn't been any abuse of the blade).

The hardness of the blade will have an effect on the edge as well. The harder the blade, the longer it will stay sharp. The hard blade also takes longer to sharpen. The softer the blade, the easier it is to sharpen, but it will then require more care to keep a good edge. There is a trade-off between edge-holding and ease of sharpening.

Once a good edge has been put on a quality blade, it usually will not require any more than occasional touch-ups on the hard Arkansas stones and strop. There is no real need to use the soft Arkansas unless the edge is chipped or otherwise heavily abused.

A quality blade deserves a good edge. A sharp knife is a pleasure to use and is safer than a dull one. There is no excuse for having a dull blade, especially a handmade blade. There are no secrets to keeping a sharp blade other than keeping the sharpening angle the same for every stroke on the stone or strop.

RECLAIMING A LOADED-UP STONE

Sometimes the oilstone will become loaded with steel grit that is embedded in the pores, rendering the stone useless. To clear out the pores, soak the stone overnight in kerosene, then bake the stone at 325 °F for several hours. Place the stone on some sort of sheeting to contain the kerosene as it seeps out of the stone. The heat from the baking will lift out the grit that has been loosened by the kerosene soaking, thereby making the stone almost as good as new.

JAPANESE WATERSTONES

Japanese waterstones are used as are oilstones, with one major difference: They are soaked in water for several hours before being used, and the more ''mud'' that is built up on the surface of the stone, the better the cutting action on the steel. The same angles and techniques are used as in oilstone sharpening, but the available grits are much, much finer than the natural oilstones. If you use the superfine grit waterstones, there is no need to strop the edge as the feather is reduced to its smallest by the stone's cutting action.

TESTING FOR SHARPNESS

The first way to see if a blade is taking an edge is to look at it, sighting down the edge of the blade. If you can see light bouncing off it, it still needs a lot of work. As the blade gets closer to sharpness, you will no longer see the light, only a thin black line of the steel.

Most people like to shave their arms to see whether the blade is sharp. Doing so is okay if you like to have hairless arms all the time, but the best way to see how sharp a blade is is to cut leather scraps. If the blade will cut leather without difficulty, it will cut just about anything.

Using wet paper is also a good way to test to see how the edge is coming — as is wet cardboard. If these are cut and not torn, the edge is fine. It really doesn't matter what object you test with (I do prefer the leather, as it can concurrently remove the burr) as long as the blade cuts.

Sometimes you will want or need the superfine, ultra-sharp ''surgical'' edge, as in skinning thin-skinned game or caping out trophy mounts. At other times, if it is general work, the extra time spent in sharpening will, for all intents and purposes, be wasted. A general-purpose cutting edge will be more than adequate.

Regardless of the use, a dull blade is a dangerous one, as you will be forcing the blade to cut and a slip can cause a nasty cut. There is no excuse for a dull blade, especially when you are making your own blades. Keep the blade sharp, and it will be a pleasure to use. Such quality isn't difficult to attain, and the time involved will be well spent.

CHAPTER 13

Leatherwork

There are numerous ways to make a sheath for a blade. Each method has its advantages and drawbacks. There are three methods that are used today in sheath making: *molded pouch, welt,* and *single seam wrap-around.* Of the three, the molded pouch and welt constructions are the most popular.

Some designs are better suited for certain blades than others. The molded pouch is best suited for single-edged blades or folding knives. The welt construction is a bit more versatile, and it can be used for just about any design of blade, single- or double-edged, straight, or curved. The wrap-around is best for symmetrically designed blades.

But before you start making the sheath, you need leather. But what kind? There are numerous grades and weights of leather, let alone the different varieties. Some leathers are better than others for certain sheaths. The main concerns are weight of the leather (expressed as the ''ounce'' weight — the actual weight of one square foot of leather, such that one square foot of eight-ounce leather weighs eight ounces), type of leather (cow, elk, deer), and tannage.

There are three different tannages of leather: chrome, oil, and vegetable (oak) tanned.

Chrome tanning uses metallic salts to drive out moisture and replace it with salts; oil tanning involves the preservation of the leather by the infusion of various oils into the leather. Vegetable tanning (oak tanning) uses various vegetable extracts to preserve

the leather and is moldable when wet.

The vegetable-tanned leather is best for molding and wet-shaping. The chrome- and oil-tanned are longer-lasting leathers, but they are ill-suited for wet-molding. These particular tannings are fine for use in the non-molded welt construction, though they can cause corrosion of the blade due to the chemicals used in their processing, but they can be used for other leather needs such as strapping and belts.

The so-called ''tooling leathers'' are usually vegetable-tanned, and are very expensive as the surface is selected for its freedom from blemishes and discolorations. The tooling leather hides are nearly perfect, and their prices reflect this fact. Unless you need the perfect hide, you can use the standard grades of leather and cut around any imperfections, or you can leave the imperfections in for a rustic look in the finished sheath.

Regardless as to what grade of leather you decide to use, get the best you can afford. A full side or shoulder is more economical in the long run than a smaller, precut strip.

SINGLE SEAM WRAP-AROUND SHEATH

This traditional sheath, used for the medieval European broadsword and dagger, is an elegant sheath that lends itself well to tooling and carving. I suggest you make this type of sheath after the blade has its crosspiece mounted and before you put the

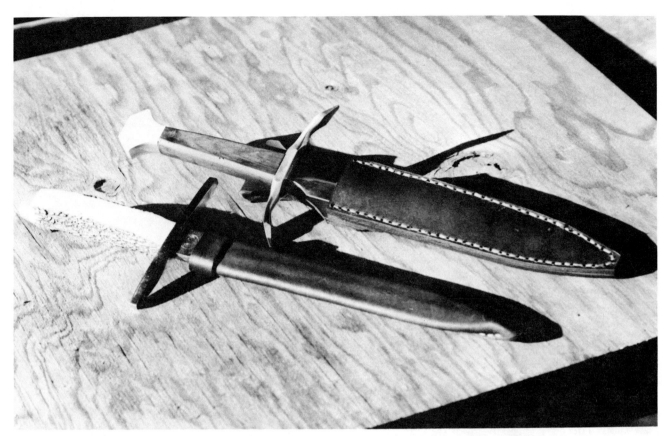

Fig. 79. At top is the welt-constructed sheath, and at bottom is the single seam wrap-around sheath.

Fig. 80. Single seam wrap-around sheath

final polish on, as you are going to be exposing the blade to moisture and solvents, and there is no sense in polishing something that is going to have its finish abused.

To start off, you need some leather in the six- to nine-ounce range. Use a piece long enough to encase the length of the blade and wide enough to wrap around the blade.

Lay the blade edge up on the *inside* (rough) surface of the leather, and trace around one side of the blade, from cross to tip. This is the centerline of the tracing. Carefully roll the blade over and away from the centerline you just traced on the leather and add another quarter-inch to that distance for swords and three-sixteenths inch for daggers, depending on the thickness of the blade. Trace around the outside edge onto the leather, and repeat the process on the opposite side.

You should now have an outline of the blade on the leather. Cut out the outline from the rest of the leather, leaving an even half-inch to three-quarter-inch margin along the outside of the tracing. Coat this margin with contact or barge cement, and let the cement dry for five minutes (or until tacky).

When the cement is dry, wet the center portion of the inside of the sheath with some acetone. Be careful not to get any acetone on the cement as this will remove the cement.

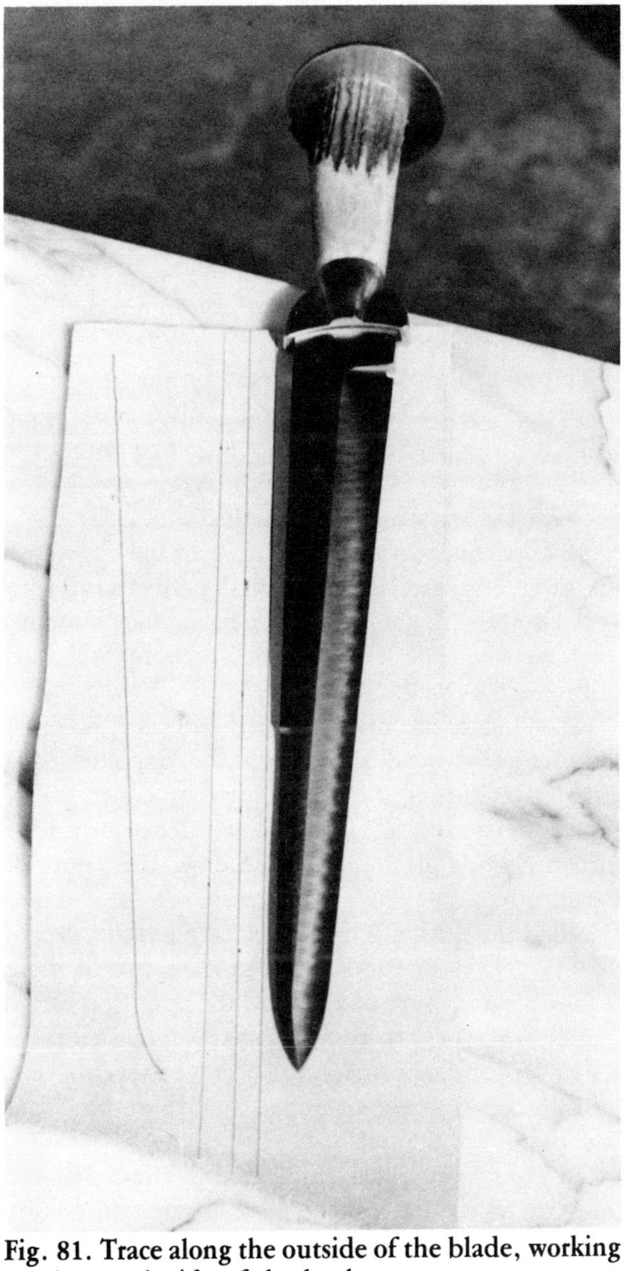

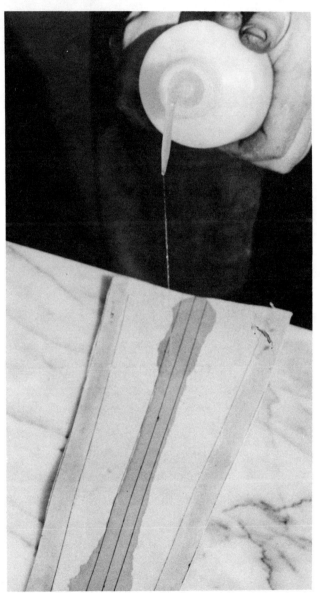

Fig. 81. Trace along the outside of the blade, working on the rough side of the leather.

Fig. 82. Acetone is applied to the leather to make it moldable, but be careful to keep the acetone away from the cemented areas as such contact will remove the contact cement, making the cement useless.

With the leather moist from the acetone, fold it so the margin edges are even. On a longer blade, you can work in sections from the point back toward the hilt end if necessary. As you are folding the leather, moisten the back of the fold with the acetone to prevent the leather from cracking.

When the sheath is folded, place the blade in the sheath and mark a line about three-sixteenths inch for daggers and one-quarter inch for swords from the edge of the blade on the excess leather.

Drill evenly spaced three-thirty-second-inch holes along this line from one end to the other. A thonging

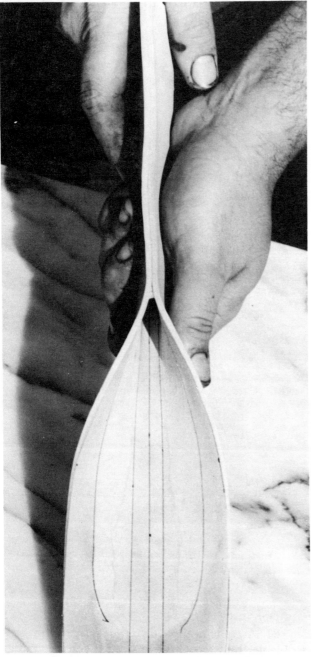

Fig. 83. Leather is folded, and cemented areas are brought into contact.

chisel (available from leather craft stores) will assist in marking the spacing.

You will want to use a double needle *saddle stitch* to do the sewing. The saddle stitch is best for the leather work you will be doing because, if one of the stitches gets cut or broken, the others will hold the leather together without unraveling.

As for thread, you can use just about anything for this type of sheath. I suggest the *artificial sinew* available from leather craft shops. It is very tough and practically unbreakable. Dental floss is also good, though expensive. Do not use linen thread as it tends to tangle, stretch, and break. You will develop personal preferences as to what you use.

After the leather is sewn, tie off the ends of the thread with a square knot, and pull the knot through the last hole so it is inside the leather seam, and trim off the extra thread. This way, there are no loose ends hanging out and the knot is protected from untying itself.

With the sheath sewn, wet it down with the acetone and place the blade into it so that the seam will run up one side of the flat of the blade. You will need to re-wet the sheath with the acetone while you work it into shape.

You can, of course, use water to do this, but water may cause the leather to shrink and discolor. Acetone will not do so, and it dries fast without corroding the blade.

Shape the sheath around the blade (known as the *casing*), paying particular attention to the edges and the mouth of the sheath. Work the edges until they are well defined, and the mouth of the sheath retains its shape when the leather dries. The point will need to be cased as well.

I have made use of a modified ball peen hammer that has a highly polished face and a very short handle, which makes the job somewhat easier to accomplish. I push the hammer down along one side of the seam while playing it up and down the length of the sheath.

When the leather is dry, the sheath is done, except for the belt suspensions. You can use two or more strips of leather wrapped around the open end of the sheath, with these strips forming attaching points for a belt loop or mounting rings, or you can make a metal locket that goes over the mouth, and a chape that protects the point.

On the two strap attachments, sew these strips to the seam on the back of the sheath through the holes that are already there. Tie off, pull through, and trim the thread.

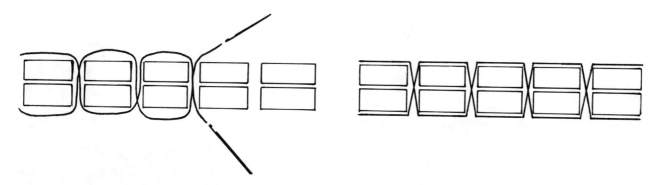

Alternate holes making two blind stitches and pull tight as you sew.

This stitching will hold better than other seams; if a thread is broken or cut, it will not unravel.

Fig. 84. Saddle stitch

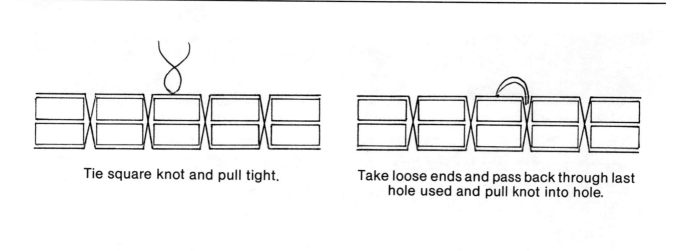

Tie square knot and pull tight.

Take loose ends and pass back through last hole used and pull knot into hole.

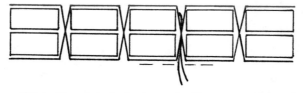

When knot is in hole, cut off excess thread level with surface.

Fig. 85. Tie off the knot and pull the knot through the hole.

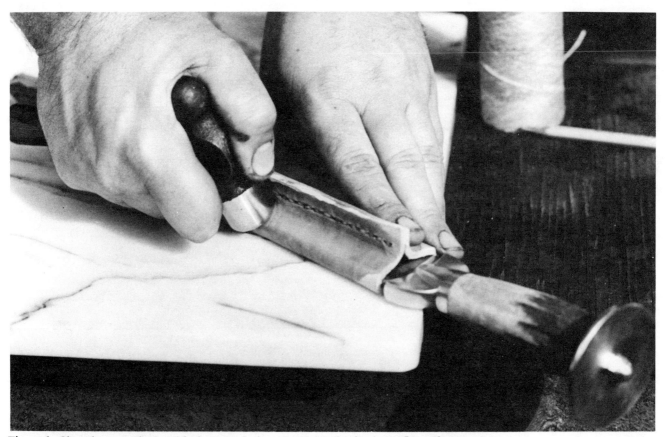

Fig. 86. Sheath must be molded around the actual blade for best fit and appearance.

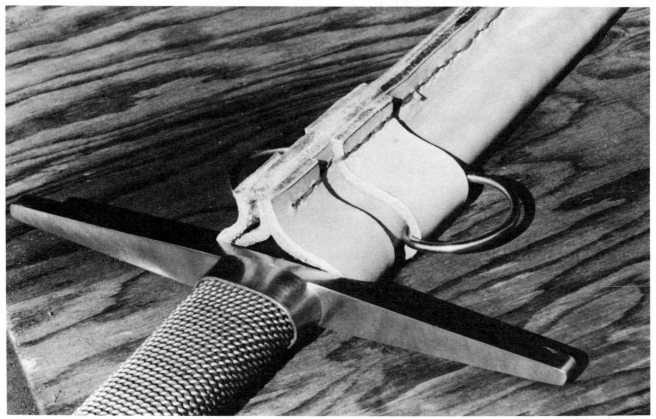

Fig. 87. The straps for the mounting rings are sewn to the sheath using the same holes as those used for the seam stitching.

MAKING A LOCKET AND CHAPE

The making of the metal sheath fittings is not as difficult as it sounds. The material used can be brass, copper, German silver, or other sheet material. Sixteen-gauge stock is best for the locket (mouth) and eighteen-gauge is the choice for the chape (tip).

For the locket, cut a strip of stock long enough to wrap completely around the sheath with a three-quarter-inch overlap. Anneal the metal until it is dead soft, and let it cool.

Place the blade into the sheath and trim the seam down around the mouth of the sheath, leaving a little "tab" of leather about one inch long, three-quarter-inch down from the mouth. This tab will be pulled through a slot to help secure both the locket and chape to the sheath.

Take the sheet of metal and bend it around the mouth of the sheath to form a collar. Mark the area where the tab will come through. Cut out a notch the same size as the tab on both overlapping sides. To aid in cutting square corners at the bottom of the notches, drill a one-eighth-inch hole, and use a coping saw and a fine blade.

Anneal the piece before proceeding. With the notch cut and the piece annealled, mark a line down the center of each edge. This will give you a centerline along which to drill the holes for the mounting rings.

Make the rings from one-eighth-inch diameter rod, in a U-shape, with the diameter of three-fourths inch to one inch. After the rings are completed, drill one-eighth-inch diameter holes to correspond to the diameter of the rings on opposite edges of the piece, along the centerline. Make certain that the top hole is no closer to the mouth than three-quarters of an inch. Insert the rings and silver-solder or braze them into the holes from the inside.

After the rings are attached, trim the two underlapped strips of the notch if they interfere with the overlapping two. Fit the metal onto the sheath and bend it tight around the mouth. Remove any excess material. Remove the piece from the sheath and silver-solder the overlap. Clean up the locket and polish it. Clean the inside, being careful to remove any loose scale, water, grease, or buffing compounds. To attach the locket, remove the blade from the sheath and coat the inside of the locket and the area covered on the sheath with contact cement and let dry.

Place the locket on the sheath and pull the tab

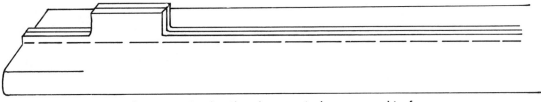

Leave extra leather in area to be covered to form
a 'key' to secure metal mountings.

Fig. 88. Cutting of the tab

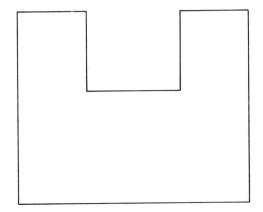

Cut notch on longer side the same
size as the leather key.

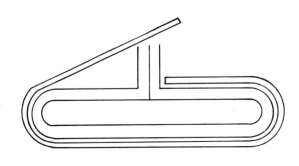

Form sheet around mouth.

Fig. 89. Notch cutting and forming

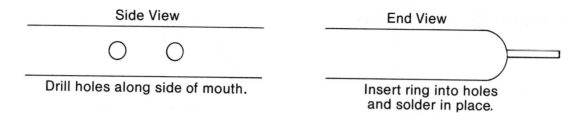

Side View

Drill holes along side of mouth.

End View

Insert ring into holes
and solder in place.

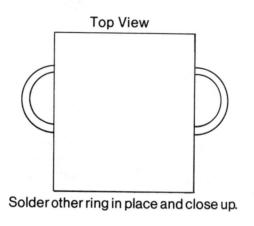

Top View

Solder other ring in place and close up.

Fig. 90. Ring attachment

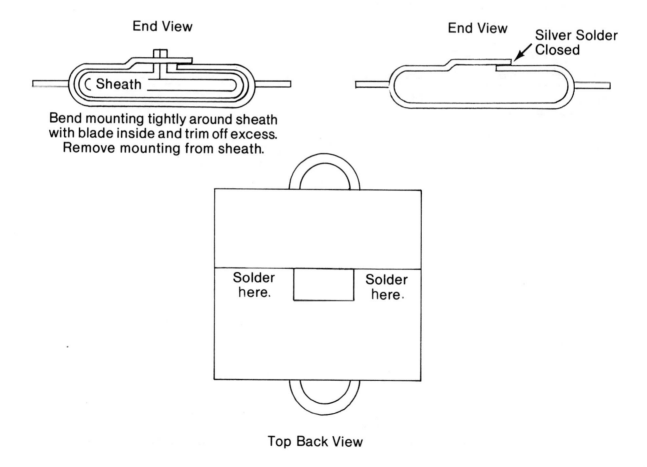

End View

Bend mounting tightly around sheath
with blade inside and trim off excess.
Remove mounting from sheath.

End View

Silver Solder
Closed

Solder
here.

Solder
here.

Top Back View

Fig. 91. Trimming, fitting, overlapping, and silver soldering

through the slot and smooth the leather out on the inside of the chape. Place the blade back into the sheath to set the bond. The piece will be held onto the sheath by not only the contact cement, but also the tab. The blade will not allow the tab to be removed while the blade is in the sheath. The contact cement will prevent the tab from loosening when the blade is removed.

The same folding/wrapping-around process that you used for the locket will be used for the chape.

You will need to cut a cone for the tip after the tab is cut. Use a heavy craft paper as a pattern, and transfer the pattern onto the sheet metal and form the metal around the tip. Anneal as required.

After the chape has been formed, do not solder. Cut a small piece of matching material and solder it to the small end of the locket. After the soldering, trim the piece even with the edge and solder the overlapping tabs. Trim the locket so the top is even across the sheath. Polish, clean, and attach the chape to the sheath.

Apply the dye to the sheath after the hardware is attached. The dye will not affect the metal, and the dye is easily removed with a quality metal polish/cleaner.

SWORD/DAGGER BELT

The European sword and dagger belt (a belt taken from an effigy, bronze, circa 1200 to 1430 A.D.) is a highly evolved way to carry the broadsword and companion dagger. There are numerous styles and designs of these belts from which you can choose.

The basis of the sword/dagger belt is a long plain leather belt fastened together with a tined buckle in the shape of a heart, the actual fastening being made by the indentation at the top of the heart with the remaining length of the belt being passed around and over the belt, and left to hang.

The suspension of the sword is made by a one-piece leather strap that is secured to the opposite side (from the sword) of the belt. The dagger's suspension strap is secured to the belt after the fashion of that of the sword, though on the opposite side. The sheaths can be attached in numerous ways from being directly riveted, sewn to the strapping, looped and buckled, or by a double ring.

The adjustable attachments were most often used as they allowed for easier riding and walking than the nonadjustable ones. The adjustable bucklings are extremely comfortable to wear, and are proper for the period throughout most of western Europe.

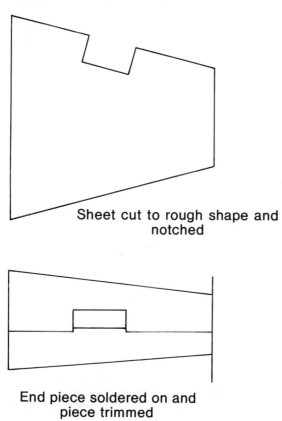

Sheet cut to rough shape and notched

End piece soldered on and piece trimmed

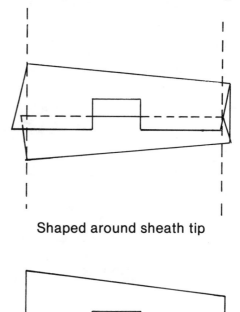

Shaped around sheath tip

End piece trimmed flush and seams soldered closed

Fig. 92. Chape construction, soldering and trimming

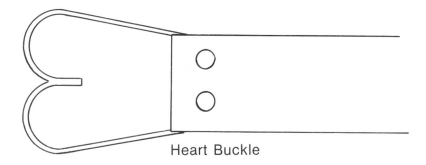

Heart Buckle

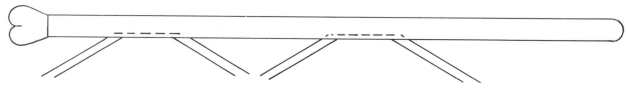

Belt laid out flat. Straps attach to
sheaths, suspending them at sides
of wearer.

Fig. 93. Adjustable attachments on sword-dagger belt

THE WELT SHEATH

The welt construction sheath is the most rugged and cut-resistant of the three sheath types. It is also one of the easiest to make as it requires no casing or molding.

You will need two pieces of leather, long and wide enough to allow the blade to be surrounded on three sides with a one-fourth-inch to three-eighth-inch welt.

Trace around the blade on the inside of one of the pieces of leather and cement a piece of leather strapping on the outside of the line.

If the blade is thicker than three-sixteenths of an inch, cement an additional piece of strapping about one-third of the length back from the opening of the sheath. Taper the inside end of the strap to aid in sewing before you cement.

After the welts are cemented, apply cement to the

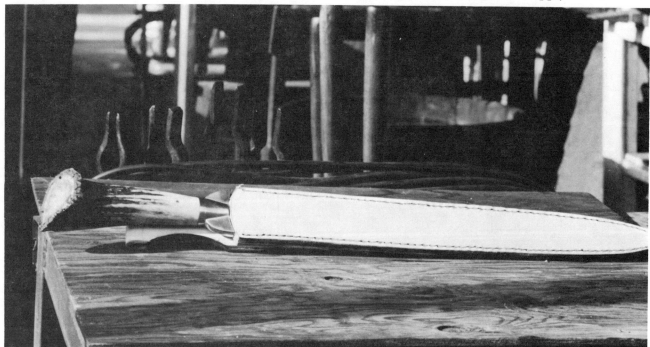

Fig. 94. The welt sheath

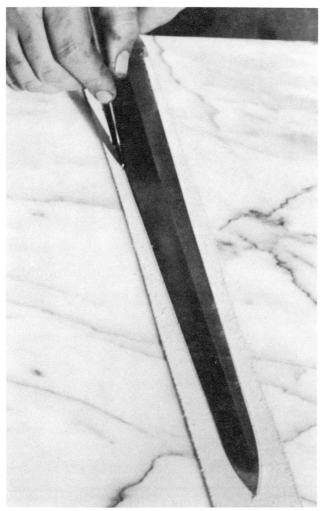

Fig. 95. Trace the outline of the blade onto the inside surface of the sheath.

rough side of the remaining piece and the top of the welts, and attach the remaining piece to the top of the welts.

Shape the sheath by trimming or sanding or using the belt grinder. Check the fit of the blade and make certain that the guard and leather meet evenly at the top of the sheath. Trim as necessary. Make a belt loop from a strip the same width as the sheath, cement the ends together, and trim even.

After the loop is made, cement a piece of scrap leather to the back of the sheath to form a spacer between the sheath and the loop. This spacer will allow for easier entry and withdrawal of the blade.

Cement the loop to the spacer, and finish shaping the sheath. Drill holes and stitch; dye and apply finish.

MOLDED POUCH SHEATH

This sheath type is a combination of the first two types of sheaths, combining the molding of the single seam and the welting of the welted seam sheath.

You will need to trace the outline of the knife on the inside of the leather as in the single seam, leaving a margin of approximately three-eighths inch around the outline. Leave an extension of leather approximately three to four inches long to form the belt loop on one side of the outline.

Next, sew the loop down to the back side of the sheath to form the loop. Moisten the top of the loop to form a better bend without cracking the leather.

Fig. 96. Loop is cemented and ready for attachment to sheath body.

Fig. 97. The finished welt sheath

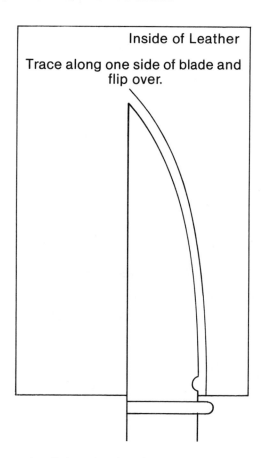

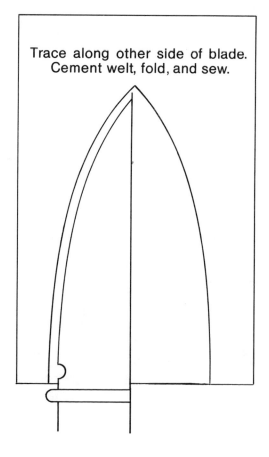

Fig. 98. Outlining the sheath

Fig. 99. Contact cement is applied to the area outside the tracing.

Apply contact cement to the outlined areas (both sides) and to both sides of the welting. Attach the welting to one side of the outline and fold, using acetone to moisten the leather.

Drill holes and sew securely. Moisten the leather with acetone, and insert the blade; form the leather around the blade to closely shape the sheath to the shape of the blade. Work the leather until it is dry. Trim the edges even and check the fit with the blade.

DYING AND FINISHING

With the sheaths finished, you are ready to apply the dye and the finish/sealer.

Dying leather is not difficult. There are numerous quality dyes on the market, and all one has to do is pick the preferred color.

Wear plastic gloves to protect your hands from the dye. If you coat your hands with liquid dish soap and allow the soap to dry on your hands before you put the gloves on, you will find that if you get a hole in the gloves, the dye will not stain your hands.

Apply the dye, using a lint-free applicator, in circular motions over the entire surface of the sheath. Pay special attention to the edges and seams as they will absorb more dye than the rest of the sheath. Make certain that the dye is evenly applied. If it takes more than one application to cover the sheath, work the edges of the dyed areas together to blend the color evenly.

Most colors will dye in one or two coats to the

Double Rings on Loops   Metal Chape   Wrap-around made by suspension straps. Sewn on sheath permanently

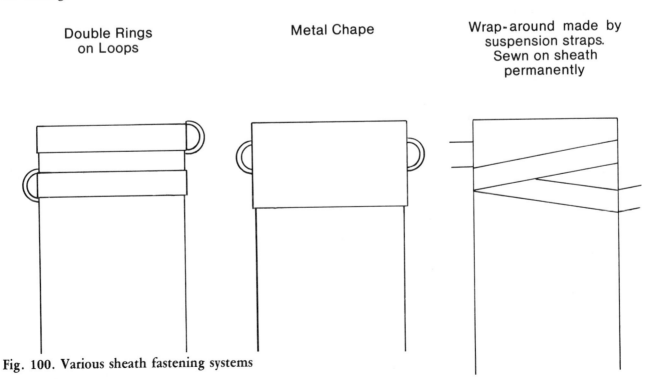

Fig. 100. Various sheath fastening systems

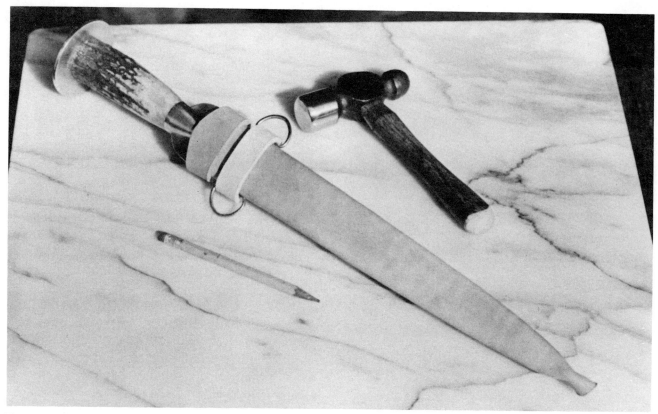

Fig. 101. The completed wrap-around sheath

desired shade; black will not. The best results will be achieved if you do a priming coat of blue before you apply the black. The blue will soak into the leather and allow the black to penetrate deeper into the surface. In this way, the black will appear to be blacker, and the results will be better than if you applied two or three coats of just black dye.

After dying the sheaths, let them dry completely before you finish. The drying time will depend on the ambient temperature and humidity, and upon the type of dye used. Three or four hours are usually all that is needed before you can apply the finish.

There are several different types of leather finishes available, and all of them say that they are best for everything. I have found that neat's-foot oil, followed by a coat of shoe polish, makes for a nice finish on most leathers.

Apply the neat's-foot oil warm with a lint-free cloth. The oil will soak into the leather almost

immediately. Apply two or three good coats and set the leather aside to dry. When dry, apply one additional coat and let it set overnight. This gives the oils some time to penetrate the leather before you apply the polish.

After the sheaths are oiled and dry, apply a coat of shoe polish (in the appropriate color), and buff the leather with a soft cloth. The sheaths will require some occasional care, amounting to a coat or two of shoe polish. The oils will preserve the leather, keeping it pliable without softening it to the point of uselessness, and the polish will seal the surface, protecting it from moisture.

Carnuaba wax, available in liquid or paste form, is also good, as it hardens and protects leather better than most other finishes, though it is harder to find. It is also harder to apply in an even coat. All in all, it is longer lasting, and it will preserve the leather.

CHAPTER 14 ——
Scrimshaw

Scrimshaw is an old, original art form used for untold centuries by the native Arctic Eskimos for decoration of their everyday implements. Originally, the materials used for scrimshaw were the various walrus or narwhal ivories that were the standard materials used by the Eskimos for most of their tools and weapons.

The art of scrimshaw spread rapidly among American whalers, who had countless hours with nothing to do on open ocean voyages. The whalers had an abundance of whale teeth, baleen, and whale bone to use as the basis of their art. Even today many Americans are familiar with the sperm whale teeth scrimshawed with various nautical scenes.

There are no more American whaling ships these days and whales are an endangered species, but the art form of scrimshaw is very much alive, both on its own merits and as an accessory to the custom knife.

One does not have to use whale teeth or baleen to scrimshaw, as today the materials that can be used are varied. Both natural and man-made materials are available that will provide a good surface that will take and hold scrimshaw designs.

Of the man-made materials, the one most often used in place of ivory is the paper-based micarta. This material is available in several colors, including white, black, blue, and "ivory." The "ivory" coloring was developed as a substitute for natural ivory and has a slight yellowish cast, mimicking aged ivory.

Some plastics can also be scrimshawed, though these materials really do not seem to have the same "glow" to them that the natural ivory imparts to this artistic technique.

Of the natural materials, ivory is the king. African elephant ivory is perhaps the most used material for scrimshaw today. It is moderately priced and readily available. Possession of whale's teeth, walrus, narwhal tusks, and most of the other materials from the "good old days" are now illegal, with only the antique forms being available.

Fossilized ivory, such as walrus, mastadon, and mammoth, are legal as these particular ivories are in excess of 5,000 years old. They are considerably harder than the "fresh" ivory, as the mineralization that occurs causes the ancient ivories to "petrify," thus preserving them over the passage of time.

Besides the preservation effect of the minerals, the ivory also derives color from the minerals. The colors vary from creamy yellow/brown to reddish brown, to dark brown/almost black. Sometimes different colors will be encountered, with the most prized colors being pinkish red, and blue.

Some bone may be used, as well as stag antler, if it is properly sealed and polished prior to the actual scrimshaw. To do this, use the same stabilization techniques as used for ivory to fill the pores in the bone surface.

Horn can also be used to create a highly dramatic piece. The horn surface will take a good line, but due to the hard nature of the horn, the tools used must be very sharp.

As I have said before, almost any material can be scrimshawed. Some accomplished scrimshanders suggest starting out using the backs of plastic spoons to test new techniques rather than practicing on the far more expensive ivories.

The tools used in this art are far from expensive. They include an X-ACTO knife with an assortment of blades, a pin vise, and several needles. Just about any type of needle can be used, but the number 11 tattoo needle works the best. A good quality oilstone is also handy to keep the needles sharp, as the ivory can dull a needle rather quickly.

There are two different ways to do the actual scrimshaw. The traditional style of scrimshaw uses multiple-scribed lines and cross-hatching. This *cut-work* lends itself toward the single-color (usually black India ink) nautical themes so often encountered in antique pieces.

The second technique is called *stippling* and involves making numerous pockmarks in the smooth, polished surface where these stipple marks hold the inks. Stippling lends itself well to multi-colored designs, using various colored inks, applied separately while the piece is being worked on.

Whichever style of scrimshaw work you choose to do, the most important factor is the surface of the piece on which you are working. The surface must be absolutely smooth, with no coarse marks to catch the ink.

To prepare the surface, work it as if you were putting a mirror polish onto a blade. Remember to keep the piece cool to prevent crazing.

Work by hand using progressively finer grits down to 600 wet/dry paper. After the paper, use a polishing creme to smooth the piece even further. You should have a very smooth and shiny surface, free from all scratches. To check the smoothness of the ivory, use an ink wash on the surface.

Apply the ink (India ink is best for this), and let the ink stand on the surface for a few moments. Wipe the ink off using a soft lint-free cloth. If there are any scratches on the surface, they will be highlighted by the ink, appearing as black lines on the surface. If there aren't any scratches, then you are ready to start cutting the design. If by chance there are some scratches left in the surface, regrind them with a 600 grit, and then polish.

With the surface prepared, you are now ready to place the design that you wish on the ivory. There are several ways to go about this: you can use a transfer, or you can draw it directly on the surface using a soft pencil.

To transfer the design, first make the original drawing on a piece of onionskin and, using *Graphite* paper as the transfer, trace over the design onto the ivory. Do *not* use carbon paper. The carbon can and will stain the ivory with bluish black lines.

After the design is transferred, a sealer must be applied to the surface as a fixative in order to prevent smudging and line erasures. Unscented, clear hair spray works best, as it is easy to acquire and, unlike the spray used by commercial artists, it doesn't require a solvent (such as acetone) to remove. Solvents can adversely affect the coloration of the piece.

Another concern is the lighting. The scratches will be very difficult to see in inadequate light. The best lighting arrangement is muted, from behind the workpiece. This way the light will be reflected off the piece and you should readily see the lines as they are being cut. Magnification will also be of some aid. There are numerous designs of illuminated magnifiers/desk lamps on the market; these can be useful in scrimshawing a piece, as they leave both hands free and provide good lighting, as well as a magnified image of what you are working on.

With the design transferred onto the ivory and the fixative applied and dry, you are ready to start. You must, at this point, know which technique is to be used for the actual scrimshaw.

The traditional line/cross-hatching is best suited for geometric and nautical themes. This technique is quick to do, as you are basically drawing straight lines over the transfer. The best tool to use for this is a very sharp X-ACTO knife or a strong and sharp needle.

Closely set parallel lines produce shading, and cross-hatching produces progressively darker areas. The finer the lines and the closer they are together, the darker the carving will become. It is very difficult to achieve a solid black background using this technique, but it can be done if the lines are fine enough and very, very close together.

The stippling technique allows for greater flexibility as far as shading, highlighting, and detail are concerned. The numerous dots on the surface allow for gradual shading and blending. However, stippling is a very tedious and time-consuming way of scrimshawing an item, as even stippling a solid line can take several thousand dots.

You must maintain sharp needles in order to achieve the best results. Stippling lends itself especially well to portraits and wildlife subjects, and it achieves a "photographic" look on a well-executed piece.

Excellent results can be had by combining the two methods and using them to their best advantage, as each has different strong points and, if combined properly, they can produce a truly beautiful piece.

It is not unusual to spend hours upon hours cutting and stippling one piece. Face it, the more elaborate the subject matter and the greater the detail and shadows, the longer it is going to take. Start out with simple, easy-to-draw designs until you get used to working the material. After you have mastered the simple stuff, advance toward the more difficult designs and shadowing/highlighting.

If by chance you make a glaring, uncorrectable error, you can erase it by fine-sanding/polishing the surface. If you do this, you will be erasing the rest of the design as well. You are, in essence, starting over from the beginning.

When you are finished with the cutting/stippling, you should wash the piece in warm, clean water, and let it air-dry. This will remove the oils from your hands that got on the piece and will enable the ink to adhere better.

There are numerous ways to color a scrimshaw. Watercolors, India ink, and oil paints are the most common. The oil-based artist's paints last the longest and come in a wide variety of colors. Watercolors are very sensitive to moisture and are best suited for display pieces that will never be handled. India ink is the most traditional of the three—it is easy to apply and very stable.

To apply the color to scrimshaw, simply wipe the pigment onto the surface, let it dry for a few minutes, and then wipe off the excess with a clean, soft lint-free cloth.

Scrimshaw is an art form in its own right. It takes considerable practice and time to master, but it can and does increase the beauty and value of a well-crafted blade.

Fig. 102. The design is cut into the surface of the ivory. Note use of magnification.

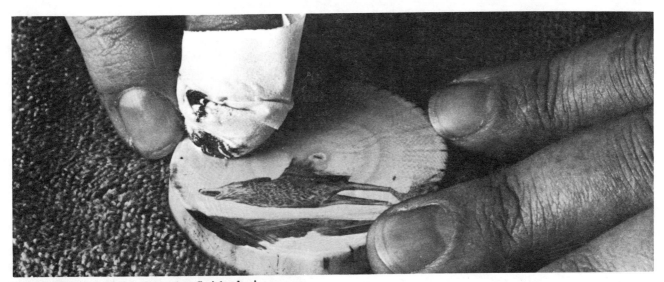

Fig. 103. Ink is applied to the finished piece.

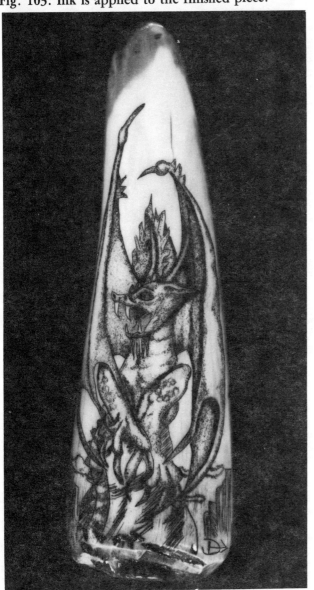

Fig. 104. *Firedrake*, by Jean de Savage, on fossil walrus ivory

Fig. 105. *Tiger*, by Bob Engnath, on African elephant ivory

Fig. 106. *Lion,* scrimmed by Bob Engnath, on African elephant ivory

CHAPTER 15
Sword Making

Making a sword is quite a different task than making a knife. I suggest that you start slow and work carefully.

The first consideration is the size of your forge. The forge will have to be big enough to be able to heat not only the area in which you are working, but the entire blade as well (for heat-treating and tempering) unless you wish to send the blade out to be commercially heat-treated. This may prove to be a problem, as most of the custom cutlery heat-treating firms cannot handle blades over twenty-four inches in total length.

The second concern is the size of your quenching tank. Mine is fourteen inches square and four feet long. It stands vertically, and I can effectively heat-treat blades up to forty-two inches in length along the cutting edge.

You can use any nonflammable material that will withstand the heat and flare-up of the quench for a large tank. It must hold enough volume of oil (or whatever quenching medium you are using) to properly cool the blade. A piece of ten-inch diameter iron pipe with a plate iron end brazed on will work, and is easily made.

If you do not wish to make your own tank, any sheet-metal shop can fabricate one from 16 or 18 gauge galvanized sheet metal. Be certain that it will be watertight and that you build a stand for it as well. If you do decide to go this route, place a piece of three-quarter-inch plywood on the bottom of the tank, and weight the wood down so that it stays on the bottom. The plywood will prevent any hole from being punched in the bottom in case you drop a blade in the tank.

FORGING THE BLADE

Start with the tang, and forge it to one inch wide at the top, and taper it evenly to a thick three-eighths-inch diameter at the end. The tang should be five to six inches long.

After the tang is forged, start at the tip and work the blade in sections of four to six inches long until the entire blade is profiled to shape. Care must be taken to keep the blade straight and true in the forging. This takes practice and is not as easy as it sounds, for the blade will have a tendency to bend from the hammer's impacts. The impacts can be lessened by using local heats, working only the hot areas, and laying the blade lengthways on the anvil surface instead of across.

With the blade shaped, you can either work on the edge bevels or fuller the blade.

Fullering the blade, or creating longitudinal grooves along the blade, serves two main purposes: it lightens the blade while making it wider without sacrificing cross-sectional strength, and allows for a more flexible blade. (The fullers were neither invented for the blood to run down nor to prevent the suction of a body binding the blade in the case of a stab. These are old wives' tales based on fantasy, not fact.)

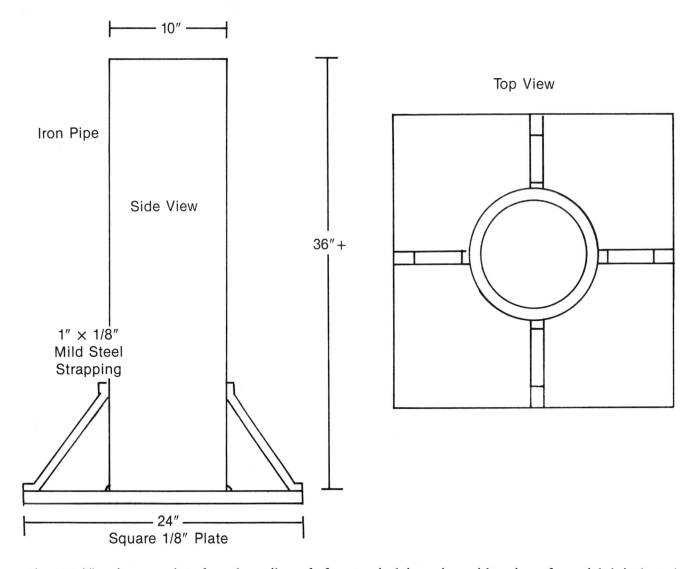

Fig. 107. The pipe quench tank can be easily made from ten-inch iron pipe, with a piece of one-eighth-inch steel plate brazed onto one end to form a liquid-tight seal. Iron strapping welded to both the pipe and bottom plate will help to steady the assembly.

Fig. 108. Lay the blade lengthwise on the surface of the anvil to aid in keeping the blade straight while forging the edge bevels.

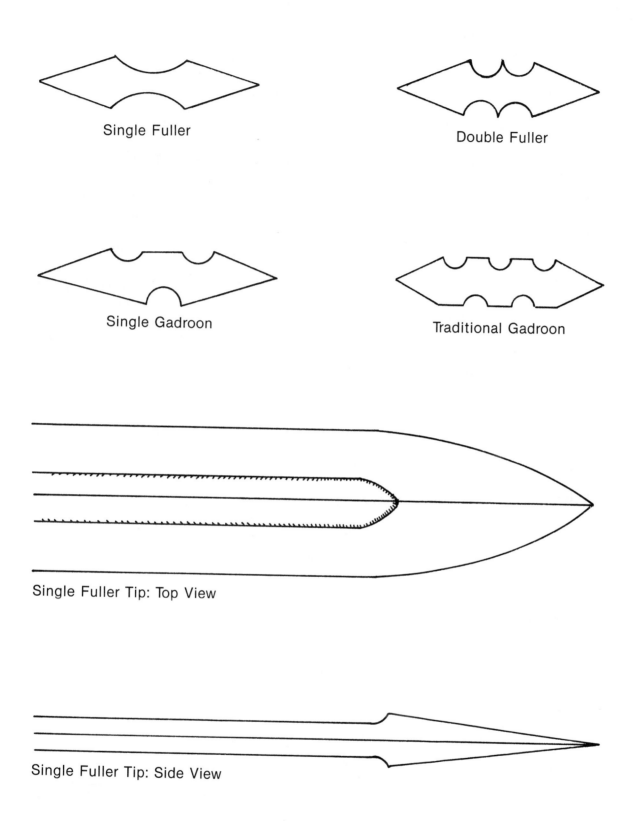

Single Fuller

Double Fuller

Single Gadroon

Traditional Gadroon

Single Fuller Tip: Top View

Single Fuller Tip: Side View

Fig. 109. Some of the more common European-styled fullered blade cross sections

Before you start to forge in the fuller grooves, lightly pack the edges of the blade to show where the edge bevels will end. This will give you a guide to follow when doing the actual fullering.

To fuller a blade, use a top fuller and a bottom fuller (see tool section) with matching radii to work both sides of the blade at the same time. Care must be taken that the fullering is straight and even for the entire length of the groove.

Work at a bright cherry-red heat, and keep the blows heavy and well placed. This operation works best with two smiths (one to hold the blade and the fuller, and the other to strike). It can be worked alone, but it takes some tricky handling.

You can create one, two, or as many grooves in the blade as you see fit. The more grooves on the blade, the narrower they will need to be and the harder it is to clean them up afterward. I have had good results with one wide groove down each side. It looks good, and it does lighten the blade.

With the fullering completed, forge the remaining edge bevels, being careful not to strike the blade on the top of the edge of the groove, as this will destroy all of the work you put into the fullering. Work with sectional heats, and be careful.

I have found that the best results come from austenite-forging the blade in the lower-red ranges, below the critical temperature of the steel. This will take a considerable length of time, but it will result in a tough and well-forged blade. Toughness and flexibility are the chief requirements of a sword. In austenite-forging, you will not enlarge the crystal structures between the forging heats. Enlarged crystal structure is one of the reasons that blades break. Keeping the crystalline structure fractures small and breaking the crystals up into small and tight cells will improve the toughness of the blade.

This is hard, time-consuming work, and the metal will feel harder under the hammer. Working time will be reduced, and the amount of material moved with each hammer blow will be smaller as well.

Count the number of blows delivered to each side. Each edge must receive the same number of blows to even out stresses and prevent warpage and twisting in

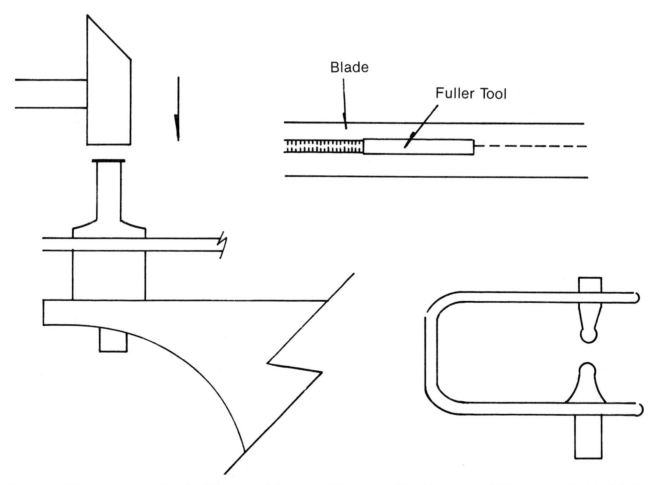

Blade

Fuller Tool

Fig. 110. Blades can be fullered with top and bottom fullers, or with this device. Either way the areas being forged must be overlapped and groove straightness must be maintained.

heat-treating.

Straightening a sword presents its own set of problems. Most of the work can be done hot, at a dark red heat. Start to straighten from the tang toward the point. Get it as straight as possible. Position the bends so the curve is on top and strike several blows on the top of the curve and check for alignment. Repeat if necessary. The more you straighten now, the easier it will be later to do the final straightening after the blade is annealled and cooled.

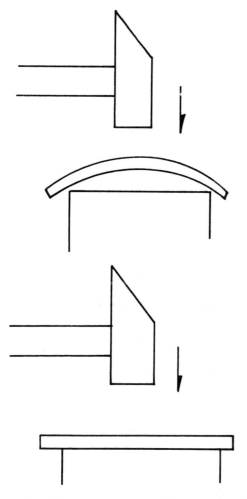

Fig. 111. Straighten any unwanted curves by placing the blade with the curve up and hammering lightly on top of the curved section.

If you plan to do a number of larger blades, then make a "straightening anvil" from a large block of steel. A piece of railroad track is excellent for this purpose. You will want to grind a depression in the surface of the track about an inch or so long. This depression should be three-sixteenths of an inch or so deep. It will aid you in straightening a blade, especially when the blade is cold. There is no need to heat-treat the face as it will not be used for forg-

ing—only straightening. The railroad track will need to be polished to at least 180-grit, with 240 being better yet.

After the blade is straightened hot, anneal and allow to cool slowly. After it is cool, any additional straightening can be done so the blade is perfectly straight. The straightening anvil will be a great aid in this step. Do not strike the blade with hard forging blows as lighter blows will suffice. All of the major straightening should be done hot, with only the very minor final alignments to be done cold, using the torch and vise. This way there will be no undue stresses placed on the steel.

With the blade straight, you are now ready to do the profiling and final shaping of the blade. This can be done with files or on the grinder. Do all of the shaping that you need at this time. The less shaping needed to be done after the heat-treating, the less the chances of ruining the temper by friction heating.

With the profiling completed, thread the tang. Use the largest thread size that the design will allow. This is the weakest part of the sword and the area most prone to harmonic vibrations. A three-eighths by sixteen-inch thread is best, with a five-sixteenths by eighteen-inch being minimum for a sword. Cut a threaded area about three-quarters-inch long so that you will have enough thread to secure the pommel and to adjust for grip fitting. When completed, the blade is ready for heat treatment.

There should be no need to rough-grind prior to heat-treating. The bevels that have been forged into the blade will take the place of the grinding. By omitting the rough grinding you will leave excess steel on the blade in case of any slight warpage. This warpage may easily be ground out after heat-treating.

HEAT-TREATING AND TEMPERING THE BLADE

You will need to build a fire that is long enough to heat the blade evenly. While the fire is burning itself clean, break up the coal into small pieces to help in the even heating of the blade. When the fire is clean, place the blade *on top* of the fire with the blast going enough to cause an even glow in the coals. Turn the blade over repeatedly to prevent warpage. When the blade is preheated, place it into the center of the fire, with the flat side down. Make certain that the tang/ricasso area is *not* in the fire. You do not want to get this area hot enough to harden or crack.

With the blade in the fire, turn it over every twenty to thirty seconds to prevent warpage. Check the blade color by using a poker to move the coals

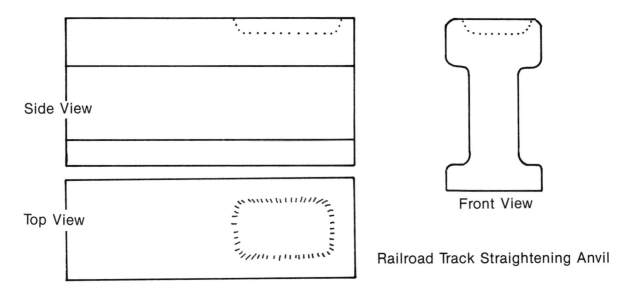

Side View

Top View

Front View

Railroad Track Straightening Anvil

Fig. 112. Depressions can be ground out to a depth of three-thirty-seconds to one-eighth of an inch. The depressions will aid in removing stubborn bends and warps in a blade.

around. The tip will be the first area to get to temperature. You can control the temperature by moving the coals away from the steel to lower the temperature, and next to the steel to raise it.

An even heat is very important. The time that the blade is at critical temperature is very important. As soon as the blade is hot enough to harden, remove it and quench. If there are any bends in the blade, they can be straightened by torquing them straight between the anvil and a poker. Push the steel straight, and before the color drops below the hardening temperature, quench.

The quench is where the warpage will occur. If you have an even heat on the blade and you quench quickly and carefully, you should have very little (if any) warpage. A point-down quenching bath is best for preventing warpage (this is especially true for swords). Place the blade into the oil as vertically as possible and totally submerge the blade.

There will be a flare-up, but this is to be expected, and the oil usually self-extinguishes after the blade is submerged. If not, it can be blown out. If the flame persists, cover the tank. Whatever you use to deal with this problem, do not remove the blade from the medium until the blade is cool. An interrupted quench can result in an improperly hardened or even a cracked blade.

There is some controversy about the movement of a blade while it is being hardened. In my experience I have found that with long blades, movement within the quenching bath can cause warpage and severe bending to occur. Keep the blade still and submerged until cool.

When the blade has cooled, remove it from the tank, and clean the blade. Acetone works well to remove oil, but make certain that you are well away from the fire before you even open the acetone container. Clean the blade so all of the oils are removed from the entire surface of the sword.

When the degreasing is accomplished, polish one side of the blade to a shiny surface, using a worn 50- or 120-grit belt. Do not touch this surface with your bare hands after it has been polished.

Temper the blade in the standard manner to a brown color. You can draw the temper back further, but you will start to lose hardness. Most swords are fine in the brown ranges, except those that are required to be extremely flexible, such as rapiers and estocs. These are best in the magenta to peacock-color ranges.

When the proper tempering color is reached, quench again in the oil, letting the blade cool completely before removing.

When the blade is cool, repeat the degreasing, polishing, and tempering step twice more. This triple tempering will assure that the temper is good.

After the last tempering quench, degrease the blade and check for warpages. If the blade is warped, straighten it by using the oxyacetylene torch; quench in oil.

With the blade straight, you are now ready to start to grind the blade.

GRINDING A SWORD
Grinding a blade as long as a sword does have some

inherent problems (mostly in the length of the reach of the maker). Otherwise, grinding a sword is pretty much the same as grinding a knife. Work in sections of six to eight inches in length. Alternate grinding from side to side and edge to edge so that you will not create any internal stresses within the blade. Remember to keep the blade cool as it has been heat-treated and tempered prior to grinding. Finish and mounts are similar to knives.

BALANCING THE SWORD

The balance of a sword is an important matter. It enables the sword fighter to move with little effort and also affects the control of the blade.

Balance is a matter of personal preference. Most swords should have a balance point of three to five inches above the quillion. This balance point is about standard for swords.

The way you control the balance of a blade is twofold. Blade design and grind both play major roles in the balance, as does the weight of the pommel.

A tapered flat-ground blade will weigh more than the same size hollow-ground blade. Hollow grinding is proper for reproduction of later period (twelfth century and later) broadswords. Hollow grinding allows for a lighter blade made from thicker steel and is also easier to control in the grinding process.

With the blade ground and all of the other steps in the making completed, you will need to decrease the weight in the pommel to bring the balance to the proper point. The more weight you have in the pommel, the closer the balance will be to the hand.

For most broadswords, a pommel of six to eight ounces will suffice. If that is not the case, either lighten the blade by further grinding or add a heavier pommel.

A heavy pommel can cause problems with the overall strength of the sword. All swords can be broken, some more easily than others. Abuse and bad materials/workmanship aside, the major problem is harmonic vibrations.

Harmonic vibrations run along the length of the blade when the blade strikes an object. Mostly they have little, if any, effect on the sword as a whole. Occasionally, they can be so severe that the blade will break at its weakest point. This point is usually at the junction of the tang and pommel. The vibration, if severe enough, will shear off the tang at this point. This is one reason that if a sword strikes a stationary object, it will break. Harmonics cannot easily be stopped once they have started, and pommel weight has much to do with the breakage factor of a sword. The heavier the pommel, the greater the chances for a problem. Use the lightest pommel possible to prevent the vibrations from breaking the blade.

Even with this "limit," sword making can be very rewarding and, although it seems difficult at first, it will get to be an easy task as you make swords more often. One must never forget that a sword is an altogether different weapon from a knife. A knife is meant to slice and cut, whereas a sword was meant to chop and cleave. All in all, a sword should be tough and hard enough to take an edge, whereas a knife should be hard, but tempered, so it will be somewhat tough.

Serviceability is the major concern. A bent sword will still be useable in a fight, but a broken one is useless.

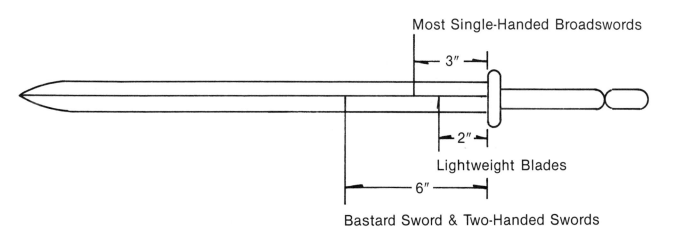

Fig. 113. Balance points will vary from blade to blade, depending on size, weight, and cross section.

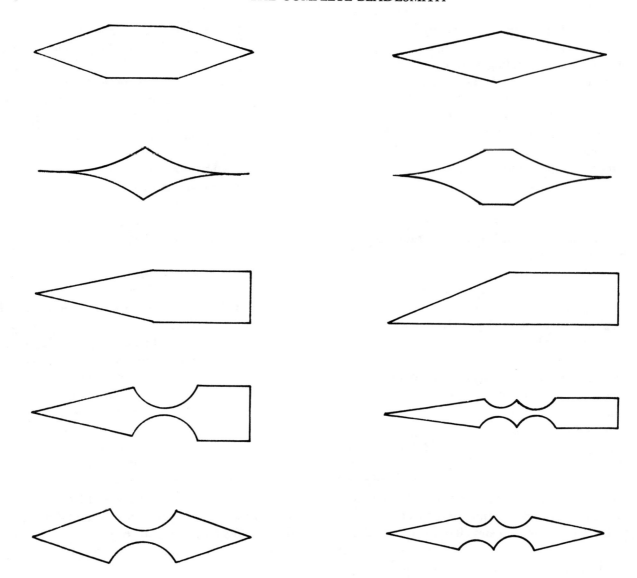

Fig. 114. Examples of traditional European cross sections

CHAPTER 16 ————
Damascus Steel

The term *Damascus steel* stirs the imagination. It conjures visions of a blade of untold beauty and cutting ability. But what is it and how can it be made?

The name Damascus steel is generally used today to refer to a material made by a process called *pattern welding*. Simply put, this material consists of laminated layers of a high-carbon-content steel and a softer weldable ferric material such as wrought iron, mild steel, or pure nickle.

The pattern-welded blade is perhaps the greatest testament to a smith's skill and experience. The basic process is simply forge-welding different materials together. It is this difference in materials, whether it be only in carbon content or other alloying elements, that causes the individual layers to stand out when acid-etched.

The history of Damascus steel is shrouded by much controversy. Contrary to popular belief, the pattern-welding process was never lost. Pattern-welded steel has been made into shotgun barrels as recently as 1920, and the Malaysian Empus (kris makers) have been using the techniques steadily for the last 900 years or so. In World War II, the Germans made use of pattern-welded material in some of the fancier presentation daggers that the Third Reich gave to "deserving" individuals. The Japanese swordsmiths have taken the process and perfected it to an art form that only a few men can rival today.

How long has pattern-welding been around? It was once thought that the earliest known examples of pattern-welded steel dated from around the fourth to sixth century A.D. These items are either Merovingian Frank or Viking sword blades. There has been a recent discovery of a pattern-welded Gladius blade at a Roman site in Great Britain dating to around the second century A.D.

So you can see, the process was not unknown in Europe. It was "lost" to the European smiths sometime around the First Crusade, for some unknown reason. It is my theory that when the need to arm a vast majority of fighting men arose, the overlords and nobles could not afford a pattern-welded blade, and the need to arm gave way to the easier-to-forge homogenous iron sword blade. I am not saying that it totally disappeared in Europe — just that the basic knowledge was lost to the vast majority of bladesmiths at that time. Of course, every now and then, a piece of Damascus steel is discovered in a bog or burial mound, throwing a wrench into all the theories.

Nevertheless, European pattern-welded steel did not make its appearance in Europe from the end of the fifteenth century A.D. until the end of the eighteenth century.

J.J. Perret started to experiment with pattern-welded material in Paris, France, sometime around 1770. Mr. Perret dealt with pattern manipulation and development; he studied not only the procedures, but also the desired results. He was so skilled with folding the metals that he made bars which actually contained readable words and sentences.

Until the last fifteen years or so, the pattern-welded blade was more of a novelty than anything else. This has since changed. There are more people doing pattern welding now than ever before.

The Damascus process has found new life in the form of the ''art knife,'' as well as the ''user'' blade. The quality of the steel being produced today, using modern materials, surpasses the work done long ago when it comes to the beauty and cutting ability.

The Damascus steel blade has been made for a rather long period of time. In fact, almost every culture that had iron-working capabilities, has, at one time or another, made some form of pattern-welded steel.

The actual technique may sound difficult, and to a certain extent it is. The major hurdle in attempting Damascus steel is the mastery of forge welding.

THE FORGE WELD

Forge welding is the process of joining together two or more pieces of iron, steel, or their related metals. It is a process as old as iron-working itself. Forge welding involves the hammering together of two (or more) clean metal surfaces that have been heated to the correct temperature. This hammering will render the surfaces of the metal semi-molten and cause them to fuse together. That is all there is to it.

The two most important considerations in forge welding are temperature and clean weld surfaces. The temperatures rely on what you are welding. The clean surface relies on flux (see compounds).

The flux acts as a cleaning agent/protective coating. The flux will melt and combine with the scale and other surface impurities and, when hammered, will squirt out from between the surfaces, taking all the junk out with it (it is hoped).

Preparation To Weld

The first thing required is an absolutely clean burning fire. Most bladesmiths prefer the closed fire, as the igloo effect tends to retain the heat better. I use an open fire because I seem to have better control as to where I can take a heat on the bar. I suggest you try both methods, and decide which one works best for you.

Preparing The Stock

Take four or five layers of mild steel bar stock (1010 or similar) or one-eighth by one by six inches or so, and clean off the excess mill scale from the surfaces of the bars. Stack the bars on top of each other and wire them tightly together. Leave one end unwired. Place

them tightly together. Leave one end unwired. Place the unwired end into the fire edgewise and heat slowly.

The reason that most welds fail is improper temperature. By placing the stacks edgewise (edges down), the heat from the fire will flow up around and between the layers instead of through one layer at a time. If the stack is placed with the flat facing down into the fire, the outer layers will reach welding temperature while the inner ones will still be far too cool to weld.

As the piece is being heated, take it out and look at it. You should see that the outside two layers are a little brighter red than those inside. Put the piece into the fire until the color is even all the way through. Make sure the blast is slow and steady.

You mustn't have the blast higher than absolutely necessary since the raging inferno of a forge will burn the outside layers of steel off while the inside layers are just starting to get hot.

When the piece is an even cherry-red, sprinkle flux along the edges and flat surfaces of the red area. It

Fig. 115. Stack wired together, prior to first weld

should melt and form a smooth glistening coating on the hot area. Place the piece back into the fire with the blast slow, until the piece is an even light cherry-red. Turn the blast up slightly until the piece is an even yellow. Let the stack of alloy heat slowly, and do not try to rush it. (This is the most difficult weld in this process as you are making multiple welds at the same time.)

As the piece nears welding heat, the flux will start to boil and bubble. Since you are welding low-carbon mild steel, you will be working at a somewhat higher temperature than if you were working with the higher carbon tool steels.

When the piece has heated up nearly to welding heat, you will notice a low hissing sound and a sparkle or two coming out of the fire. This means that the piece is singing to you, telling you it is ready to weld.

When this singing and sparkling is seen, take the piece out of the fire and quickly place it, flat side down, on the anvil (you should see the piece sparkle, and it should be hissing steadily as you are doing this). With the two-pound double-ended jack, strike the piece firmly, but not hard, at the very end. You should be able to "feel" the metal stick together.

Keep hammering back from the end until you are either done hammering the hissing section or the metal has ceased to sparkle. When hammering, use overlapping blows so that the entire surface is struck.

Note: There will be some splattering of the flux and impurities out of the weld surfaces. These are quite hot and care should be taken to remove any flammable materials that may cause a hazard if struck by these hot sparks.

Examine the weld. If it is not sound, immediately replace the piece back into the fire and try again. If the weld has taken, remove the wires and flux the next section to be welded and replace the piece so the next section (with a little overlap on the first) will get heated. Repeat the welding process until the entire bar has been properly welded.

I like to reverse ends and go back over the entire bar with an additional weld series just to be sure that the welds have taken. In this way, I don't have the unpleasant surprise of a weld delaminating on me as I am forging the piece down.

When finished, place the bar someplace where it can cool slowly and then examine the bar.

When the piece is cold, grind the ends and edges off the bar and take a close look at the sides. If

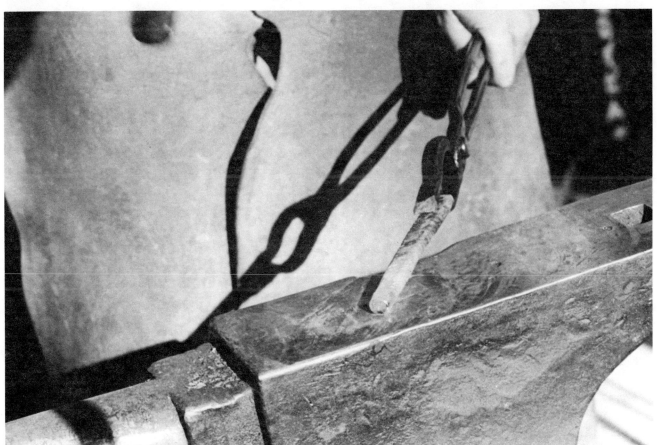

Fig. 116. First welding series completed

Fig. 117. Bar is chiseled three-quarters of the way through to aid in folding the bar in half.

Fig. 118. The fold is started. The cut surface of the bar on the outside makes the fold tighter and easier to accomplish.

Fig. 119. End view of the fold. Note that laminations are visible on the chiseled surfaces.

Fig. 120. The second series of welds are now ready to be done.

everything went well, you should not see anything but bright metal. If you made a mistake, the mistake will show up as black lines or pits; it will have a spider-webbing effect. Some surface oxidation should be expected, but this is very easily ground away.

Making a forge weld takes experience and practice. Sometimes problems do arise, the most common of which are:

Cold shuts are caused by a section not welding due to uneven temperatures. A cold shut appears as a very thin dark line. It is possible to reweld the bar to correct the problem, and you should expect to see a lot of these phenomenon when you are first learning the trade.

Slag inclusions are the products of a dirty weld surface and appear as pockets and pits. Slag, scale, and clinkers are trapped between the weld surfaces, and there is nothing that can be done to correct these problems. This problem *can be* prevented by welding with a good flux and in a clean, clinker-free fire.

Cracks are caused by striking the steel when it is not within the welding-heat range and above the upper temperature limit for forging. This is a very common problem when welding high-carbon steel. It cannot be corrected. This is a common occurrence on the very end of a bar, and the affected area must be

cut off to salvage the bar. To prevent the problem, do not strike the steel when it is below welding temperature.

As I have stated before, to forge-weld takes experience, practice, and skill. It is important to know when the temperatures are correct and to have the surfaces to be joined, clean.

Make sure your hammer blows are rapid and well placed. "Strike while the iron is hot" is no mere saying around the smithy. I strongly suggest that you do a lot of practice welding low-carbon steel to low-carbon steel and, when that is mastered, weld low-carbon to high-carbon. In so doing, you will get a feel for the different materials and how they react under the hammer. After you have made several successful pieces, you should be ready to try your hand at pattern welding.

THE PATTERN WELD

The first consideration when making a pattern-welded blade is the materials you are going to use. Remember that if the blade is to hold an edge, at least half of the blade needs to be made from a high-carbon steel to allow the blade to harden.

Materials To Be Welded

1095 and 1010. These are easy to weld together, and will have subtle watering when etched. In coarser laminations (less than 300 layers per one-quarter-inch of thickness), it will harden in oil. In finer laminations (more than 450 layers), it will harden in brine.

0-1 and 1010. This is probably the most used combination in pattern welding. These two are rather easy to weld as long as you remember the forging range of 0-1. The watering will be rather subtle as the coloring will be based on differences in carbon content. Heat-treat as if for 0-1 in the coarser laminations, and harden in brine in the finer layers.

W-1, W/2, and 1010. This is another old-time-favorite combination. Be careful, as it will red-short if struck above its upper forging temperature and below welding heat. It also has a tendency to burn due to the carbon content of the tool steel. This combination makes a good blade, gives subtle watering, and will harden in brine.

Of course, these are not the only materials that can be used for a pattern-welded blade. I have used recycled plowshares (1065), tool steel shim stock (1095), worn-out files (annealled and ground smooth; W-1 or W-2) and old leaf springs (5160) as the high-carbon layers. I have had great success with 1075 carbon-steel sheet in the 0.050-inch thickness and pure-nickle sheet. I have covered some of the other materials at the end of this chapter. Feel free to use various materials and experiment.

Preparations For Welding

After you have chosen the materials that you are going to weld (and after you are confident in your forge welding abilities), the bars must be stacked and the edges ground flush and wired together.

Depending on the raw materials used, you can start with as few as five layers or as many as thirteen. A good starting point is five to seven layers of one-eighth by one by six inches. (This size will be easy to handle and is made up of "standard" bar-sized material.)

I suggest that you use two layers of the low-carbon on the outside of the stack, with the high-carbon steel on the inside and the remaining low-carbon in the middle.

The mild steel is less prone to burning than the higher carbon tool-steel, and it will withstand more heat and oxidation. By placing the low-carbon steel on the outside, a better first weld is achieved, along with the prevention of surface cracks, carbon runs, and other difficulties that could arise from having the carbon steel on the outside of the bar. Do not worry about the mild steel being folded into the center of the bar since by the time you are done with all of the weld/forge/fold/weld processes, the mild steel will be scaled off from the outside surfaces and the high-carbon/low-carbon laminations will be welded into the center where the edge will be. You can, of course, always add a layer of high-carbon steel between each fold to prevent the mild steel from coming together and to increase the volume of the material.

If you are using salvaged raw materials, make certain that the surfaces are clean and that all edges are ground flush. I have found that if you clamp the pieces together with C-clamps, the grinding will be much easier to accomplish. No matter what your materials are, wire the bar together as in the forge-welding exercises.

Build a large fire, and let it coke down until it is clean and burning well. Place the stack into the fire edgewise and let it heat to cherry-red. Then flux the bundle and return it to the fire.

With the piece back in the fire, bring the temperature up slowly and take your time. You are now dealing with two different materials with two different welding temperature ranges. You must get the temperatures correct or the materials will not weld.

When the carbon content of steel is raised, the burning temperature is lowered as is the welding temperature. In order to accomplish a good weld, you must find that narrow range in which the mild steel is ready to weld without burning the high-carbon steel to a useless, slaggy mess. Expect to burn the first few pieces on which you work.

When using a high-carbon/mild steel, the welding temperature for both will be lower if you use a good flux. Anhydrous borax is best for this. When you apply the flux, make certain that it coats the blade evenly. If the blade is well coated, the weld will take in the orange range and not be as prone to the cracking which occurs at the higher ranges. Also, the use of a flux will help prevent decarburization and material loss.

To get a good weld using different materials, bring the temperatures up slowly, with a gentle blast in a clean fire, and wait until the steel is up to temperature. It takes practice. Flux the area at a cherry-red; when the steel is ready (usually at an orange color), take it out of the fire and strike rapid and firm blows to set the weld. Remember to overlap the heat and hammer-strikes from one area to the other. Also, if you hit the metal too hard, it will shatter, "mush-up," or crumble and crack. Do *not* strike the steel when it is below the welding temperature as this will also cause cracking and the piece will be ruined. Perhaps the easiest way to tell if the piece is up to a welding heat is to look at the flux. If it melted, evenly coating the piece and bubbling away, then the piece should be hot enough to have the weld take. You will need to become familiar with the particular materials you are using.

When you are satisfied with the welding, let the steel cool slowly, grind the edges flush, and check the welds. You will know when the weld is sound or not. If the weld is not sound, replace the bar into the fire and reweld.

After the first weld is complete, forge the bar down to twice its present length, maintaining the same width, but reducing the thickness by half.

If, by chance, you cause a weld to shear during the forging process, wire-brush the split clean, flux the breach, and weld it closed. To fold the piece, mark the center of the bar on the top side (the hammered surface) and take a heat in the center. Use the hot chisel and cut three-quarters of the way through the bar and fold so the *uncut* surfaces (the anvil side) are in the center of the billet.

Some blade makers will cut the billet into two or three pieces and then stack, wire together, and reweld. I have found that folding the bar makes the weld easier to start. In doing this, you will cause one lamination to be a little thicker than the others, as you may be welding the same layer materials together. To me it really does not matter, as these layers are compacted to the point where they will appear to be almost the same thickness anyway.

At this point, I usually clean out my fire and set in additional green coal to coke down. When the fire is clean and ready to weld in, place the bar into the fire and bring it up to a cherry heat and then flux. Repeat the weld process. You will need to repeat the weld, forge fold, and weld sequences until the desired number of layers is achieved.

But when do you stop welding? There has been much controversy as to how many layers are needed to give a superior blade. For a straight (untwisted) pattern, anything around 200 to 550 layers in three-sixteenth to one-quarter inches will give a very good edge. Actually, I have found that as few as seventy-five layers can give a decent edge if the blade is forged and heat-treated properly. The total layer content is up to the individual smith, but one must remember that the finer the layers get, the more difficult it is to see the pattern. Carbon migration may occur as the laminations become finer, and this can really cause a problem.

To figure out the total, take the number of layers that you started out with and then double the number for each fold that you welded (for example: a ten-layer billet folded four times will be 160 layers or 10 x 2 x 2 x 2 x 2 = 160). This will give you the approximate number of layers in the bar.

For the twisted patterns, the number of layers needed will vary as to which pattern you wish to make. We will be going over patterns further in Chapter 18.

There will be a problem with material loss due to the repeated welding. You can always weld two or more equally layered billets together to bring the volume up or, if you want to have wider layers within the bar, weld a piece of one-eighth to three-sixteenth-inch thick tool-steel between the folds (this really looks great in a ladder-patterned blade). If you are going to do this, do not do it on the last fold, but stop on the second to the last. By doing so, you will have the patterned section along the edge with a thicker band running along the sides of the blade.

Problems Usually Encountered

Cracking. As was mentioned above, this is due to the piece being struck below the weld temperature and above the upper forging limit. Nothing can be done to repair the damage.

Crumbling and breaking up (red short). This is caused by striking the steel harder than is required to weld. The steel will mush up and crumble like cottage cheese. The damage is irreparable.

Carbon migration. Carbon will migrate from areas of greater carbon content to areas of lesser content. This process is a result of heat and time. It can be prevented or decreased by welding in the least amount of heats and watching your forging temperatures. If carbon migration occurs to an extreme degree, the piece may be able to be hardened satisfactorily by using a faster quenching medium and lightly tempering (if at all).

EXOTIC DAMASCUS STEELS

There are materials other than plain high-carbon/low-carbon that can be welded together to make a blade. Some of them are common (like stainless steel) or rare (like meteorite iron). Nevertheless, the techniques are pretty much the same, but these materials do present unique problems.

The mixture of *high-carbon steel and pure nickle* will have the most brilliant watering of all of the combinations, because the nickle will not be affected by the acid etch and will retain the polish, whereas the carbon steel will etch away into a smooth satin gray. If you apply a cold-bluing solution after the acid etch, you will bring out even more contrast and beauty of the pattern.

The nickle will not easily compress and form thinner layers, as it will alloy with the surface of the steel and appear to be thicker. Since this will affect the appearance of the bar, use thicker carbon-steel layers, one-eighth-inch steel and nickle sheet in 0.063-inch-thick sheets. The number of layers you can achieve may be limited; 200 to 250 layers are about the maximum you can see in a three-sixteenth to one-quarter-inch thick blade.

Another problem that will arise is due to the oxidation of the nickle in the fire: the nickle will not weld to itself. To get around this problem, you will need to put an extra carbon steel layer between the two weld surfaces so that the nickle will weld to steel and not form any voids or cold shuts.

Nickle is also quite sensitive to sulphur and will quickly absorb it from the fire. This sulphur absorption can cause nothing but trouble since it will affect not only the nickle but the steel as well, weakening the structure of and imparting brittleness to the blade. If at all possible, use a charcoal fire to prevent this from happening.

Nickle flows at about 2,600° F and will weld easily to carbon steels. You will need to use a strong brine for hardening since nickle has a very high thermal conduction rate. Nickle is easy to grind and etch.

You can get the most brilliant contrast if you cold-blue the blade after etching and then remove the blue from the nickle with a polishing compound and a soft cloth.

440-C and 1010. Some makers will say that you cannot weld 440-C in a forge. You can, however, if you use a very clean coal or a charcoal fire. The welding temperature is in the light-orange/yellow range, and 440-C welds reasonably well to the low-carbon steel. Use a good flux, and be aware of the fact that 440-C is a little red-hard, and of the usual problems one encounters with forging stainless steel.

The problem nickle suffers with oxidation will also prevent the 440-C from welding to itself, so you will have to insert a layer of either high-carbon or low-carbon steel to get around this.

Heat-treat this pattern-weld like 440-C, including the subzero quench. The watering will be strong and will respond well to the acid/bluing finish used on nickle. The blade will be tougher than any stainless blade.

Meteorite iron and high-carbon steel. This mixture sounds exotic, rare, and difficult to work and then there's the problem of finding the meteorite. Actually, meteorite iron can be obtained from mineral supply houses that specialize in specimens for collectors. The majority of the meteorite comes from either the Meteor Crater (Barringer) near Winslow, Arizona, or the Odessa Fall in Texas. Meteorite is expensive, and prices vary widely, so shop around.

The use of meteorite iron was quite common in the Malaysian area of the South Pacific. This material is known as *pamir,* and was (still is) a very important part of the kris knife.

For the modern-day smith who wants to try working with meteorite, it presents some interesting problems in forging; namely, the meteorite pieces can be riddled with vesicles, impurities, and fissures.

The best way to start is to heat a piece of meteorite to a light cherry-red and place it on the anvil and hit it. If the meteorite shatters, well, there're plenty of others where it came from. If it does not shatter, flatten it out into a bar. Use a low heat of dull cherry to do this.

The iridium content of this material can cause red-short and red-hardness as well. The quality control of this stuff is terrible. When the bar is forged, sandwich and weld the bar between two pieces of low-carbon steel.

Welding meteorite takes skill and practice; it is not for beginners. It will weld anywhere from an orange to a yellow heat, depending on the individual piece. Use a borax flux and take your time.

With the piece welded, forge the bar down, and cut it into two pieces and include these into the billet of high-carbon and other material.

Heat-treat meteorite in the same manner as the high-carbon steel used in the blade, and etch.

Due to the nickle content of this material (from 3 to 7 percent), it will respond well to acid. Meteorite is a very rare and unique material that can be quite rewarding to work with in terms of the accomplishment. I have made a good number of blades with meteorite, and I can honestly say that each one was entirely different from all the others.

Super Damascus

There is a unique way to make a pattern-welded blade that will outcut all other Damascus steel blades: pattern-weld 0-1 and 1050. Welding these two materials will allow for a very sharp edge as all of the laminations involved will harden and temper. You will need to draw the blade back to relieve any brittleness in the steel.

Forge as you would high-carbon steel, and heat-treat in oil. Temper the blade to a full straw-yellow/brown. The blade will take an edge like a fine high-carbon steel blade, but due to the differences in the alloy, it shows some very distinct watering.

The ultimate Damascus steel blade can be forged from vasco wear and 1050/1060. This blade will be a bit more difficult to work as the vasco wear is highly wear-resistant, and can dull new belts rapidly. Forge this combination like Vasco wear, and heat-treat and temper it like carbon steel.

There are two good reasons to make the Super Damascus. First, the blades will out-cut all other Damascus steel, and, second, carbon migration will be all but eliminated due to the fact that you are welding a high-carbon steel to a tool steel.

These are not the only materials that are forge-weldable into a pattern-welded blade. There are numerous alloys on the market, and experimentation is the only way to find out if the newer steels are truly pattern weldable. The limits are your imagination.

CHAPTER 17
Heat-Treating Damascus Steel

The pattern-welded blade presents several new problems when it comes time to heat-treat the blade. Heat-treating Damascus steel is a different process from heat-treating high-carbon steel. Start out using a light oil quench.

With the oil quench, use the same procedures as for a nonlaminated high-carbon steel blade. If you cannot get a good hardening using oil, go to a brine quench.

This nonhardening in oil can be caused by several factors, most notably carbon migration and the alloys used in the welding.

A brine quench will usually solve the problem. Use it hot, at approximately 130° to 160° F. If you still cannot get a good hardness, use the brine at room temperature.

MIXING THE BRINE

Take five gallons of boiling water and dissolve as much rock salt (available in most grocery stores) in it as it will melt. This is what is known as a saturated solution. Keep this liquid at a temperature of 130° to 150° F. When this is done you are ready to harden the blade.

HEAT TREATMENT

With the blade at the proper temperature for hardening, remove it from the fire and quench the blade point first until the entire blade (including tang) is submerged below the surface. There will be a considerable amount of steam generated by the hot

steel hitting the water. Move the blade around slightly to help in the cooling and to prevent any stress cracks from forming. You will also feel the steel vibrate as it cools. When the steel stops vibrating, it should be cool enough to handle.

When the steel is cooled, you will notice that the scale will have blown from the hardened portions of the blade due to the quench. If the blade develops any cold shuts, inclusions, or cracks, these will be quite visible. They will either open up or cause a blister-like bump in the surface of the blade.

If you have used a nonhardening material for half of the laminations, there is no need to draw a temper in the blade. The reason behind this is the fact that the softer, nonhardened laminations will hold the blade together and support the hardened tool-steel layers. When I use 1010 and 1095, I do not temper at all, but only heat to 300° F in order to equalize stress within the blade.

If you want to have a supertough blade, draw a temper as if the blade were made of carbon steel. The toughness resulting from this tempering will be amazing.

If the materials used are a hardenable material and a nonhardenable material (such as wrought iron or pure nickle), draw a temper that will be a little harder than usual, a light-yellow instead of a straw-yellow/brown. The unhardened material will hold the blade together. I have proven this many times with breakage tests; while these blades will, like all others break, they will withstand more abuse than any one mortal man can subject them to, even under the worst possible conditions.

If you have used all heat-treatable materials (such as 0-1 and 1050), temper as you would normally for a straight high-carbon steel blade.

If the blade fails to harden properly using the brine hot, try it with the brine at room temperature. If the blade still fails to harden, try using water with some soap added to it as a last resort. If you still cannot get a good hardening, then you have either welded up nonhardening materials, or there has been considerable carbon migration within the blade and it is useless as a cutting instrument.

OTHER QUENCHING MEDIUMS

Now, I am sure that we have all heard about taking a flaming sword out of the forge and plunging it deep into the body of some poor unfortunate slave to heat-treat it. I say *nonsense!* It won't work for the simple fact that the human body is not a homogeneous medium. First, the steel is very soft and will bend and not penetrate the skin easily. Second, since the human body is so internally varied, the cooling rate will be considerably different from point to point. Hence, warpage, cracking, and stresses will be built up within the blade. It just won't work.

I have tried some of the more traditional mediums such as wine and lamb's blood and have found that they give a very nice hardness and temper to the blade. This may have something to do with the lower boiling point of the alcohol in the wine and with the nitrogen content of the lamb's blood.

Another traditional quenching medium is urine. It sounds horrible, but it works. The results are very close to using brine. It is a slightly faster quench. It was believed that only urine from a red-haired holy man was to be used for heat-treating a blade as this was supposedly the best type of urine available. Another formula states that urine from a goat, fed only ferns for three days, is best. I really haven't studied this in depth, and I really cannot say why these two formulae are so specific. All I can say is that the techniques I have tried do work.

Heat-treating Damascus steel is like heat-treating high-carbon steels. As long as the steel cools quickly enough to harden without cracking, the quenching medium will work (whether it is simple brine or a secret mixture full of bat wings and owl droppings). If the quenching medium allows for a fast cooling that doesn't crack the steel, then whatever it is, it will work.

So you can see, there are no secrets to the heat-treating, and it is not as difficult as some people would lead you to believe. It is the old adage once again: It's easy if you know how.

CHAPTER 18
Damascus Patterns

Making various Damascus steel patterns takes time, patience, and understanding of the limitations of the materials that you are using.

The patterns most commonly used today in the custom knife are *ladder, pool and eye, waterfall, maiden's hair,* and *Persian,* to name a few.

These patterns are all made from a basic straight-laminated billet. Some patterns work best with fewer layers than others. Usually, the more layers the better, within reason.

Basically, the types of patterns can be grouped into two categories: surface manipulation and material manipulation. Surface manipulation is just that—you work with the surface in various ways. If you are not careful with the finish grinding, you can wash out sections or totally erase the pattern you are attempting to put into the bar. Material manipulation is when you use the characteristics of the material for your benefit, and the pattern will run all the way through the bar. The various twisted patterns are good examples of this technique.

Whichever technique you decide to use, you will be using a larger volume of the laminated materials than you would think. The twist-based patterns are quite wasteful in this regard, but the results are worth it.

The best results in patterning this material will be obtained by using materials that have a great deal of contrast. A billet made with various high-carbon tool steels, layered with a chrome-or nickle-bearing alloy, or pure nickle will be best.

Beware of the pure nickle, as it must be worked slowly when patterning. Be certain that there are no cold shuts or inclusions in the billet before you even start to work it, or you can ruin the piece.

LADDER PATTERN

The ladder is a classic pattern and is rather easy to make when compared to all of the others. The ladder is a surface manipulation pattern that should be put into the blade after the blade is forged to profile, but before the bevels are put it.

The more layers used in this pattern, the better. I suggest that you use upward of 300 layers, depending on the materials used. A billet of 150 to 200 layers of pure nickle/tool-steel laminations is quite dazzling when done in this pattern.

Then again, any material that contrasts reasonably well can be used. This pattern can produce a good edge with as little as 70 layers and an excellent edge with 175.

There is a variety of different styles of ladder patterns. The patterns depend on the amount of layers, the distance between the cut grooves, and whether it is single- or double-edged.

To start, weld a billet of not less than seventy layers and forge the blade to shape—but leave it 25 to 30 percent thicker than the finished blade. In so doing, you will have enough thickness to put the pattern in. Do not forge the edge bevels or do any final profiling on the blade.

Cut a series of evenly spaced grooves along both

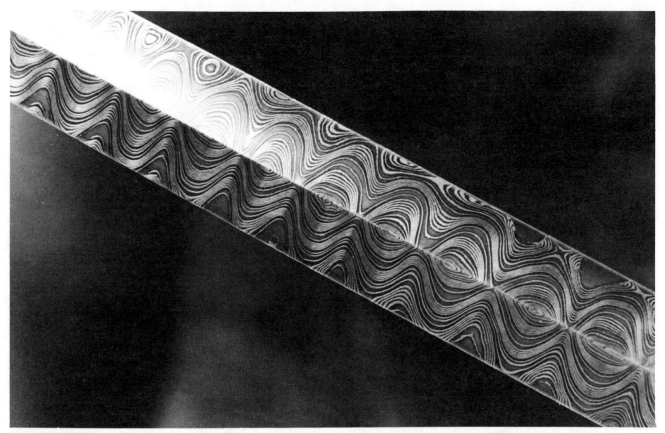

Fig. 121. Close-up of a ladder pattern blade made by author. Materials used: 1095 and pure nickle sheet.

sides of the blade. Space the grooves out so they alternate from side to side so that they do not align on top of one another.

Cut the grooves about one-third to one-half the depth of the piece. The closer together you make the grooves, the tighter the pattern will be, but the less definition you will get of the "rungs" of the ladder. The farther apart the grooves are, the better you will be able to see the "rungs," but you will not get as good an edge. If you are using three-sixteenths to one-quarter-inch wide grooves, space them one-to one-and-a-half groove widths apart (this is measured center to center of the grooves).

The way you cut the grooves will also affect the pattern. If you cut a V-shaped slot, the pattern will be even with the majority of the layers of the same width when the blade is finished. If the groove is U-shaped, the layers at the bottom of the U will seem to be a bit thicker in the finished blade. This is due to

the way that the layers are cut. The rounding of the bottom of the groove will be somewhat parallel to the laminations and cause the number of layers that are revealed to be less than on the sides of the groove. A small difference, but a difference none the less.

After the grooves are cut, forge the blade flat until all of the grooves disappear from both surfaces of the blade.

What this forging flat does is to cause the bottom of the grooves to come up to the surface of the bar, bringing the edges of the cut laminations to the surface as well. The pattern that is seen is caused by the ends of these laminations being forced to the surface. This in turn causes a "wave" to be seen along the edges of the bar.

The pattern that will be seen in the unfinished blank will look like a straight laminated piece, crossed by a series of lines at a 90-degree angle.

When the piece is flattened, forge it to shape and

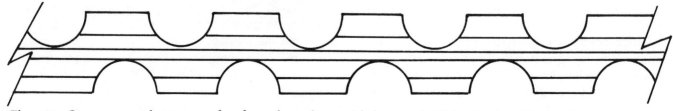

Fig. 122. Grooves must be staggered and cut through one-third to one-half the depth of the bar for best results.

Fig. 123. Note wavy appearance of the laminations on the edge.

rough-grind/heat-treat, and finish.

If the blade is single-edged, it will appear to be a wavy pattern, with the pattern going up and down away from the edge. If it is a double-edged blade, the wave should be even on both sides of the center spine.

This wavy pattern enables more laminations to cross the cutting edge on the blade; the more laminations that cross the edge, the better that particular blade will cut.

The ladder pattern is one of the better-cutting steel patterns.

BUTTERFLY PATTERN

The butterfly pattern is a modification of the ladder pattern, though instead of cutting grooves straight across the billet, you cut a series of Xs on both sides of the billet and forge flat. The more layers, the better for this pattern. A word of caution: You can erase this pattern easily by grinding this pattern too deeply. Do as much of the forming and edge packing as possible at the forge and keep grinding to a minimum.

POOL-AND-EYE PATTERN

This pattern is started after the first fold is made. The pattern is a bit on the random side, but still attractive. Start from a billet of not less than sixteen layers, and drill a series of one-quarter-inch holes through one-third of the depth of the bar, and forge the billet flat. There will be a small bull's-eye pattern anywhere you drill a hole. When the billet is flattened, fold the billet, weld, and repeat the drill/flatten/fold process.

As the billet is forged, the first holes that were

Fig. 124. The pool and eye pattern in a hunting knife made by the author.

drilled will be stretched out into long oval "pools," with the next series of flattened holes forming smaller and smaller pools. The last series of holes will be the "bull's-eye" patterns seen in the finished blade.

You will get the best results if you do not align the holes on top of each other. This pattern is somewhat subtle when compared to the others, but it can be quite pretty in its own way. It will cut like a flat-laminated blade, so the more layers you have, the better the edge will be. I have had good results from approximately 300 to 360-plus layers.

TWISTED PATTERNS

The twisted bars can produce a very different pattern from a flat-lamination-based pattern. They can form patterns that look like feathers, spirals, or stars. The spiral twists will impart a different pattern to the surface as you remove material from the twisted bar due to the bar's physical makeup.

As you grind away material, the pattern will look like a spiral twist. As you get closer to the center of the bar, the twist will affect the laminations less and less, and that is what causes the stars or crosses to appear in the bar. Also, if you flat-grind a billet, the results will differ from a hollow grind. Flat-grinding removes a minimum amount of material when compared to hollow grinding.

The more layers that are cut through, the greater the amount of the laminations that are seen. It is the laminations that cause the patterns, and some material manipulation patterns are best when flat-ground (i.e., maiden's hair and waterfall), while others will benefit from hollow grinding (such as the chevron and ribbon-type patterns).

If you do a lot of forging of the bar after it is twisted, the pattern will be dramatically changed. The forging will have a tendency to straighten out the twist along the axis of the forging. The forging will not cause the bar to untwist; it will elongate the twist in the direction of the material's movement. This characteristic can be taken into account before starting and can result in some very interesting patterns in a blade.

The best patterns are usually a result of twisting bars three-eighths to one-half-inch square, consisting of anywhere from sixteen to 200-plus layers. I have used smaller diameter bars (one-quarter-inch) for the ribbon patterns, and have had good results. Usually, the smaller the diameter of the bar, the easier it is to get a good tight twist without shearing apart the welds. Some material will twist with better results than others.

Be certain to round the sharp corners of the squared bar. Smooth corners will help prevent any stress cracks from developing while the twist is being made. I have seen bars that were so cracked that they were, for all intents and purposes, useless. Also, make certain that there are absolutely no cold shuts or inclusions in the bar before you do any twisting. If there are any of these irregularities in the bar, the twisting will open them up to the point where they are irreparable by welding.

Do all of the twisting at a full cherry-red heat. You can twist clockwise or counterclockwise (deocil or widershins for you old-timers). I have found that a reworked pipe wrench (monkey wrench) with an extra handle brazed or welded on makes twisting a lot easier, and helps in controlling the amount of twist that is placed into a bar as well.

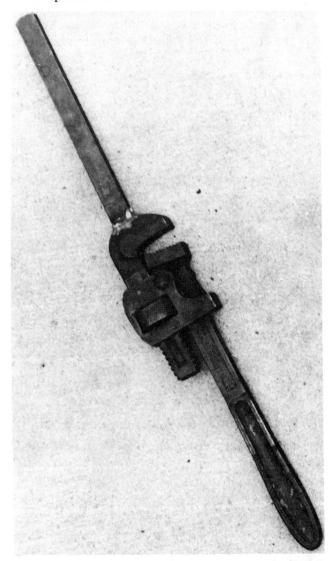

Fig. 125. The extra handle on the reworked pipe wrench aids in twisting billets and with other forge work.

Expect a lot of heavy scaling as you twist the steel. Wire-brush away the scale to enable you to see the condition of the bar. There will be some minor surface cracking regardless of the roundness of the corners. This is to be expected and will in no way be detrimental to the bar. These cracks may go in only a few thousandths of an inch, and are easily removed. The surface will be ground away after the twisting, in preparation of the next step in the forging process.

For a bold pattern, try fewer layers, with a chrome or nickle content in one of the basic materials. For the finer patterns, such as the Persian ribbon, use a greater number of layers to get the most out of the effect.

The final cutting abilities of these patterns vary greatly. Some will outcut all the other patterns, while others will be outcut by the straight-laminated blade. As with the other patterns, the more layers that are crossing the edge, the better the blade will cut.

Fig. 126. The bar has been twisted and flattened and is ready to be ground true prior to further forging.

WATERFALL PATTERN

This is a twisted pattern made from one twisted rod of laminated material. For the best definition, use a billet of not more than 100 layers, forged into a round rod of one-half to three-quarter-inch. Twist the rod into a slow spiral of a twist or two to the inch. The round rod will give a different pattern than will a square rod.

The resulting twisted rod is then forged flat and into the blade shape. The pattern will be slightly twisted, with the layers running in a slow spiral down the blade. Do as much shaping as possible in the forge to keep material removal to a minimum. Flat-grind the blade to bring out the best possible patterning.

This pattern will cut a little better than a flat laminated blade, but not as good as a maiden's hair pattern.

MAIDEN'S HAIR PATTERN

The maiden's hair pattern is similar to the waterfall, as it is a simple single twist. The major difference between the two is the greater number of layers and the bar being square in the cross section.

Construct a bar of 160 to 300-plus layers, of one-half to three-quarter-inch square cross section. Round the corners and twist tightly. Use localized heats if required to get an even twist. Do not force the material to twist more than it wants to during any given heat. If a greater amount of resistance is felt, back off and reheat. Wire-brush as needed to clean off the scale.

The actual number of twists is up to the individual. Three twists per inch is minimum, with seven or eight being about all that you are going to be able to do. The more twists in the bar, the better the blade will cut, the better this pattern will look, and the less it will appear to have straightened out during the forging.

After the bar is twisted, grind or file the corners of the twist down and forge flat. When the bar is flattened, forge the blade and forge the edge bevels. Do as much shaping as you can in the forge, as the less material you remove from the blade in the grinding, the better the pattern will come out. This pattern will work best with a flat grind since the hollows of the hollow grind will penetrate into the interior of the twist and start to form stars, which are not desirable in this particular pattern.

This pattern will outcut the waterfall pattern and is comparable to a good ladder pattern in terms of edge holding.

SINGLE-TWIST STAR PATTERN

The single-twist pattern is made along the same lines as the maiden's hair or waterfall patterns. The amount of forging is less, but the depth of the grinding is greater.

Make a rod of one-half to three-quarter-inch square cross section of not less than thirty layers or more than 250. The more layers, the better the blade will cut, but the less the stars will come out.

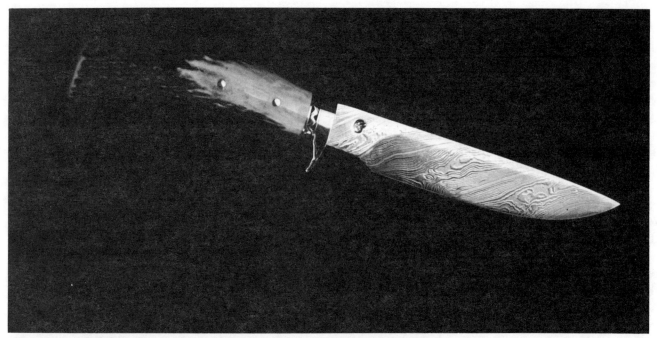

Fig. 127. A maiden's hair pattern hunter by Sean McWilliams; stag grip.

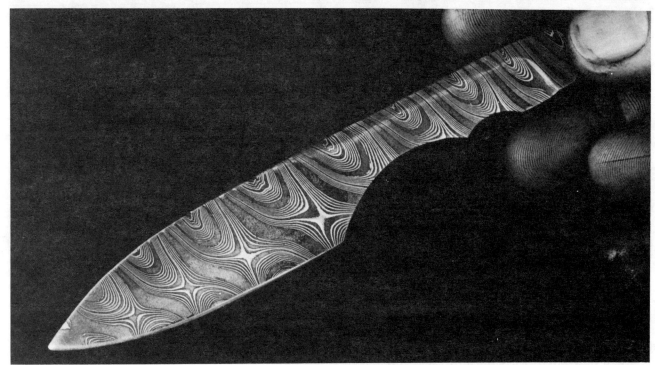

Fig. 128. A star pattern leather worker's knife made by the author. Materials used: 1095 and pure nickle sheet.

Twist the bar tightly, but not as tight as you would a maiden's hair bar. Round off the corners after twisting and forge the bar flat. Form the blade from the billet, but do not forge in the edge bevels, as you want to remove a considerable amount of material when the blade is ground. This pattern works best with a deep-hollow grind.

The more material you remove from the bar, the better the stars will come out. The reason for the dif-

ferences in this pattern from the maiden's hair is basically the depth of the grind. As the grind gets deeper into the bar, the less the laminations are twisted, and they appear to be flatter than the outside of the ground area. It is this difference that causes the starring effect.

This pattern can be best brought out by a double-edged blade with deep-hollow grinds. It will cut like an equivalent layered maiden's-hair-pattern blade.

MULTIPLE-TWIST PATTERNS

The multiple-twist patterns offer some of the most beautiful and time-consuming patterns that can be made. You will find them addicting and engrossing, but they do present problems, most of which are based on the materials used for the blade. If you use pure nickle, stainless steel, or any other material that doesn't weld well to itself, you will have to shim the weld surfaces with a piece of high-carbon steel in order to get a sound weld. This will affect the pattern, but it makes these patterns possible with the more exotic materials.

You will also find that the more contrast between the materials, the better these patterns will appear and the easier the etched patterns will be seen. This is especially true with the ribbon patterns.

DOUBLE-TWIST CHEVRON PATTERNS

The double-twist patterns can be manipulated to form patterns that resemble either the maiden's hair or star patterns, depending on the depth and type of grinding done to the blade and the direction of the twist.

To make the double-star chevron, use two square rods of three-eighths to one-half-inch diameter with layers of not less than thirty or more than 120 for the best pattern. Twist the rods tightly, with one rod twisted clockwise and the other counterclockwise (twist the bars in opposite directions).

Once twisted, cut or grind off the untwisted sections of one end of the bar. The remaining untwisted end will form the tang section of the blade. With this done, grind or file a flat surface on one side of each

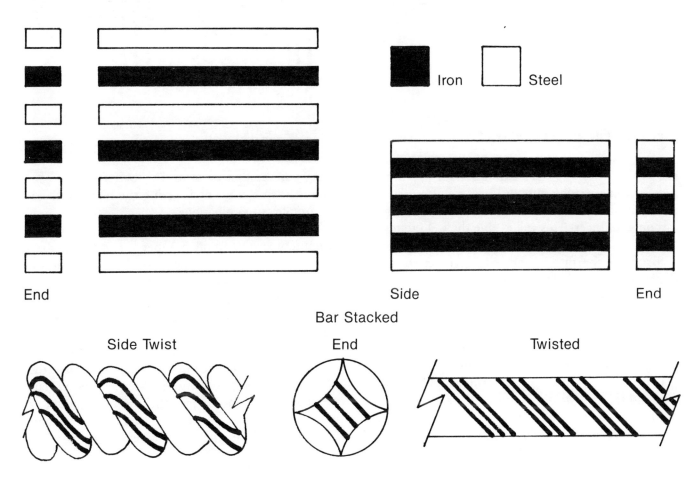

Alternating striped sections caused by flat and edges of the bar being twisted about center axis

Fig. 129. Single twisted rod construction, side and end views

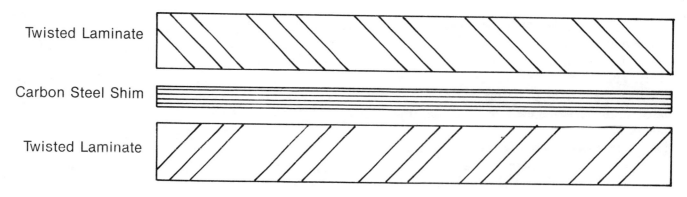

Twisted Laminate

Carbon Steel Shim

Twisted Laminate

Wire end and center of billet to allow easier welding of unwired end.

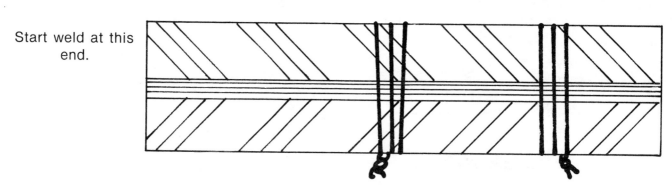

Start weld at this end.

Fig. 130. Wire end and center of billet to allow easier welding of unwired end.

rod. This will form a flat welding surface to join the rods. If you are using pure nickle or stainless steel in the laminates, shim the weld with a piece of high-carbon steel sheet. This will enable the weld to take, as these materials do not weld well to themselves.

Sandwich the pieces, and wire together to keep them in place during the welding process.

Start the weld on the untwisted end. If the layers shift at the start of the weld, you will not lose any patterned material. Flux heavily and work with light blows to prevent any shifting of the pieces. Straighten the alignment as is required as you work.

Once the piece is completely welded together, take a second series of welding heats, and strike the blade on the flat section of the billet. This will ensure that any sheared welds caused by the twisting will be rewelded, helping to prevent any future problems such as cracking or cold shuts opening up while you are forging the blade.

As you are working, the pattern on the surface of the bar should look something like a feather, with the bottom of the V being in the center of the bar.

Forge the blade to shape and lightly pack the edge bevels on the billet. Use a heavy hollow grind to bring out the best pattern. This pattern can be enhanced even further by fullering the blade to reveal even more cut laminations.

The cutting ability of the blade will depend on the amount of layers and the number of twists in the bars used. The more of both, the better the blade will cut.

DOUBLE-TWIST MAIDEN'S HAIR

This pattern is very similar to the star pattern—the only difference is in the way the bars are twisted and the amount of forging done to the finished bar.

Twist the rods in the same direction and forge the blade as much as possible to the finished shape. Flat-grind the blade and remove the minimal amount of material. A blade made in this fashion will cut basically along the lines of a maiden's-hair pattern.

PERSIAN-RIBBON DAMASCUS

This is perhaps the most beautiful of all the Damascus steel patterns. It is very time-consuming to do, uses a tremendous amount of material, and is one of the most difficult to make due to the numerous rods that are welded together.

This pattern uses three or more tightly twisted rods

Fig. 131. Note the feather pattern visible on the ricasso of the blade.

Fig. 132. Double star or chevron twist blade made by the author. Materials used: 1095 and pure nickle sheet.

(five to seven being about average) consisting of a greater number of layers than in the other twist patterns—175 to 250 layers in a one-quarter-square-section rod. Use materials which contrast sharply without washing out after a couple of hundred layers and which will forge weld to themselves without difficulty.

Make all the rods as identical as possible so you will end up with a more or less uniform pattern in the blade.

Twist the bars as tightly as possible, alternating the direction of the twist from bar to bar. When the bars are twisted, grind the weld surfaces smooth and stack the bars so that the twists alternate direction from row to row and wire together. This alternating twist will bring out the best pattern with numerous stars all up and down the blade.

If you are using more than four or five rods, break them up into two or three groups, welding these together first, then welding the resulting conglomerate bars to make the billet. This will be easier to manage than trying to maintain proper alignment on half a dozen bars while they are at a welding heat.

Once the pieces are welded, grind the surface until

it is more or less smooth and forge the blade as usual, leaving the blade slightly thicker than normal. A deep-hollow or flat-grind will bring out the best results in this pattern. This is perhaps the best cutting of all the patterns, both surface and material manipulation, due to the greater number of layers with the tighter twist, all of which cause a surprising number of laminations to cross the cutting edge.

PATTERN-WELDED NORSE BROADSWORDS

The pattern-welded blade was taken to its highest form by the Norse, who spent hours upon hours to make their finest broadswords. The majority of the Norse patterns were based on the use of twisted material and fabricated from three to nine (or more) pieces of previously welded/twisted material and homogenous iron.

The workmanship and quality of these early blades are unbelievable, especially when you think that most of these blades were made before the ninth century. Multiple welds with pattern-welded material was the most common method of construction. I have estimated that 100 to 125 hours or more of forge time would not be unusual for some of the more elaborate

Stacked

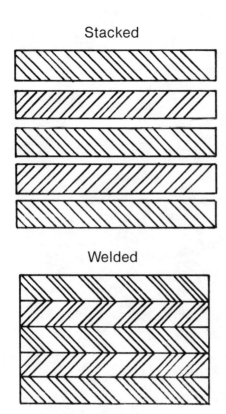

Welded

Fig. 133. Twisted bars must be stacked with twists running in opposite directions.

patterns found in these blades.

The Norse broadsword is the best example of period European pattern-welding available to date. The legendary quality, beauty, and workmanship is silent testimony to the fact that the Vikings were not the horn-helmed, murderous raiders that Hollywood would have us believe. They were some of the greatest swordsmiths and metal craftsmen the world has ever seen. Their blades were in great demand and worth a small fortune in their day. A pattern-welded sword was a sword fit for a chieftan or a king, a sword that would not break like the softer, steeled iron ones were prone to do. It was a mark of rank and high birth, a symbol of quality.

The patterns within the steel were a guarantee that the blade was made in the proper way. The pattern-welded sword was in such demand in Europe during the Migrationary Period (from the fourth to the ninth centuries A.D.) that for a time, plain steeled-iron blades were often inlaid with silver, latten, or bronze to simulate the pattern-welded finish. This fact is attested to by the numerous amount of such blades that still survive to this day.

The patterns within the blade varied from simple laminations to complex twists. The basic blade shape

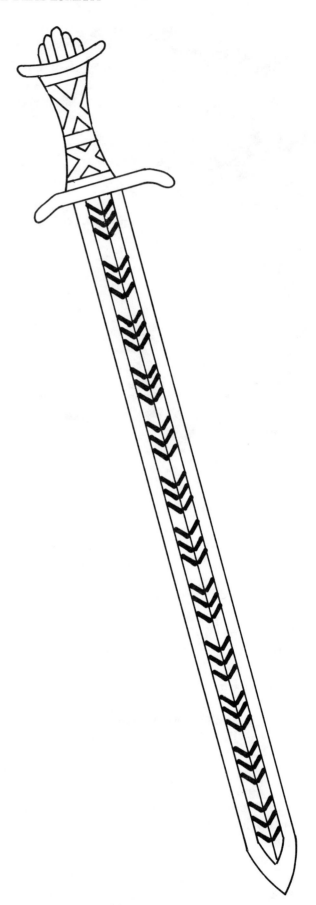

Fig. 134. The classic Norse broadsword

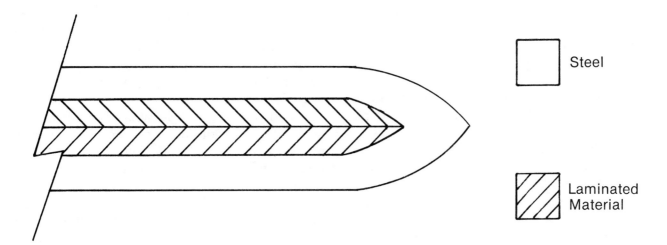

Fig. 135. Simple Norse construction

was relatively wide with very little taper, a thin cross section, and a narrow edge bevel. More often than not the blade had one wide, shallow fuller down each side, starting from beneath the grip and ending a

1	2	3
4	5	6
7	8	9

1	2	3	4
5	6	7	8
9	10	11	12
13	14	15	16

Fig. 136. Rods need to be arranged in a square prior to twisting.

short distance from the tip. This was a blade designed to chop and slice, not to thrust.

The most often used simplest pattern consisted of two bundles of small-diameter rods twisted together and welded between two pieces of steel that formed the cutting edges.

Blades made in this fashion showed open cold shuts in the center rods that did not weld together during the forging process. As far as I can tell, these were very common and were planned into the construction of the blades. The individual strands of the rods will flex independently from their counterparts and will enable the blades to withstand tremendous shocks, both on the flats and the edges.

This blade can be easily reproduced by obtaining small cross-section mild steel (one-eighth-inch-square) barstock and arranging the barstock into a larger square. Nine bars arranged in a square, of three by three, will work, as will sixteen bars arranged in four by four.

Make two bundles, heat the rods, and twist tightly, alternating directions of the twist on the different rods (one rod clockwise and the other counterclockwise). Make the twists as even and as uniform as possible. Let the rods cool slowly.

When the rods are cool, round off the square sections of the twists, being careful not to remove too much material or else you will start to cut through the smaller rods and will have to start over.

When the rods are rounded off, wire them together and weld. You will need to flux them heavily to get the flux to penetrate the areas between the rods. Remember that mild steel welds at a higher heat than high-carbon steel.

Overlap the weld areas and make certain that the

welds are sound. This is important, for the welds must take and support the strands of the twist. With the pieces welded together, forge a point onto one end of the bar. This point will form the tip of the blade.

Use a piece of medium-carbon steel (60 to 70 points) for the edge. You can attach the steel to the core in two ways: You can sandwich the core between the two edge pieces of carbon steel or fold the steel around the core. The majority of the period blades were made in this latter fashion.

Wire the bars together and weld. The welding temperature will be similar to pattern welding since the carbon content of the carbon steel will lower the welding temperature.

With the piece welded, forge to shape, and fuller. Heat-treat and finish as usual. The blade will show subtle watering, and will be tougher than all hell due to the iron core.

The Norse also went to great pains to work patterns into the swords. These higher-grade swords used twisted sections that were split lengthwise, folded open, welded along the fold, and then assembled around an iron core. These blades showed a different watering due to the splitting of the twists.

The use of the split twist can open up a variety of new possibilities for the bladesmith. The patterns will be different on both sides; since these patterns were usually welded around a softer iron core, the fact that they are different did not present any problem. Then again, why should it? Whose place is it to decide that both sides of the blade should match? More often than not, Norse blades had two, three, or more different patterns, all up and down the blade's length.

This variety in the patterns was brought about not only by the splitting of the twists, but also in the methods used in the working and forging of the materials after they were welded.

If the twists were bent into a tight "wave" shape and then ground down in a flat bar, the resulting

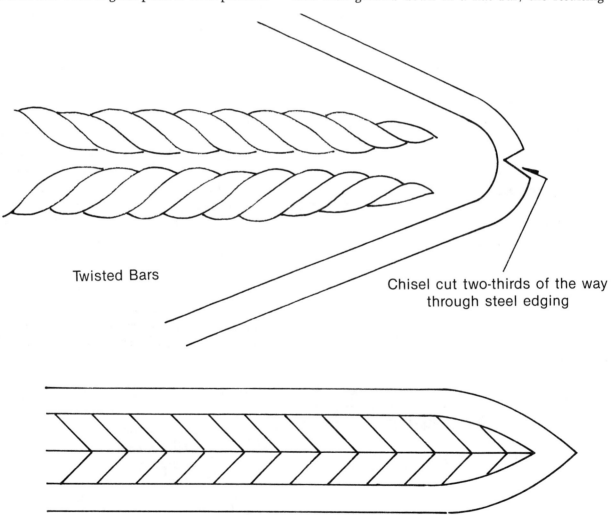

Twisted Bars

Chisel cut two-thirds of the way through steel edging

Fig. 137. Simple Norse construction breakdown

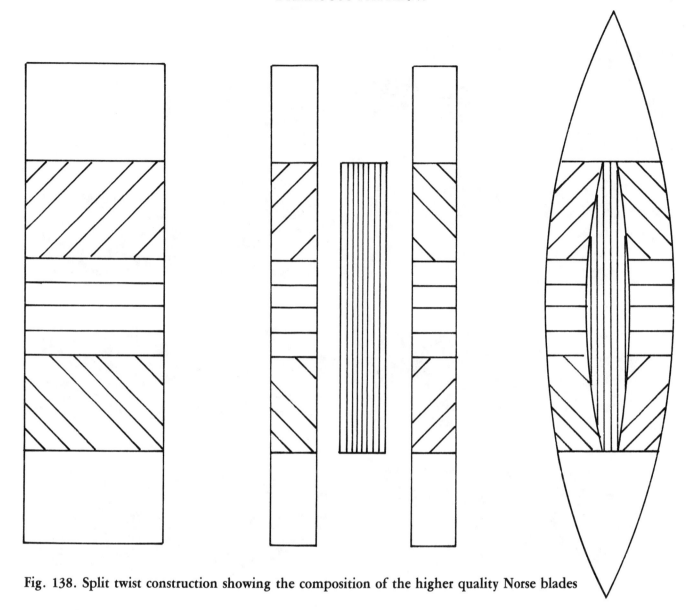

Fig. 138. Split twist construction showing the composition of the higher quality Norse blades

pattern would be considerably different than just a plain split twist.

The amount of time involved in making a blade along these lines will be greater than most of the other patterns. The forging techniques are quite sophisticated and indicative of an advanced metalworking culture. The Norse bladesmiths had a feeling for their craft and spent endless hours making their finest blades. Not bad for a so-called barbaric culture!

All in all, some of the finest blades in preRenaissance Europe were made by the Norse. These blades have stood the test of time for over fourhundred years. The medieval culture was a knife culture; blades were a part of everyday life. The blades had to cut, hold an edge, and be able to withstand constant everyday use. They were beautiful as well as functional, bearing silent testimony to the art of the medieval bladesmith.

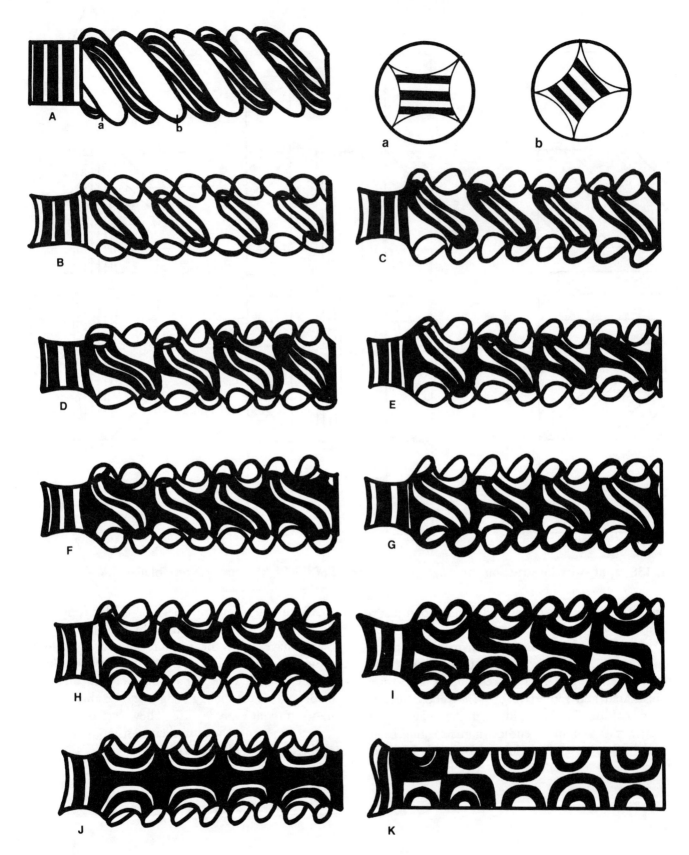

Fig. 139. Variation in pattern as the bar surface is ground and split.

CHAPTER 19 ———

Cable Blades

There is another way to obtain the "watered steel" patterns in a blade. It is a different and unusual technique: forge-weld wire rope (steel cable).

The welding of a steel cable into a blade has been done for at least the last eighty to 100 years. I remember watching a blacksmith from northern California do it when I was a child. It was done, but not as widespread as pattern-welding. In all practicality, the art was, for a period of time, all but lost to common knowledge. This is no longer the case.

There has been a revival in interest in welded cable, and it is making an impact in the custom-knife realm. The resulting blades are tough, durable, and different. They have a considerably different watering pattern than the majority of the pattern-welded steels made today.

The water pattern is more along the lines of a "spider web" or lizard-skin pattern, somewhat random, but to a degree controllable. Due to its nature, it is best suited for the various twist patterns.

The only material required is all-carbon steel wire cable. There are various types of this cable available, but you will need the all-steel (nonstainless, nongalvanized) kind.

Usually, the material used is referred to as "plow-share steel," which is the oil-hardening 10XX series steel.

Types of Wire Rope

Plow steel	1065
Improved plow steel	1075
Extra improved plow steel	1095

The available sizes range from one-quarter inch to over one and a half inches in diameter. The number of strands used in a cable will vary from seven to over 300, depending on the type of cable you are using (see the last section of this chapter for more information). Be certain that you get the all-wire-rope type of cable. Do not use wire rope that has a plastic or fiber core. These will not weld, but will make a horrible mess.

But what causes the pattern in the blade if it is all the same material? The pattern achieved is caused by the cold drawing of the wires used in the cables. This cold drawing causes the crystalline structure to align itself along the axis of the drawing direction. When welded, the surface decarburization of the weld will cause a "line" around the weld seam. It is the difference in crystal structure and the decarburization along the seam that causes the watering to be formed. The resulting blade will be stiff and very tough. I have done tests to destruction of such blades, and have found that this material is almost as tough as pattern-welded material. This toughness may be due to the presence of the wirelike structures within the blade, which is quite evident if you break a billet.

Granted, though this watering will be rather dull and plain when compared to the laminated Damascus, it is still interesting. The costs are low and the materials readily available.

As far as I know, all of the wire rope has a petroleum/asphalt-based lubricant/rust-preventative coating. This coating should be removed before start-

Fig. 140. Cut cable section prior to welding and twisting (top). Completed weld/twisted section (bottom).

ing in order to get the best results. I have tried all sorts of solvents, grease removers, and other cleaners (from acetone to carbon tetrachloride) and have found that nothing is really effective in removing the coating. Gasoline does a decent job, but due to its volatile nature and the hazards of a fire, it should be done in the open, away from any flames or sparks.

To start, cut a section of three-quarter or one-inch wire rope about six to twelve inches long. Next, arc or gas-weld the ends over so they will not fray out and burn when the first forge weld is being made. I have found that you will get a better weld if you use a deep closed fire with a good bed of active coke on the bottom. You will then be able to see what is going on within the chamber and not burn the small steel wires as you are taking a heat.

Start out the weld with a very low blast and make sure the heat is even. When the heated section is a bright cherry-red, flux with anhydrous borax and return the cable to the fire. Turn the blast up to a slow weld heat and bring the piece up to weld temperature slowly. Keep turning it in the fire to prevent any wires from burning. When the piece is welding hot, start the weld. (Remember that this material is all high-carbon steel. It will weld in the orange color ranges, not in the higher colors that are needed to weld the lower carbon steels.)

When the piece is ready, you will need to strike first on one side and then rapidly turn the cable one-quarter of a turn to strike it again. This alternate turn/strike/turn will cause the round cross section to become a square one.

You will notice that the volume of the area will be dramatically reduced. A three-quarter-inch round wire rope will forge down to a three-eighth to one-half-inch square section. This reduction is caused by all of the airspace between the round strands being closed by the welding process.

There will be a great deal of slag and scale that will be hammered out of the cable as you hammer the welds closed. It is important that you overlap the weld areas and flux with borax. In so doing, you can prevent any cold shuts or inclusions.

Note: If you encounter problems with the cable untwisting, twist the cable tighter before starting to do the first weld. It is easier to twist if the ends are tack-welded together first. When twisting, take a cherry-red heat, flux the entire length of the cable, and then twist. Fluxing before the twisting will allow better penetration of the flux into the cable.

Be very careful with the working ranges of the steel since it is all high-carbon and is quite prone to being red-short.

You can ruin the steel by rushing the welding and working the steel when it's above its upper working-temperature limits.

After the first welding process is completed, the surface of the bar should appear to be streaked by the spiral groove patterns of the strands. I strongly suggest that you take a second series of welding heats, and strike the corners of the bar to be certain that they are welded.

To improve the appearance of the pattern, take a cherry-red heat and twist the bar in the same direc-

Fig. 141. Twisting the cable tighter prior to first weld. Note the two-handled wrench used in the twisting procedure.

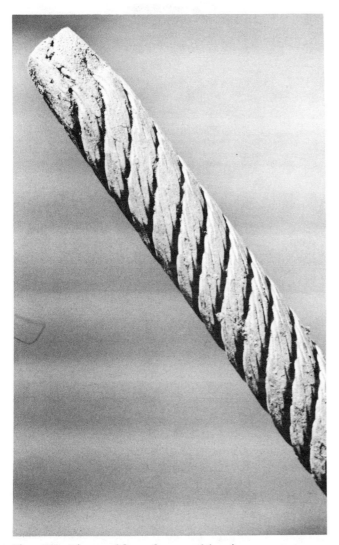

Fig. 142. First weld made on cable piece

tion that the spirals are going. (Five to nine twists per inch will suffice.) This twisting will enhance the pattern and has a positive effect on the cutting ability. Be very careful with the forging after the twisting as it will have a tendency to straighten itself out in the process.

After the twisting is completed, forge the bar down and get ready to fold. Fold the bar and weld it. You do not have to twist the steel, but the pattern will be straight and rather plain. I have had a great deal of success with chevron-like patterns using two, three, or four pieces, with each piece having an alternating clockwise/counterclockwise twist.

Once the piece is completely welded, forge and heat-treat the blade like 10XX series steel. The water pattern will not readily show until the blade is fully hardened and tempered.

Do not be discouraged if you encounter cold shuts and inclusions when first starting out using this material. This is a very tricky type of welding and does take some practice.

To etch the blade, polish to 400-grit, follow with a crocus buff, and clean. Etch with a mild nitric acid solution or ferric chloride until the pattern is visible. (Ferric chloride is available in the form of printed circuit etch at most electronic supply sources.) Aqua regis also works well. In some steels, it reveals the best patterns.

It seems that the welding temperature has an effect on the pattern's visibility. The lower the temperature at which you weld, the less the pattern will be seen. To bring out the most pattern, use the ferric chloride

Fig. 143. Second twist to tighten the pattern after the first weld

Fig. 144. Welding the cable into one piece

and let it etch for a considerable period of time, up to half an hour, making certain that you check on the etching process often.

A lot of experimenting can be done using wire rope as a basic material. It doesn't take the usual hours-on-end to weld a blade-size billet using the wire rope. The welded wire cable can open up a great deal of creativity in the pattern-welding process.

Types of Wire Ropes

There are various types of strands and twists within the strands. This can (and does) get quite confusing to someone who has no idea at all about what kind of wire to get. I suggest that you start out with plain, all-steel wire rope of seven-strand construction. Do not get ''Lang Lay'' cable, as the airspaces between the strands are greater than in the regular cable.

Fig. 145. Close-up of cable blade made by the author

The wire ropes listed below are all-steel (no fiber cores), have bright, uncoated (nongalvanized) finishes, and are those most commonly encountered. Some of the military specifications for the more common wire ropes indicate that the materials used should be of improved plow steel, that the finish should be bright steel (nongalvanized), and that the lay (twist direction) should be a right regular lay, unless otherwise specified.

Type I General Purpose, Class 3, construction 2, 6 by 37: 1 core with 6 surrounding strands of not less than 33 nor more than 43 wires each. Total wires: 198 to 301.

Type I General Purpose, Class 3, construction 4, 6 by 37 (filler wire): 1 core with 6 surrounding strands of not less than 29 nor more than 37 wires each. Total wires: 203 to 259.

Type I General Purpose, Class 4, construction 2, 8 by 19, (Warrington-Seale): 1 core with 8 surrounding strands of 19 wires each. Total wires: 152.

Type II Elevator, Class 2, construction 4, 8 by 19 (filler wire): 1 core strand with 8 surrounding strands of not less than 21 wires nor more than 25 wires in each strand. Total wires: 168 to 200.

Type II Elevator, Class 2, construction 5, 8 by 19 (Warrington-Seale): 1 core strand with 8 surrounding strands of 26 wires each. Total wires: 208.

The total number of wires used varies greatly. The more wires, the finer the pattern. If you fold the bar, the patterns will be finer yet, and quite subtle. Experiment with the different cables to see which ones you like best.

CHAPTER 20

The Japanese Blades

Japanese swordsmiths elevated the craft of pattern-welding into an art form. They dealt with not hundreds of laminations, but hundreds of thousands. The edges the Japanese achieved are legendary (but not as fantastic in real life). But what did the Japanese smiths do that was so remarkably different from Western smiths?

The basic difference in the Japanese blades is in the manufacturing. The Japanese smith used several different methods of assembling the steels and irons that went into their swords. Some methods were haphazard, at best, while others produced a blade of extremely high quality and beauty.

The poorest blades were made in a process called *kataha*, which involved welding a piece of steel on top of a piece of iron. The result was a bar with one hard side and one soft side. This process was used to make kitchen knives, tools, and as a basis for the better quality swords. Some of the Kozuka blades were made in this fashion as well.

The Japanese process one degree higher in quality is called *suyeha*, which involved welding a steel bar along the edge of an iron one. The blade was forged with the steel becoming the cutting edge. This was also a very haphazard way of making a blade.

The *wariha* process was quite similar to the suyeha technique in result. The iron body of the blade was split open, and a steel insert was welded within, closing the split. It is interesting to note that this process was used in Europe and was thought by Europeans to produce a good quality blade. The Japanese smiths thought differently.

The *kobushi* blades were made from two pieces also, but the steel was formed into a V-section and a softer iron spine inserted into the steel V, which was then closed. The blade was then forged so the bottom of the V formed the cutting edge.

The *uchimaki*, or *awase ni mai*, method involved the doubling over of a kataha bar so the steel side of the bar was folded back over itself to form the center of the bar, and then welded. This center was then forged to form the cutting edge.

The *moroha* blades were formed by wrapping a soft iron jacket around a steel center section in a manner from end to end (not around the sides), and then welded. The uncovered edges of the bar were then formed into the cutting surfaces of the blade.

The above-mentioned bladesmithing methods all involved two pieces of material in their construction. The Japanese looked at these blades as somewhat uncertain, and a little below first class. If done correctly, the kobushi and moroha processes would produce very tough blades, and these processes were used in other cultures around the world as well.

The *ori awasi san mai* process was looked upon as the only method that produced top quality blades using nonlaminated outer layers. This method involved the making of a suyeha bar and sandwiching it between two pieces of iron and welding the three together. The steel section along the one edge was then formed into the cutting edge of the blade. This process sometimes used a pattern-welded section for the sides, instead of the iron, for a quite dramatic effect (see *shihozume* below).

155

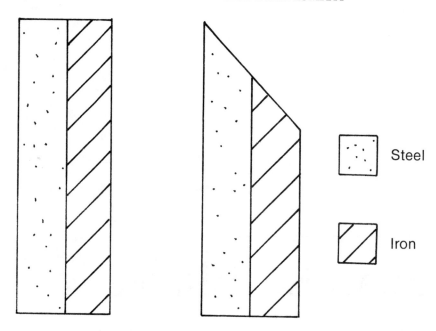

Fig. 146. For the kataha construction a piece of steel is laminated to a bar of iron and forged to form a single-edged, chisel-beveled blade.

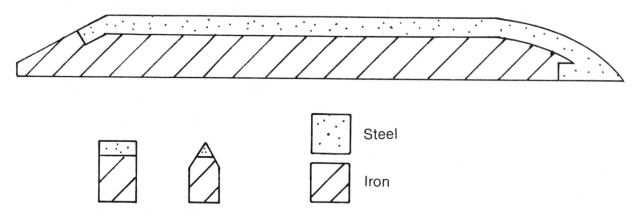

Fig. 147. For the suyeha construction a piece of steel is butt-welded to a bar of iron to form the cutting edge.

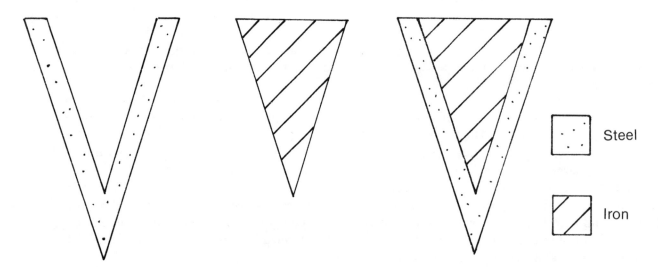

Fig. 148. The kobushi construction is formed when a soft iron triangular bar is sheathed by a thin-walled V-section steel skin that forms the cutting edge and two sides of the blade.

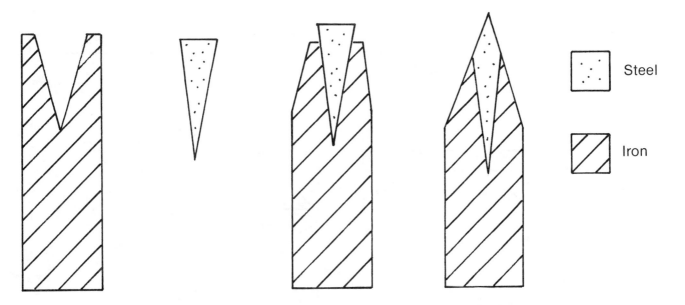

Fig. 149. In the wariha construction the iron bar has a V-shaped split forged into its length, and a steel insert is placed in the split to form the cutting edge.

Fig. 150. For the uchimaki construction a kataha bar is folded over with the steel side becoming the center of the bar, welded and forged, forming the cutting edge.

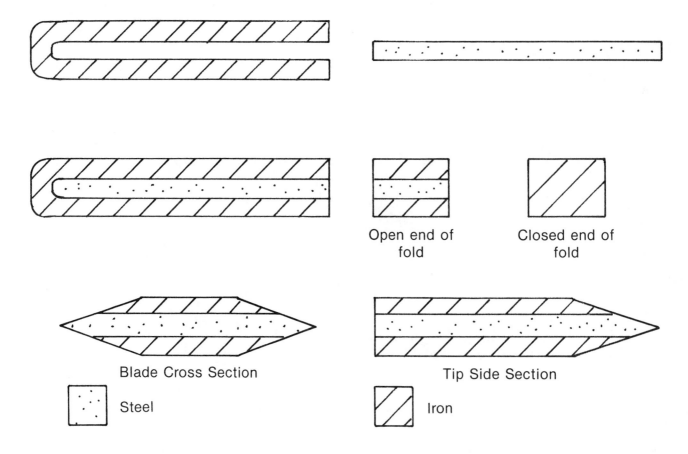

Fig. 151. The moroha construction consists of a U-shaped iron bar which is folded around a steel core, the two being forge-welded together. This softer iron sheath around the steel core is then forged into the blade with the iron supporting the harder steel.

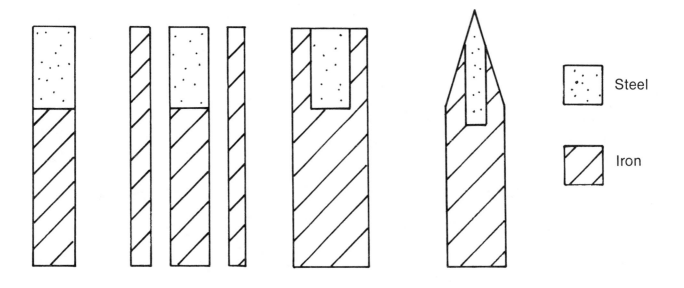

Fig. 152. For the ori awasi san mai construction a suyeha bar is welded between two pieces of iron that form the sides of the blade.

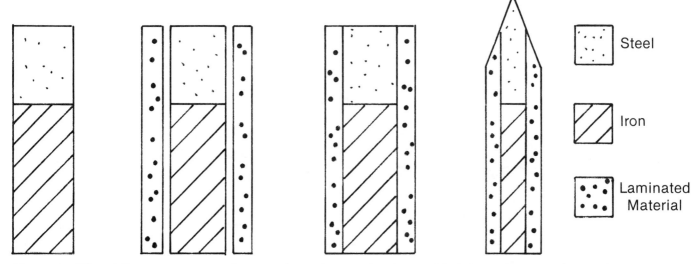

Fig. 153. The shihozume construction consists of a suyeha bar welded between two pieces of pattern-welded/laminated material that form the sides of the blade.

The following process involves the repeated folding and welding of the same bars. The Japanese smiths considered these techniques to produce a blade of very high quality. There are some strong similarities between these processes and pattern-welding.

Shihozume is very similar to the ori awasi san mai method, with the exception that two side plates were made from two kataha bars that were doubled over and welded fifteen times each bar. This results in approximately 32,000 layers in each piece. There will be no discernible watering caused by the actual layers visible on a piece made in this fashion. There may be weld lines that are visible, giving the effect of numerous layers within the piece, but these lines will be far less numerous than the actual number of layers in the blade.

The Japanese smiths would literally spend days at the forge, welding, forging, and rewelding these blades until the blades were, in the smiths' opinion, perfect in construction and purpose.

For the Western mind, the task seems endless and difficult. Take it from me, I have done these procedures, and they are not that difficult—but they are time-consuming. They also eat up a considerable amount of raw materials. I have used upward of fifteen pounds of steel and iron to make one twenty-six-inch katana in the shihozume tradition.

The methods produce quite beautiful blades, but this is not a blade that you can produce in an afternoon or two. It is quite labor-intensive and nerve-wracking, but worth it.

The resulting surface will be quite different when polished in the traditional Japanese methods. There will be areas of clouds and slight color variations.

These are quite attractive and, to the Japanese, show the quality of the blade.

WESTERN VS. JAPANESE TECHNIQUES

There are several differences between the Japanese methods and the Western ways of welding, and these are in the fuels used, the basic materials, and the flux.

The Japanese did not have the usual coal fires that we Western smiths are so familiar with, since they used wood charcoal (usually red oak or pine; teak was also used when available). These fuels burn very clean, very hot, and quite fast. Since the impurities were already removed in the charcoal-burning processes, the fuels were clean and ready to use as soon as they were added to the fire.

The Japanese smith used vast amounts of charcoal to forge even a small blade. The quantities were in the several-hundred-pound range. Charcoal burns away to a clean ash that will not impart any adverse effects to the forging or to the steel's structure. In fact, this ash has a very beneficial effect on the steel as it acts as a flux and helps to remove any impurities from the steel, while imparting some trace elements of silicon into the steel. (Silicon has a tendency to toughen the steel and is a beneficial trace element.)

The basic materials were also different from those used by the European smiths. The Japanese obtained their raw iron from several sources, the most notable being the use of magnetite iron (black sand) obtained from a riverbed or beach sand. This unrefined iron ore was then melted into the basic materials. The smelting processes were very similar to the Western methods. The iron ore and fuel were placed into the

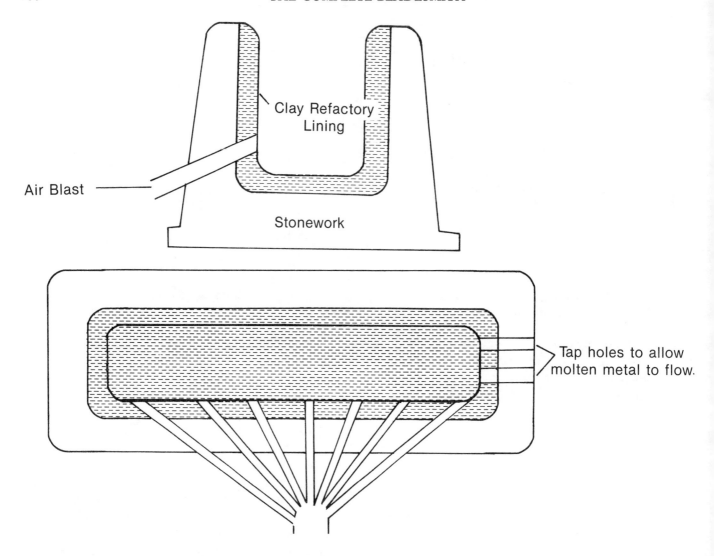

Fig. 154. The Japanese forge. Note the numerous side blast tuyeres, located along the side of the forge in place of the more common European style bottom blast tuyere/air grate.

Japanese forge and the fire started.

As the fire burned, it melted the iron ore, and the molten ore filtered down through the fire and formed a pool in the bottom of the forge. It is interesting to note that since the charcoal burned away to a clean ash, these ashes actually formed a protective coating on the surface of the molten metal and prevented any free oxygen from burning the surface of the molten pool.

As the fire burned and the forge started to absorb heat, the sides of the forge would melt, and the clays used in the construction of the forge formed a flux that imparts silicon and other trace elements into the steel. I have no idea as to the formulae the Japanese used in the mixtures of the refractory clays, as these were and are still a secret.

After the steel was smelted, the forge was allowed to cool and the metal removed.

The Japanese smith, like his European counterpart, relied on his experience in selecting the right sections of the metal to make his blades.

The metal would range from almost pure iron to cast iron, mild steel, and carbon steel. The Japanese smith obtained the same basic materials as the European smith, except that the Japanese material was purer, with fewer impurities and harmful trace elements than European steel. (This was a far better way to obtain the basic materials.)

After the smith chose the raw material to suit his purpose, he started to make the blade. The pieces were welded together into solid bars and stacked together to form the basic pieces of construction.

The Japanese used a different fluxing technique than Occidental smiths. The Japanese used straw ash, not wheat straw, but rice straw. The ash was applied in several different ways, depending upon the school in which the smith was trained. Sometimes it was brushed into the weld, and at other times it was spread between the layers in a thick mass. The ash acted as a flux by preventing oxidation and by imparting a little extra carbon into the weld as well. You can actually see the welding line as a bit of brilliant color in the steel. Borax-based fluxes usually will not cause these lines. The Japanese, with their love of the simple and intricate as well, seem to appreciate the subtle differences these weld lines make in the traditionally made blade.

The working methods were basically the same in Japan as in the West. Drawing out, folding, and welding are all basically the same, no matter from which culture you learned the art.

The Japanese swordsmith used a tool very similar to the European draw knife to do the final shaping of the blade. This tool is called the *sen* and was made of a fully hardened piece of steel. The sen would shave and cut the softer, unhardened steels before they were heat-treated.

The Japanese also had a unique way of hardening the blades by placing a refactory material on the non-cutting surfaces that resulted in a variable hardening and a visible temper line (*yakiba*). I will go into deeper detail later on in this book (see Chapter 21).

To reproduce the Japanese blade, use a plain 10XX series carbon steel (1085 or 1095 is best) laminated with either wrought iron or 1010/1020. You do not want any impurities (such as chromium, nickle, tungsten or other alloying elements so common in modern steels).

Weld the blade using either a borax flux or the traditional straw ash.

The straw ash is just that—straw burned to ash. Rice straw is quite difficult to obtain, but the more common wheat straw is usable. Burn the straw down to an ash and add the resulting powder to the weld surfaces at a higher heat than you would add the borax.

Layer and weld the steel/iron laminates as you would pattern-welded materials. Draw out, fold, and weld until the desired number of layers is reached.

Assemble your blade along the lines of one of the various styles of Japanese construction. The basic blade shapes varied somewhat from one school to another and from one time period to the next.

The Japanese blades were generally single-edged, slightly curved, and quite thick when compared to their width.

Forge the blade to shape, with less curvature than you want in the finished blade, and heat-treat the blade using the Japanese heat-treating techniques described in this book. There will be some warpage during hardening, and this warpage should put the remaining curve that is wanted into the blade.

Polish and finish the blade to bring out the temper line using progressively finer abrasives (see Chapter 21).

Contrary to popular belief, these blades will not perform feats of legendary cutting ability. I have yet to see one of the machine-gun barrels, rifles, helmets, and other objects that these swords were supposedly able to cut in twain without even slowing down. Steel is steel. It will behave like steel will behave, regardless of whether it is American, Japanese, or Swedish.

Some metal-working techniques (like lamination) will produce a tougher blade than others, but all blades will eventually break. The Japanese blades were not very flexible compared to their European counterparts. Japanese blades broke, chipped, and shattered, but they were well suited for the purpose for which they were designed—cutting.

These blades have an extremely hard edge and a softer back that holds the blade together. This combination is almost unbeatable when it comes to slicing and cutting. Remember that a harder edge will stay sharper than a softer and tougher one. This was the combination that the Japanese chose for their blades, a full hard edge and soft back. The European smiths, on the other hand, chose a "spring" temper throughout their blades.

Unlike the European broadsword, the Japanese sword did not have to encounter a shield very often. The sword was the "last ditch" weapon of the Japanese warrior, who relied heavily on the bow (*yumi*), the spear (*yari*), and the Japanese version of the pole weapon—the *naginata* (or the *nagimaki*)—to do the job in combat.

But the Japanese blade will cut, and cut well. The edges tend to nick since they are full hard, but they will hold a sharp edge longer than most other blades. The real beauty of these Japanese blades comes from the subtle watering, the character of the temper line, and in their design.

The clean lines of the blade's shape, free from all the "new" ideas as to what a blade should be, are quite pleasing to the eye. These blades are more than a weapon—they are objects of beauty and works of art that should not be judged by their intended purpose alone, but also for the work and inherent beauty of the steels.

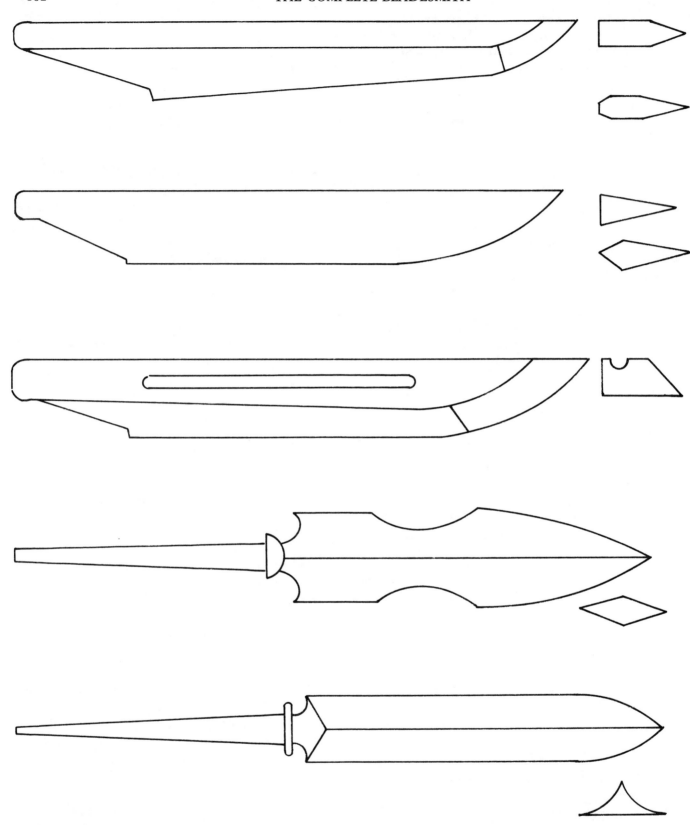

Fig. 155. Some of the more common shapes and cross sections of Japanese blades. Note that the bottom two blades are *yari* (spear) points.

CHAPTER 21

Japanese Heat-Treating and Polishing

The visible *temper line (yakiba)* on a Japanese blade was accomplished by not only the type of steels used, but also the way the blades were heat-treated. You do not need to laminate upwards of 3,000-plus layers in a blade to get a nice, visible line. This hardening technique will work with most of the simpler water-hardening steels and some oil-hardening steels as well. This works best with a flat- or a convex-ground blade. Most of the Japanese blades were a modified flat/convex hybrid grind. They were flat-ground almost to the edge, and then a convex section was put in to bring the blade down to a sharpenable thickness. You can use a temper-line heat treatment on a hollow-ground blade, but the blade will be considerably more difficult to polish than with the flat grind.

In order to achieve a temper line, one must first use a shallow-hardening, plain carbon steel of about sixty to sixty-five pts. carbon; 1065 carbon steel is ideal. The reason for using such a low-carbon-content steel is that the temper line will be more pronounced and easier to control. Stay away from any deep-hardening steels such as 5160, 0-1, or the like as the temper line will be quite difficult to obtain. You can use W-1 or W-2 steel, but these are quite prone to cracking during the hardening quench. You can get around this problem by using a light-oil quench for the water-hardening alloys.

Since this technique was developed for use on the traditionally made Japanese steels, the results will be quite dazzling if used on a laminated blade. You will

not attain all of the crystalline structures on a nonlaminated blade, but the lines will show up very well after they are polished.

You should mix the refactory coating ahead of time. The following formula (developed by Bob Engnath of the House of Muzzle-Loading in Glendale, California) consists of easily obtained materials and is quite easy to prepare.

Japanese-Type Blade Clay
6 parts finely ground fire brick
5 parts superfine iron/steel filings
2 parts silica sand (white sand available at foundry suppliers)
1 part finely ground charcoal
1 part CMC compound (available from ceramic supply houses)
Enough water to mix to a consistency similar to thick cake frosting.

I prefer to do about 90 percent of the necessary grinding before heat-treating the blade. I strongly suggest that you anneal the blades one additional time before the refactory is applied so that no residual hardness is left to spoil the process. After the blade has fully cooled, apply the clay with either your finger or a spatula.

The blade should be covered along the sides, back, and anyplace else you wish to have remain unhardened (this should be all of the blade save the cutting edges). The thickness should be approximately three-eighths of an inch. The cutting edge is now scraped clean. If you wish to have a wavy line, cut matching waves on both sides of the blade running along the edge. Be as adventuresome as you wish. What you get after heat-treating will depend on what you do now. The temper line will be similar, but not identical to the designs that you scrape into the clay.

It is a good idea to do three or four blades at a time in this manner and experiment with different scraped designs. I have come out with stunning lines doing this. It is all in how the clay is scraped and how long the blades remain in the fire.

After you are satisfied with the designs you have created, let the blades dry for twenty-four hours. By doing so, the water will evaporate and the clay will adhere to the blade surfaces better. I prefer to hang the blade vertically so it doesn't bump into anything. Do not worry about any cracks in the clay, as these are easily repaired by adding more clay and letting it dry.

After the blades are dry, build a fire long enough to heat the entire blade evenly. A good even heat is critical, for without it the results will be less than what they could have been.

When the fire is burning clean, place the blade edge-down into the coals and slowly bring the blade up to the critical temperature. Be very careful about bringing the blade up to temperature, as it is very easy to burn away part of the edge. The clay is a heat sink and will take considerable time to heat up. When the edge is at the proper heat, remove the blade and quench, point-down (vertically), into a light oil. (Do not worry if the portion of the blade covered by the clay is still dark. You really don't want that section very hot anyway.)

After the oil ceases to boil and smoke, wait an additional ninety seconds, and then remove the blade and place it into a warm water and dish-soap bath until completely cool. Remove the clay (if the clay is stubborn, use a wooden stick to scrape it off).

You will find that the best lines will come about if you heat evenly and to the critical temperature. If you go a little below or above this temperature, the lines will appear different in coloration and crystalline structure. The closer you get to the lowest temperature in the critical temperature range, the greater the crystalline contrasts will be, and the yakiba will be prettier and easier to see.

Fig. 156. Close-up of blade covered in the heat-treating clay

Note: Do *not* keep the blade in the fire any longer than required to get it to critical temperature, or grain growth will start to occur.

There is no need to draw a temper as this step was accomplished by the clay. The edge is fully hard, and the portion covered by the clay, if everything worked out right, is soft. If you wish to temper the blade, do so in your kitchen oven set at 350° F. Let the blade bake for two and a half hours, then let it cool slowly to room temperature.

After the blade is cool, you are ready to perform the finish grinding and hand-polishing.

FINISH GRINDING

The one thing to remember is to keep the blade cool. Do not allow the blade to get too hot to hold, or you can ruin the line by annealling the hardness out. The final polish on the machine should be 360- or 400-grit. As you work, you should start to see the line coming out in the machine polish. Make certain that all of the rougher grind marks are removed and that you have a perfectly flat surface on all sides of the blade (with no ripples or waves). These surface imperfections will be difficult, if not impossible, to remove in the hand-polishing.

Hand-Polishing To Reveal The Yakiba

The yakiba will be easier to see if the proper method of hand-polishing is used. The basic difference in hand-polishing and power-polishing (buffing) is the surface finish that is achieved on the metal.

In the Western methods, various types of polishing compounds are used on a power buffer. These compounds start out coarse and get progressively finer. The compounds are applied to a high-speed buffer and are used to remove the scratches left by the previous abrasives, leaving a smoother, shinier, and brighter finish.

By using such compounds, the crystal structure along the surface of the metal is somewhat "smeared" across the surface of the steel. The amount of metal that is removed is small, and the crystals are "closed over" by the buffing action.

In the Japanese technique, the amount of material removed is greater than the Western methods and the crystalline structure is "open" on the surface and not smeared over like a buffed surface. It is the open crystal structure that causes the line to become readily visible.

Traditionally, polishing in the Japanese fashion was accomplished using various natural stones, starting with a very coarse sandstone and finishing with a very fine and soft limestone. The amount of time involved is considerable when compared to power polishing—but the results of hand-polishing are worth the effort.

Today, the availability of the natural stones is very limited and, in general, quite rare. However, you can achieve the same basic appearance using readily available modern abrasives.

With the blade final-ground to 400-grit, *sharpen* the blade to the 400-grit stage with a convex edge. To do this, use a slack belt section and rock the blade into the belt edge-up until the edge is formed. You will need to alternate the sides of the blade every few passes to get a centered cutting edge.

The reason for sharpening is that you will be polishing the surface right to the cutting edge and honing the edges as well as polishing the blade. This is one of the "secrets" to the edge-holding abilities of a Japanese blade.

With the blade sharpened, you are ready to start the hand-polishing. Work slowly and carefully and *always* from the *back* side of the blade. The blade will get progressively sharper as you polish, and it can remove a lot of skin from careless fingers.

Start with 360- or 400-grit wet/dry sandpaper backed with a block. I have found that a micarta block works best as it does not get waterlogged and softer as it gets wet. Wet the paper, and with even pressure, start to polish the surface on which you are working. I have found that you can remove a lot of material by using small circular motions. This really helps to remove scratches on the hardened portion of the blade. Also remember to keep contact with the entire surface under the paper so you do not wear away the blade unevenly and ruin all the work you have done so far.

Replace the paper as required and be very careful when doing the tip and edges of the blade since it is quite easy to cut yourself or run the tip into your hand while you are doing this.

I strongly suggest that you use magnification to examine the surface for tiny scratches and other problems. All of the scratches must be removed prior to going on to the 600-grit. You will be surprised how stubborn the scratches can be. The ones on the hardened sections are sometimes very nasty to get out. If you leave a few in, they will show up very clearly when you are doing the 600-grit polish.

After you are sure that all the coarser scratches are gone, proceed to the 600-grit wet polish. This will

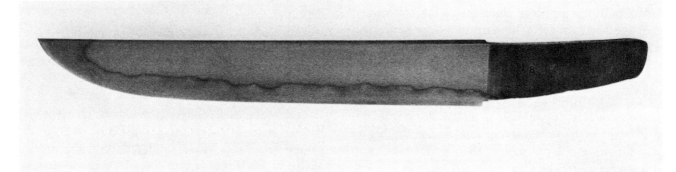

Fig. 157. Japanese-style tanto by Bob Engnath using Japanese heat-treating and polishing techniques

take considerably more time and a lot more paper. About halfway through with the polish, the line will start to stand out from the rest of the blade.

You will notice that the line will achieve a mirror-like appearance, and the unhardened portions of the blade will remain a frosty silver-gray.

To aid you in polishing, I suggest that you work at a 45-degree angle to the 400-grit marks so you can see any coarser marks easier. After you have removed *all* of the 400-grit scratches, it is best to finish off the polish going along the length of the blade until all of the 600-grit marks are running in the same direction.

By now you should see the yakiba. To bring this line out to a better contrast, take the following steps.

Make a tray from aluminum foil that will hold the blade. Place the blade into the tray and cover it with household cider vinegar. There will be a very rapid color change in the blade to a dark gray. After the blade turns color, rinse the vinegar off and dry the blade.

Polish off this discoloration, using a leather hand buff and a mixture of cerium oxide and water. (These items are available at lapidary supply stores.) If there are no lapidary supply stores in your area, you can use an automobile rubbing compound.

Polish slowly and carefully until the blade is clean and back to its original color. Keep the cerium oxide and water very wet so the abrasive action will be active. Repeat the vinegar/polish steps several times

until you are pleased with the contrast. By the third repetition, the polishing will be to the point where continuing will not improve the appearance.

The key to the entire process is patience. Take your time and do not rush any of the procedures. You will be very surprised as to the quality of the polish if you are careful to remove all of the coarser marks before going on to the finer abrasives.

Hand-polishing is not difficult, but it does take a lot of time. Figure on spending at least eight to ten hours when hand-polishing an eight-inch blade. Hand-polishing swords tends to be a slower process, but not as slow as you may think. Be patient and do not rush the process.

The preservation of this finish is entirely different from that of a buffed finish. Since the crystals of the steel are "wide open," they can start to rust almost as fast as they are polished. This corrosion can be retarded by applying a light, nonacidic, nonpetroleum-based oil. The best oils to use are clove oil or magnolia oil. The Japanese preferred these two over all others as these oils do not "gum," or evaporate to nothingness, and they remain active for a long period of time. Clove oil is available from specialty tool suppliers. Either one is good, but no matter which you choose to use, try to stay away from any of the aerosol (spray can) oils since they have a volatile propellant that can cause corrosion on some steels.

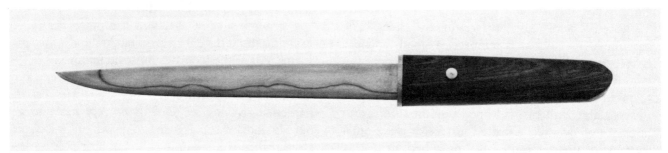

Fig. 158. Another Bob Engnath tanto showing the effects of the Japanese-style heat-treating and polishing techniques

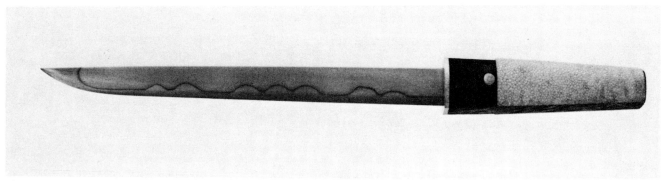

Fig. 159. A third Bob Engnath tanto

APPENDIX A——
Compounds

There are numerous books available that have been published in the last century which deal with bladesmithing, and much of the information therein is still useful, especially those texts dealing with the use of different compounds in the hardening/ tempering and finishing processes.

There is, though, a "fly in the ointment," as they say, and that is this: The names of most of the compounds used are the more colorful colloquial names like "dragon's blood" or "horn silver." These names are probably unknown to most people, so I include below a glossary to aid those who wish to recreate some of the older formulae.

Old Name	Chemical Composition
acid of potassium sulphate	potassium bisulfate
acid of sugar	oxalic acid
alcali volatil	ammonium hydroxide
alcohol sulphurus	carbon disulfide
alumina	aluminium hydroxide
ammonia	ammonium hydroxide
antimony black	antimony trisulfide
antimony bloom	antimony trioxide
antimony glance	antimony trisulfide
antimony red	antimony oxysulfide
antimony vermillion	antimony oxysulfide
aquafortis	nitric acid
aqua regia	nitric and hydrochloric acids
baking soda	sodium bicarbonate

Old Name	Chemical Composition
bichromate of potash	potassium dichromate
bitter salts	magnesium sulfate
black oxide of manganese	manganese dioxide
blue copperas	copper sulfate
blue salts	nickle sulfate
blue stone	copper sulfate
blue vitrol	copper sulfate
bone ashes	impure calcium carbonate
bone black	animal charcoal
borax	sodium borate
brimstone	sulphur
butter of antimony	antimony trichloride
butter of tin	stannic chloride hydrated
butter of zinc	zinc chloride
calomel	mercurous chloride
caustic soda	sodium hydroxide
chile nitre	sodium nitrate
chile saltpeter	sodium nitrate
chromic acid	chromium trioxide
copperas	ferrous sulfate
corrosive sublimate	mercuric chloride
corundum	aluminium oxide
cream of tartar	potassium bitartrate
dragon's blood	cannet root
ferro prussiate	potassium ferricyanide
flores martis	anhydrous ferric chloride
flowers of sulphur	sulphur
gallic acid	3,4,5, trihydroxybenzoic acid
grain alcohol	ethyl alcohol

Old Name	Chemical Composition
green vitrol	ferrous sulfate
hard oil	boiled linseed oil
horn silver	silver nitrate
iron perchloride	ferric chloride
iron pernitrate	ferric nitrate
iron persulphate	ferric sulfate
iron protochloride	ferrous chloride
iron sulfate	ferrous sulfate
ivory black	burnt, ground ivory
jeweler's etchants	3 g silver nitrate
	3 g nitric acid
	3 g mercurous nitrate
	100 cc distilled water
killed spirits	zinc chloride
lime	calcium oxide
liver of sulphur	potassium sulfide
lunar caustic	silver nitrate
muratic acid	hydrochloric acid
muriate of mercury	mercuric chloride
nitre	potassium nitrate
nordhausen acid	fuming sulphuric acid
oil of mars	deliquescent anhydrous ferric chloride
oil of vitrol	sulfuric acid
orthophosphoric acid	phosphoric acid
oxymuriate of mercury	mercuric chloride
oxymuriate of potassium	potassium chlorate
peach ash	potassium carbonate
pearl ash	potassium carbonate
plumbago	graphite
potash	potassium carbonate
prussic acid	hydrocyanic acid
purple crystals	potassium permanganate
quick silver	mercury
red prussate of potash	potassium ferrocyanide
sal ammoniac	ammonium chloride
sal volatile	ammonium carbonate
salt of hartshorn	ammonium carbonate
salt of lemon	5% solution potassium acid oxalate
salt of sorrel	5% solution potassium acid oxalate
salt of tartar	potassium carbonate
salt of vitrol	zinc sulfate
salt of worm wood	potassium carbonate
saltpeter	potassium nitrate
slaked lime	calcium hydroxide
soda	sodium carbonate
spencer's acid	3g silver nitrate
	3g nitric acid
	3g mercurous nitrate
	100cc distilled water

Old Name	Chemical Composition
spirits of hartshorn	ammonia water
spirits of nitrous ether	ethyl nitrate
spirits of salt	hydrochloric acid
spirits of wine	ethyl alcohol
sugar of lead	lead acetate
sulphuric ether	ethyl ether
sweet spirits of nitre	ethyl nitrate spirit
tetrachloromethane	carbon tetrachloride
tin salt	stannous chloride
tincture ferric chloride	ferric chloride/ethyl alcohol
tincture of steel	ferric chloride/ethyl alcohol
verdigris	copper acetate
vitrol	sulfuric acid
water glass	potassium silicate
yellow prussate of potash	potassium ferrocyanide

As you can see, the names are quite colorful and can be also quite confusing. They are especially confusing since several names are often given for the same compound in one given formula.

TEMPERING OILS

The oil in which one tempers blades can be as simple as plain olive oil, or as complex as one wishes, with all the "secret ingredients" one wants to add.

Using oil as a quenching medium may raise some alarm because of the fire flashes which can threaten safety. These oils will burn some when the metal is quenched, but the flash fire is easily dealt with by either covering the tank or simply blowing out the fire. Nevertheless, as with any fire, reasonable care and caution should be exercised at all times. One foolish, thoughtless act could be quite calamitous.

As a safety measure, always keep on hand either a CO_2 or a powder-type fire extinguisher. Never attempt to put out an oil fire with water, as this will cause the fire to spread. Also, common sand will be a great aid in cleanup of a spill as the sand tends to absorb the oil.

Natural Oils Suitable For Tempering

Olive oil is usable, though expensive. Olive oil is light oil, and as such may be too fast a quenching medium for some alloys. It does smell nice when heat-treating a blade.

Fish oil is, like olive oil, expensive, rather light, and hence a quicker quenching medium. It smells rather fishy.

Petroleum-based tempering oil formulae

The petroleum-based oils are by and large the best ones to use. The ingredients are easy to get, rather low in cost, and easy to formulate. Petroleum-based oils also can be made lighter or heavier to suit the quenching speed of the alloys you are heat-treating.

LIGHT OIL FORMULA 1
one (1) part diesel fuel
two (2) parts automatic transmission fluid
one (1) part motor oil

LIGHT OIL FORMULA 2
one (1) part automatic transmission fluid
one (1) part diesel fuel
two (2) parts motor oil

The light oil formulae are rather fast in quenching speed and should be used for the water-hardening type of steels.

Quenching a water-hard steel in the light oil instead of water will prevent cracking, warping, and excessive stresses from building up in the steel, along with thwarting other problems. It will not affect the cutting abilities of the blades.

HEAVY OIL FORMULA 1
one (1) part diesel fuel
three (3) parts motor oil

HEAVY OIL FORMULA 2
six (6) parts diesel fuel
eight (8) parts motor oil
two (2) parts automatic transmission fluid
one (1) part melted paraffin, mixed into the motor oil

The above two heavy oil formulae are recommended for most of the carbon-steel alloys that you are probably going to use. Feel free to experiment with other mixtures and compositions to find out what works best for you. As you can see, the mixtures are simple and easy to mix, using ingredients which are easy to obtain.

BLUING SOLUTIONS

Bluing can be an attractive finish on some blades. I have included the following formulae to give you the option of using this technique.

BLUING SOLUTION 1
8 fl. oz. water
8 fl. oz. denatured alcohol
2 fl. oz. hydrochloric acid
2 oz. ferric chloride

BLUING SOLUTION 2
1 gal. boiling water
3 oz. sodium thiosulfate
2 oz. lead acetate

The two solutions above are to be used when hot. Clean the surface to be blued of all oils, grease or foreign compounds, and place the item into the solution until the desired color is reached. Rinse the blade in hot water, dry, and oil.

ETCHING SOLUTIONS

The use of etching solutions is essential in producing pattern-weld (Damascus) steels. In order to see the pattern developed, the surface must be treated with a chemical etchant. There are several commercially available substances that may or may not work, depending upon the materials that you use in the blade.

Commercially Available Compounds

1. Naval Jelly brand rust remover is available from most hardware stores.
2. Printed circuit etching solutions are handled by most electronic supply houses, and are usually ferric chloride.
3. Swimming pool acid is a solution made from hydrochloric or muratic acids.

If you wish to make your own etching solutions (you will find it a great convenience to do so), please try the following formulae, as I have found that on the whole these work better than any of the ready-mixed ones.

A word of caution: When mixing an acid with water, remember to add the acid to the water, *not* the water to the acid. Wear a full-face shield *and* safety glasses. In case of an acid spill, keep a large open container of baking soda and plenty of water at hand to neutralize the acid, and wear an apron and rubber gloves.

ETCHING SOLUTION
8 fl. oz. reagent grade nitric acid
8 fl. oz. distilled water

ETCHING SOLUTION 2
4 fl. oz. sulfuric acid
4 fl. oz. hydrochloric acid
8 fl. oz. distilled water

ETCHING SOLUTION 3
4 oz. ferric chloride
16 fl. oz. distilled water

ETCHING SOLUTION 4 (aqua regia)
8 fl. oz. reagent grade nitric acid
16 fl. oz. distilled water
You will probably find that solutions one or four will work the best for most of your needs. All of these solutions should be stored in a heavy glass container and loosely stopped in a cool and well-ventilated place where it will not be knocked over. Remember to always have on hand a large open container of baking soda and a large volume of water in case of a spill.

These etching solutions can be made to work faster by warming them slightly. Remember to use proper safety precautions, and to do all etching out-of-doors, in a well-ventilated area.

WELDING FLUXES

The use of welding flux will aid you in obtaining good solid welds in your pattern-welding. There are a few fluxing compounds on the market for forge-welding and all of them, to a certain extent, work. The following mixtures are quite easy to make, and will work quite well.

The basis of the flux compounds is anhydrous borax, which is very easy to make. Take a package of Borateem laundry borax, place it in a crucible, and melt it down. It will bubble up white and "cook" into a dark glassy substance. Let it cool and grind it up into a reasonably fine powder. Next, either use the flux as is, or add one or more of the following: clean white silica sand, iron filings (low carbon steel, *not* tool steel), and/or sal ammoniac.

I prefer just to use the pure borax, as I feel that I am otherwise simply adding another chance for an impurity to be caught in the weld if I add anything else to the flux. Experiment, and see what works best for you.

Name	Symbol	Atomic Number
actinium	Ac	89
americium	Am	95
aluminum	Al	13
antimony	Sb	51
argon	Ar	18
arsenic	As	33
astatine	At	85
barium	Ba	56
beryllium	Be	4
bismuth	Bi	83
boron	B	5
bromine	Br	35
cadmium	Cd	48
calcium	Ca	20

Name	Symbol	Atomic Number
carbon	C	6
cerium	Ce	58
cesium	Cs	55
chlorine	Cl	17
chromium	Cr	24
cobalt	Co	27
columbium (niobium)	Nb	41
copper	Cu	29
curium	Cm	96
dysprosium	Dy	66
erbium	Er	68
europium	Eu	63
fluorine	F	9
francium	Fr	87
gadolinium	Gd	64
gallium	Ga	31
germanium	Ge	32
gold	Au	79
hafnium	Hf	72
helium	He	2
holmium	Ho	67
hydrogen	H	1
indium	In	49
iodine	I	5
iridium	Ir	77
iron	Fe	26
krypton	Kr	36
lanthanum	La	57
lead	Pb	82
lithium	Li	3
lutetium	Lu	71
magnesium	Mg	12
manganese	Mn	25
mercury	Hg	80
molybdenum	Mo	42
neodymium	Nd	60
neon	Ne	10
neptunium	Np	93
nickle	Ni	28
nitrogen	N	7
osmium	Os	76
oxygen	O	8
palladium	Pd	46
phosphorus	P	15
platinum	Pt	78
plutonium	Pu	94
polonium	Po	84
potassium	K	19
praseodymium	Pr	59
promethium	Pm	61

Name	Symbol	Atomic Number	Name	Symbol	Atomic Number
protactinium	Pa	91	technetium	Tc	43
radium	Ra	88	tellurium	Te	52
radon	Rn	86	terbium	Tb	65
rhenium	Re	75	thallium	Tl	81
rhodium	Rh	45	thorium	Th	90
rubidium	Rb	37	thulium	Tm	69
ruthenium	Ru	44	tin	Sn	50
samarium	Sm	62	titanium	Ti	22
scandium	Sc	21	tungsten	W	74
selenium	Se	34	uranium	U	92
silicon	Si	14	vanadium	V	23
silver	Ag	47	xenon	Xe	54
sodium	Na	11	ytterbium	Yb	70
strontium	Sr	38	yttrium	Y	39
sulfur	S	16	zinc	Zn	30
tantalum	Ta	73	zirconium	Zr	40

Weights and Measures

I have obtained these tables over the years and am constantly referring to them. I am certain they will aid you in numerous ways.

Decimal Sizes of Numbered Twist Drills

No.	Size	No.	Size	No.	Size	No.	Size
1	0.228	21	0.159	41	0.096	61	0.039
2	0.221	22	0.157	42	0.093	62	0.038
3	0.213	23	0.154	43	0.089	63	0.037
4	0.209	24	0.152	44	0.086	64	0.036
5	0.205	25	0.149	45	0.082	65	0.035
6	0.204	26	0.147	46	0.081	66	0.033
7	0.201	27	0.144	47	0.078	67	0.032
8	0.199	28	0.140	48	0.076	68	0.031
9	0.196	29	0.136	49	0.073	69	0.029
10	0.193	30	0.128	50	0.070	70	0.028
11	0.191	31	0.120	51	0.067	71	0.026
12	0.189	32	0.116	52	0.063	72	0.025
13	0.185	33	0.113	53	0.059	73	0.024
14	0.182	34	0.111	54	0.055	74	0.022
15	0.180	35	0.110	55	0.052	75	0.021
16	0.177	36	0.106	56	0.046	76	0.020
17	0.173	37	0.104	57	0.043	77	0.018
18	0.169	38	0.101	58	0.042	78	0.016
19	0.166	39	0.099	59	0.041	79	0.014
20	0.161	40	0.098	60	0.040	80	0.013

DECIMAL SIZES OF LETTERED DRILLS

Letter	Size
A	0.234
B	0.238
C	0.242
D	0.246
E	0.250
F	0.257
G	0.261
H	0.266
I	0.272
J	0.277
K	0.281
L	0.290
M	0.295
N	0.302
O	0.316
P	0.323
Q	0.332
R	0.339
S	0.348
T	0.358
U	0.368
V	0.377
W	0.386
X	0.397
Y	0.404
Z	0.413

CONVERSION TABLES

Fraction	Decimal	Millimeter
1/64	.0156	0.396
1/32	.0312	0.793
3/64	.0468	1.190
1/16	.0625	1.587
5/64	.0781	1.984
3/32	.0937	2.381
7/64	.1093	2.778
1/8	.1250	3.175
9/64	.1406	3.571
5/32	.1562	3.968
3/16	.1875	4.762
13/64	.2031	5.159
7/32	.2187	5.556
15/64	.2343	5.953
1/4	.2500	6.350
17/64	.2656	6.746
9/32	.2812	7.143
19/64	.2958	7.540
5/16	.3125	7.937
21/64	.3281	8.334
11/32	.3437	8.731
23/64	.3593	9.128
3/8	.3750	9.525
25/64	.3906	9.921
13/32	.4062	10.318
27/64	.4218	10.715
7/16	.4375	11.112
29/64	.4531	11.509
15/32	.4687	11.906
31/64	.4843	12.303
1/2	.5000	12.700

TAP AND DIE THREAD SIZES

(National Fine *[NF]* SAE)

OD Tap	Threads	Size Drill
1/4	28	No. 3
5/16	24	I
3/8	24	Q
7/16	20	25/64
1/2	20	29/64

(National Course USS) [NC]

OD Tap	Threads	Size Drill
1/4	20	No.7
5/16	18	F
3/8	16	5/16
7/16	14	U
1/2	13	27/64

COMPARISON OF STANDARD METAL GAUGES
(calibrated to thousandths of an inch)

Gauge No.	Brown & Sharpe (American Wire)	British Imperial Standard	Millimeter
1	0.289	0.300	7.346
2	0.257	0.276	6.543
3	0.229	0.252	5.829
4	0.204	0.232	5.189
5	0.181	0.212	4.618
6	0.162	0.192	4.111
7	0.144	0.176	3.670
8	0.128	0.160	3.264
9	0.114	0.145	2.906

Gauge No.	Brown & Sharpe (American Wire)	British Imperial Standard	Millimeter
10	0.101	0.128	2.588
11	0.090	0.116	2.304
12	0.080	0.104	2.052
13	0.071	0.092	1.829
14	0.064	0.080	1.629
15	0.057	0.072	1.450
16	0.050	0.064	1.290
17	0.045	0.056	1.151
18	0.040	0.048	1.024
19	0.035	0.040	0.912
20	0.031	0.036	0.813
21	0.028	0.032	0.724
22	0.025	0.028	0.643
23	0.022	0.024	0.574
24	0.020	0.022	0.511
25	0.017	0.020	0.445
26	0.015	0.018	
27	0.014	0.016	
28	0.012	0.014	
29	0.011	0.013	
30	0.010	0.012	

Size	Rounds	Squares	Hex.	Oct.
3/8	0.376	0.478	0.414	0.396
7/16	0.511	0.651	0.564	0.539
1/2	0.668	0.850	0.737	0.704
9/16	0.845	1.076	0.932	0.891
5/8	1.040	1.328	1.150	1.100
11/16	1.260	1.607	1.393	1.331
3/4	1.500	1.913	1.658	1.581
13/16	1.760	2.245	1.944	1.859
7/8	2.040	2.603	2.256	2.157
15/16	2.350	2.988	2.588	2.476
1	2.670	3.400	2.944	2.817
1 1/16	3.010	3.838	3.324	3.180
1 1/8	3.380	4.303	3.727	3.565
1 3/16	3.770	4.795	4.152	3.972
1 1/4	4.170	5.314	4.601	4.401
1 5/16	4.600	5.857	5.072	4.852
1 3/8	5.050	6.428	5.567	5.352
1 7/16	5.517	7.026	6.085	5.820
1 1/2	6.010	7.650	6.625	6.338
1 9/16	6.519	8.301	7.189	6.887
1 5/8	7.050	8.978	7.775	7.438
1 11/16	7.604	9.682	8.385	8.021
1 3/4	8.180	10.414	9.018	8.626
1 13/16	8.773	11.170	9.673	9.253
1 7/8	9.390	12.000	10.355	9.902
1 15/16	10.024	12.763	11.053	10.574
2	10.700	13.600	11.780	11.267
2 1/16	11.360	14.463	12.528	11.982

TROY WEIGHT
(used to measure precious metals)

24 grains = 1 pennyweight
20 pennyweight (480 grains) = 1 ounce
12 ounces (5,760 grains) = 1 pound

AVOIRDUPOIS WEIGHT

27.343 grains = 1 dram
16 drams (417 grains) = 1 ounce
16 ounces (6,679 grains) = 1 pound
2,000 pounds = 1 short ton
2,240 pounds = 1 long ton

APOTHECARIES' WEIGHT

20 grains = 1 scruple
3 scruples = 1 dram
8 drams = 1 ounce
12 ounces = 1 pound

WEIGHTS OF CARBON STEEL BARS
(in pounds per foot of length)

Size	Rounds	Squares	Hex.	Oct.
1/4	0.167	0.213	0.184	0.176
5/16	0.261	0.332	0.288	0.275

WEIGHTS OF FLAT CARBON BAR STOCK (RECTANGLES)
(in pounds per foot of length)

Thickness	Width	Weight per Foot
1/8	1/2	0.213
1/8	3/4	0.319
1/8	1	0.425
1/8	1 1/4	0.531
1/8	1 1/2	0.638
1/8	1 3/4	0.774
1/8	2	0.850
1/8	2 1/4	0.956
1/8	2 1/2	1.063
1/8	2 3/4	1.169
3/16	1/2	0.319
3/16	3/4	0.478
3/16	1	0.425
3/16	1 1/4	0.531
3/16	1 1/2	0.956

Thickness	Width	Weight per Foot	Thickness	Width	Weight per Foot
3/16	1 3/4	1.116	5/16	1 1/4	1.328
3/16	2	1.275	5/16	1 1/2	1.275
3/16	2 1/4	1.434	5/16	1 3/4	1.859
3/16	2 1/2	1.594	5/16	2	2.125
3/16	2 3/4	1.753	5/16	2 1/4	2.391
1/4	1/2	0.425	5/16	2 1/2	2.656
1/4	3/4	0.638	5/16	2 3/4	2.922
1/4	1	0.850	3/8	1/2	0.638
1/4	1 1/4	1.063	3/8	3/4	0.956
1/4	1 1/2	1.275	3/8	1	1.275
1/4	1 3/4	1.488	3/8	1 1/4	1.594
1/4	2	1.700	3/8	1 1/2	1.913
1/4	2 1/4	1.913	3/8	1 3/4	2.231
1/4	2 1/2	2.125	3/8	2	2.550
1/4	2 3/4	2.338	3/8	2 1/4	2.869
5/16	1/2	0.531	3/8	2 1/2	3.188
5/16	3/4	0.797	3/8	2 3/4	3.506
5/16	1	1.063			

NONMETRIC TO METRIC CONVERSIONS
(measures)

1 inch = 2.54 centimeters (cm) (25.4 mm)
1 square inch = 6.451 cm²
1 cubic inch = 16.387 cm³
1 foot = 30.48 cm
1 square foot = 929.03 cm²
1 cubic foot = 28,317 cm³
1 yard (3 feet) = 91.44 cm (0.9144 m)
1 square yard = 0.8361 m²
1 cubic yard = 0.7646 m²
1 mile (5,280 ft. or 1,760 yds.) = 1,609.3 m

METRIC TO NONMETRIC
(measures)

1 millimeter (mm) = 0.039 inch
1 centimeter (cm) (10 mm) = 0.393 inch
1 square centimeter = 0.1549 square inches
1 cubic centimeter (cc) = 0.061 cubic inches
1 meter (m) = 39.37 inches, 3.280 feet or 1.093 yards

1 square meter = 10.763 ft², 1.196 yds²
1 cubic meter = 35.314 ft³, 1.307 yds²
1 kilometer (km) (1,000 m) = 1,093.61 yds, 0.621 miles

AVOIRDUPOIS TO METRIC
(weights)

1 ounce (oz.) = 28.349 grams (gm)
1 pound (lb.) (16 oz.) = 453.6 gm
1 ton (2,000 lbs.) = 907.19 kilograms (kg)
1 lb. per in. = 178.6 gm per cm
1 lb. per ft. = 1.488 kg per m

METRIC TO AVOIRDUPOIS
(weights)

1 gram = 0.0022 lbs.
1 kilogram = 2.204 lbs.
1 gm per cm = 0.0056 lbs. per in.
1 kg per m = 0.671 lbs. per ft.
1 metric ton (1,000 kg) = 2,204 lbs. or 1.102 av. ton

Bibliography

The books listed here are suggested reading for those who wish to study further on bladesmithing.

Andrews, Jack. *Edge of the Anvil*. Emmaus, PA: Rodale Press, 1977.

Ashdown, Charles Henry. *European Arms and Armour*. New York: Brussel and Brussel, 1967.

Boye, David. *Step by Step Knifemaking*. Emmaus, PA: Rodale Press, 1977.

Kallenberg, Lawrence. *Modeling in Wax for Jewelry and Sculpture*. Radnor, PA: Chilton Book Co., 1981.

Lungwitz, A., and Adams, Charles. *The Complete Guide to Blacksmithing*. New York: Bonanza Books, 1981.

Mayes, Jim. *How to Make Your Own Knives*. New York: Everest House Publishers, 1978.

Meilach, Dona Z. *Decorative and Sculptural Ironwork*. New York: Crown Publishers, 1977.

Neumann, George C. *Swords and Blades of the American Revolution*. Harrisburg: Stackpole Books, 1973.

Oakeshott, R. Ewart. *The Archaeology of Weapons*. London: F.A. Praeger, 1960.

Oakeshott, R. Ewart. *European Weapons and Armour*. North Hollywood: Beinfeld Publishing, 1980.

Oakeshott, R. Ewart. *The Sword in the Age of Chivalry*. London: Arms and Armour Press, 1981.

Pack, Greta. *Jewelry Making by the Lost Wax Process*. New York: Van Nostrand Reinhold, 1975.

Rawson, P.S. *The Indian Sword*. New York: Arco Publishing, 1968.

Smith, Cyril S. *A History of Metallography*. Chicago: University of Chicago, 1960.

Stone, George Cameron. *A Glossary of the Construction, Decoration and Use of Arms and Armour in All Countries and in All Times*. New York: Jack Brussel, 1961.

United States Government Federal Specifications. *Wire Rope and Strand*, RR-W-401D. April 25, 1984.

United States Steel. *The Making, Shaping and Treating of Steel*. Pittsburgh: United States Steel, 1957.

Untracht, Oppi. *Metal Techniques for Craftsmen*. Garden City: Doubleday and Company, 1975.

Wallace, John. *Scottish Swords and Dirks*. Harrisburg: Stackpole Books, 1970.

Weygers, Alexander G. *The Modern Blacksmith*. New York: Van Nostrand Reinhold, 1974.

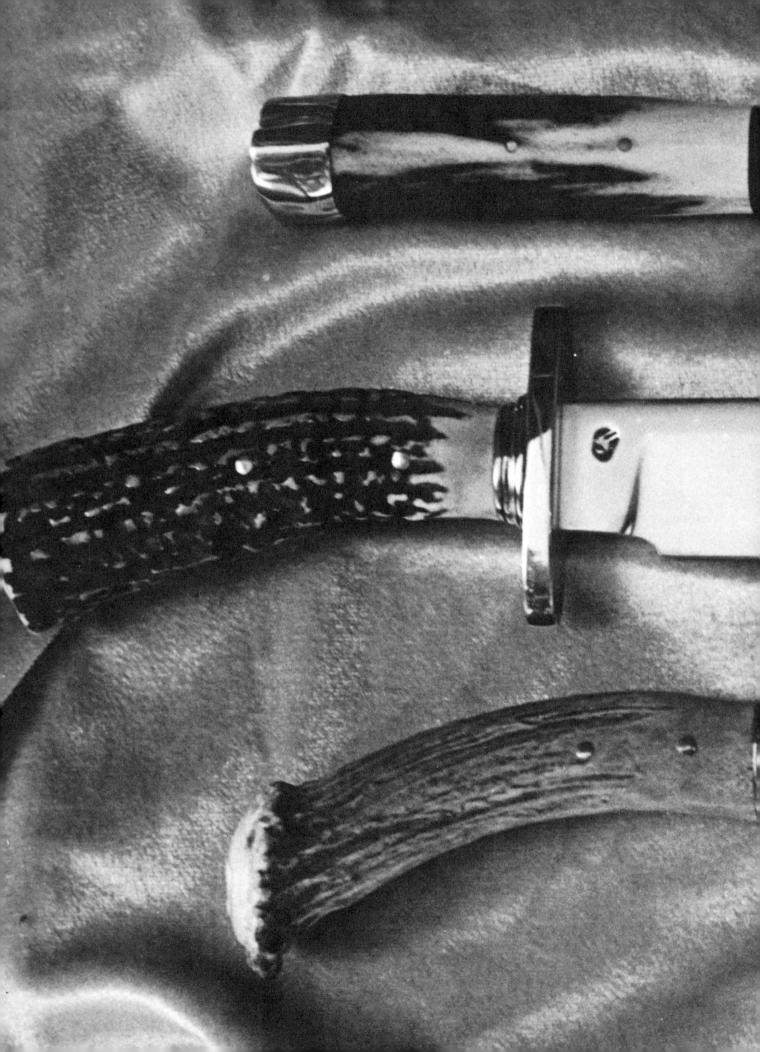